The life story of Jackie Robinson

. . . . WAIT
TILL
NEXT
YEAR .

by Carl T. Rowan with Jackie Robinson

Wait Till Ne
The Story of Jac

by Carl T. Rowan
with Jackie Robinson

ISHI PRESS
INTERNATIONAL

Wait Till Next Year
The Story of Jackie Robinson

by Carl T. Rowan
with Jackie Robinson

First published in 1960 by Random House

Copyright © 1960 by Carl T. Rowan
and Jack R. Robinson

This Printing in June, 2015 by Ishi Press in New York
and Tokyo with a new introduction by Ken Thomas

ISBN 4-87187-684-5
978-4-87187-684-1

Ishi Press International
1664 Davidson Avenue, Suite 1B
Bronx NY 10453-7877
USA
1-917-659-3397
samhsloan@gmail.com

Printed in the United States of America

Introduction by Ken Thomas

WAIT TILL NEXT YEAR . . .

The story of Jackie Robinson

by Carl T. Rowan with Jackie Robinson

Introduction by Ken Thomas

The Brooklyn Dodger's last decade:

In 1947 I became a Brooklyn Dodger fan. No doubt about it. I loved "Dem Bums!" To me Flatbush Avenue was hallowed ground and Ebbets Field was more beautiful than the Taj Mahal. Brooklyn fans knew that Pee Wee Reese was the best shortstop in baseball and the best center fielder was Duke Snider. These "facts" were strongly disputed by other baseball fans in New York City.

Ken Thomas

More than anything, I loved Jackie Robinson. I was nine year old and Jackie was my hero. My baseball skills were only fair, but in my back yard I pretended to be Jackie Robison and felt like an All Star. I became a Brooklyn Dodger fan the day that Jackie Robinson became a Brooklyn Dodger.

In 1946 my family moved from a small town in the Texas panhandle to central New Jersey. My dad was an unemployed carpenter and the Southwest was an economically depressed area. A post war building boom came to the Northeast and the Thomas family came there also.

My dad loved baseball and the St. Louis Cardinals were his team. For years he had "watched" the Cardinals on the radio, but he never had the money to travel to St. Louis for a game. Now everything changed. When the 1947 season started he took me to Ebbets Field to see his Cardinals in person for the very first time. The Dodgers won that game and I was hooked, but not on the Cards. My team was the Dodgers and Jackie Robinson soon became my favorite player.

During the next ten years I lived and died with the Dodgers. I knew everything about them. I knew their names, their uniform numbers and their batting averages. I knew all their statistics and their daily results. I always knew where the Dodgers were in the National League standing. Every August I started counting down the magic number.

Over all, during those years, The Dodgers were the best team in the National League. Unfortunately, it was their destiny to disappoint their fans. Every year the New York Yankees of the American League, who were a much better team, waited like a spider in its web to entrap the National League winner.

A season pattern soon developed. It started each spring with bright expectations of victory. Next came the summer and an exciting pennant race. The Dodgers were always on top of the National League, or near it. Sadly, October brought bitter disappointments. At season's end it was always the Dodger fans promising, "Wait till next year."

The Dodgers were defeated three times at the very end of the season. First time was in 1948. The Boston Braves beat them in the last few games. Two years later the Phillies "whiz Kids" won in the last inning in the final game of the season.

The ultimately shocker, however, was in 1951 and the famous "shot heard round the world." The Dodgers and their arch-rival, New York Giants, were tied at season's end. They needed a three games play off to break the tie. With the Dodgers leading in the ninth inning of the third game and the Giants down to their last out, Bobby Thomson hit that heroic walk-off homer.

Losing the pennant when you are expecting to win is hard for a kid to take, but there are worse ways to end a season. Five times the Dodgers actually won the National League Championship and were beaten by the powerful New York Yankees.

The Dodgers, Giants and Yankees were cross-town rivals. The New York City fans knew each other and strongly supported their own team. The media was shared and covered all three teams. A subway system connected the boroughs where the teams played. The Giants and the Dodgers were in the National League and played each other 22 times each year. Most likely there were some rabid fans who attended every single game between them. It was so exciting. The fans always expected victory, but expecting the Dodgers to beat the Yankees was not realistic. There was only, "wait till next year."

It is a fair to say that the New York Yankees of that era were the best baseball team in baseball history. They won the American League pennant nine out of ten years. They also won the World Series five consecutively times.

Some believed that the "legendary" 1927 Murderers Row Yankees were better, but that is a seriously flawed idea. For one thing, most of the 1927 team played together for seven years from 1925 to 1931. It was essentially the same Yankee personnel during those years as the 1927 team. It is true, they did manage to win three consecutive pennants,

Introduction by Ken Thomas

but they only won two World Series. In 1927 most of the Yankee lineup had their best season of their personal careers. They were far from great in the other four years. In fact those Yankees teams finished far behind the American League pennant winners by a whopping 28, 18, 16 and 13.5 games. One year they even finished seventh in the eight team league.

The Jackie Robinson decade:

In retrospect, I view this period as the "Jackie Robinson" decade. It lasted from 1947 to 1956. I grew up during those years and watched Jackie's great success as a player. Most of the time he was a dominate force. He was a fierce competitor.

His exciting base running was a new style. He stole home plate 19 times and did it famously in game one of the 1955 World Series. None of these steals were the double steal variety, which would have made them easier. They were all just Jackie Robinson charging down the third base line like a freight train.

His goal was to rattle the opposing pitchers. That he did. His method was to take huge risky leads and entice bad throws or other errors. He kept the pitcher from concentrating on the batter which resulted in more walks and hits by his team mates. His strategy worked. According to Baseball historians, he alone changed baseball to a base running strategy. For twenty years from the 1920's to the 1940's baseball had relied on the long ball. Jackie Robinson was simply the most exciting player in the game.

Age is the enemy of professional baseball players and teams. Most major leaguers have reached the Big Leagues by age twenty. They are usually finished by thirty-eight or forty. Jackie Robinson started his career late. In 1947 he was already twenty-eight years old. By 1955 he was starting to slip a little. His critic said he was washed up. The New York Yankees were aging too. They were still powerful, but showed signs of weakening. As such, in 1955 to 1958 the Yankees won four consecutive American League championships, but lost the World Series twice to the National League winners.

That was good news for the Brooklyn because in 1955, next year had arrived. They won their first World Series and were finally World Champions. Brooklyn was ecstatic and so was I. We found the Holy Grail.

Amid the great victory celebrations there was a twinge of sadness. The Dodger manager had benched Jackie Robinson in the seventh game, for poor hitting. Even though he had stolen home plate in game one of the series, His skills had diminished. It was younger players like Sandy Amoros who beat the Yankees in game seven. Jackie's critics were correct. After the next year Jackie Robinson was out of baseball. He retired to accept a great job as Vice President of Chock full o'Nuts Company.

Soon after Jackie left Brooklyn, the Dodgers left Brooklyn also. Walter O'Malley, the team owner, moved the Dodgers west to Los Angeles California. The Jackie Robinson decade was over. The Brooklyn Dodgers were no more. Brooklyn was crushed. I never saw them play again.

Dodgers are dead:

In 1947, at age nine, I had no idea what was going on in this country. Social issues were not part of my thinking. Of course I knew Jackie was black, but I did not think about it. Other black players soon came into baseball. Larry Doby played later in 1947 and Willie Mays still later. They both were good, but Doby was in the American Leaguer. Who cares about them? Mays played for the hated Giants. The idea that Jackie was somehow connected to either of them playing baseball did not occur to me.

When Roy Campanella and Don Newcombe came up they were just new Dodgers. They were our guys. In a few years I became aware the Jackie had "broken the color barrier." I thought, 'Good for him," nothing more.

It was not until I overheard family members discussing the 1954 Supreme court and "Brown vs. Board of Education" that I perked up. My uncle said, "That Jackie Robinson guy started all this." He said it like Jackie had done something bad. As a teenager at that time I knew enough to stay out of adult discussions, but I did start to pay attention. I learned a lot from then on.

After the shock of losing my beloved Dodgers, I dropped baseball completely, except for occasionally reading book about the "old Dodgers." There is much literature written about them. Roger Kahn's excellent book, "The Boys of Summer" is among the best Dodger books ever. It covers growing up in the shadow of Ebbets Field and the Dodgers last years in Brooklyn. He reports also what became of the most popular players after they retired. It was about sports and covered few social issues.

The same is true about "The Last Good Season" by Michael Shapiro. It also is well written, but very narrow in scope. It covers only 1956 season. So it gives exactly what the title promises, the last baseball season in Brooklyn. He researched the book well.

Wait Till Next Year, the book:

Introduction by Ken Thomas

Up to this point, my narrative concerns the Brooklyn Dodgers as a young fan, myself, saw them. The actual novel Wait till next year, is more than a sports story. It is the life story of a great baseball player. That man, Jack Roosevelt Robinson, in a ten year period fundamentally changed life the United States forever.

This book, Wait till Next Year, is a life story of Jackie Robinson. It is far better than other Robinson biographies. Two reasons set this book apart from others on this topic. The first of course is that this is the only book that Jackie Robinson completely collaborated in writing. Second the Author, Carl T. Rowan is not only a great writer, but was a complete participant in the civil right movement.

The facts described in Wait Till Next Year are incredibly detailed and personal. It starts with Robinson's childhood and takes the reader all the way to his career after baseball. Family background and history are covered in complete detail. Jackie was usual was candid and brutally honest in public and this retelling here give many private facts.

Many conversations and facts are provided by Jackie himself. Carl Rowan, and Jackie Robinson became best friends. They worked together and closely with Dr. Martin Luther King Jr. during this historic period of United States History. Dr. King was generous in praise for Robinson.

Some information could only have come from Jackie Robinson himself. For instance, previously unknown were details of Jackie's abandoned mother, Mallie, how she moved him and his four siblings from the share cropper's cabin in Cairo, Georgia to Pasadena, California.

Many of the family's trials and hardships are revealed. As Jackie grew up he joined a neighborhood gang and had problems with the law in Pasadena. Jackie's older brother, Mack who won a silver medal at the 1936 Olympics encouraged Jackie to become an athlete. This Jackie did with tremendous results.

His athletic career was beyond Mack's wildest dreams. The first year that Jackie was at John Muir Tech High School he lettered in four sports, football, basketball, track and baseball. He played on the tennis team also. The next year he won the boys Pacific Coast Negro Tennis champion. Jackie went on the Pasadena Junior College and had continued success in all sports particularly in baseball. He was named to the All-Southland Team for baseball and region's Most Valuable Player.

His Success at UCLA is beyond any expectation.

Wait Till Next Year, as written by Carl Rowan, gave the above fact for the first time. In today's internet world, facts concerning Jackie Robinson are easily found, but the way he felt and most details are found only in this rendering.

Who broke the color line?:

The America of the 1940s had a tradition of segregation and it was especially true in sports. Blacks had their own separate sports leagues. Jackie Robinson broke that color line, but Branch Rickey empowered him. Rickey was the Dodger Club President and General Manager and one of many baseball men trying to bring in Blacks players. It was Rickey's plan first, but Jackie Robinson was to implement it. The 75% Dodger owner, Walter O'Malley, was not for Rickey's plan unless there was a profit in it. He often referred to Jackie Robinson as, Rickey's Prime donna.

Introduction by Ken Thomas

Segregation was in other sports as well. Jackie Robinson's impact on the culture and the civil rights movement of the time was powerful. As far back as the mid-1940s Branch Rickey and the BILL Veeck, the Cleveland Indian President were working together and searching find an ideal Black player to bring up. In 1942 Veeck proposed integrating baseball, but this was flatly rejected by Baseball Commissioner, Kenesaw Mountain Landis.

Rickey after searching and weighing his options chose Robinson. Veeck chose Larry Doby. There was much contact and discussion between the two. Sadly, Bill Veeck and many Indian players, including the great Bob Feller, resented the credit given to Rickey and Robinson at the expense of Doby who followed Robinson by only eleven weeks.

The 1947 Indian players did not accept Doby well at all. Only four white players would talk to him. The others including Bob Feller, who was a nasty man at best, turned their backs on Doby as he passed by rather than talk to him. On his first day Joe Gordon befriended Doby and became one of his closest friends on the team. In his first major league at bat Doby struck out. It is said that Joe Gordon came up next and intentionally struck out on three swings just to save face for his new teammate. When Doby was listed to play first base in the second game of the double header, he had no first baseman' glove. None of his teammates would lend him one. Joe Gordon ask and got a glove from a friendly White Sox player. In the 1948 World Series, Doby lead all batters in the Series at .318 batting avg. to help the Indians beat the Braves. He was clearly the reason the Indians won. Non-the-less, Doby on road trips stayed in a Black hotel and not with the other players, for most of his years in Cleveland.

Introduction by Ken Thomas

The American League may have been the more difficult task for Doby than the National would have been. The Yankees and Red Sox ownership was clearly anti-Black, and racist according to Robinson's accusations in an interview. Later, he was proved correct when they failed bring Blacks in their huge farm systems or to the majors. It took Boston fourteen years to do so.

Actually many baseball people, especially Black, believed Robinson and Doby were the wrong ones selected for the honor of breaking the color line. The two great Black players, Satchel Paige and Josh Gibson were considered more talented. Later Paige did play in the majors for a short time, but Gibson did not and died a disappointed man.

The Author:

Carl Thomas Rowan born on August 11, 1925. He graduated from Oberlin College in 1947 and received a master's degree in journalism from University of Minnesota 1948.

In the late 1950s he reported extensively on the Civil Rights Movement including the 1955 Montgomery bus boycott. Rowan made special friendship among the boycott's leaders, including Dr. Martin Luther King Jr.

The bus boycott resulted from Rosa Park's refusal to relinquish her bus seat to a white passenger. Note that in 1942 Jackie Robinson, then in the Military, refused to accept segregated seating and was court-martialed for it. In August 1944 he was acquitted by an all-white panel of nine officers, mostly because President Harry Truman had stopped segregation in the Military.

He wrote nine books. In 1960 Carl Thomas Rowan wrote,

Wait Till Next Year, The life Story of Jackie Robinson.

Shooting Controversy:

Carl Rowan in 1988, by then a well off senior citizen and famous person, shot and injured an unarmed teenager neighbor who was trespassing and skinny dipping in his pool. The gun was unregistered. Rowan was charged for firing a gun that he did not legally own. He was called out for hypocrisy, since Rowan was a strict gun control advocate.

Rowan was arrested and tried but the jury was deadlocked. The mistrial was not retried. He died on September 23, 2000 in Washington DC.

Jack Roosevelt Robinson was born on January 31, 1919 in Cairo, Grady County, Georgia on Jim Sasser's plantation=James Madison Sasser. On 10 February 1946, he married Rachel Annetta Isum in Los Angeles California. She was born on July 19, 1922. They had four children. Unfortunately, the eldest, Jackie Robinson Jr., died on June 17, 1971 in a car accident. Jack Roosevelt Robinson Senior died on October 24, 1972 in North Stamford, Connectcut. He is buried in the Cypress Hills Cemetery Brooklyn, New York. In 1973, the year after Jackie Robinson died, his widow formed the Jackie Robinson Foundation, which has since awarded 450 college scholarships to minority students who were needy and demonstrated leadership potential.

Jackie Robinson has been honored so many times in so many ways it would be impossble to name them all. He has been awarded the Congressional Gold Medal and Presidential Medal of Freedom. Perhaps the most remarkable honor is he has a major highway, the **Jackie**

Introduction by Ken Thomas

Robinson Parkway, named after him.

The Jackie Robinson Expressway is five miles long and goes from Central Brooklyn near where Jamaica and Pennsylvania Avenues intersect and connects with the Van Wyck Expressway in Queens near to the entrance to JFK Airport. He is the only sporting figure with a major highway named after him.

Ken Thomas
Hackettstown NJ
USA
June 4, 2015

Wait Till Next Year
The Life Story of Jackie Robinson
by Carl T. Rowan with Jackie Robinson

Wait tell Next Year is the inside story of one of the most dramatic personalities of our time and a re-creation of many of the most exciting moments in modern baseball.

If nothing else had counted but hits, runs and errors, Jackie Robinson wouldn't have had many problems during his years as a major figure in the sports world. But his great ability as a player was often over-shadowed by the fact that he was the first Negro in major league baseball. He was - and still is - a man of burning pride and, above all, courage. He is a man who plays to win, on and off the baseball diamond.

Jackie Robinson was born in a share-croppers cabin in Georgia. He first won national fame as a college and basketball star at U.C.L.A. And later played in the Negro Baseball leagues. Then, at twenty-six backed by Branch Ricky's tough support, he joined the Brooklyn Dodgers organization. During his controversial record-breaking years with the Dodgers – and the important years since his retirement from baseball in 1956 – he has fought constantly for Negro equality and an end to racial antagonism and discrimination.

WAIT TILL NEXT YEAR then is much more than a narrative of Jackie Robinson's brilliant sports career. The whole story is here, including the problems that confronted his mother and his wife and children, and the dramatic scenes when Robinson refused to submit to prejudice in the Army, in housing for his family, in baseball training camps. Robinson himself describes for the reader some of these crisis in life, and his wife speaks of the events which especially affected her. Carl Rowan one of the country's finest reporters has written this biography of a great athlete with warmth, sympathy and full awareness of its value as a spirited American document.

ABOUT THE AUTHOR

In 1956, at the age of thirty, Carl T. Rowan became the only newspaperman ever to win three consecutive awards from Sigma Delta Chi, the nations foremost professional journalist organization. He won its coveted medallion for the best foreign correspondence of 1956 for his articles on Southeast Asia and his coverage of the handling Bandaung Conference. A year earlier he had won the foreign correspondence medallion for his articles on India. (These foreign experiences were described in his second book, *The Pitiful and the Proud*.) Sigma Delta Chi had also, in 1954, cited his articles on the school segregation cases then pending before the United States Supreme Court as the nations best general reporting of 1953. In 1952, his first book, *South of Freedom*, was published. In *Go South to Sorrow*, 1957, he evaluated the progress of integration since the historic Supreme Court decision.

Since 1950, when he became a staff writer for the Minneapolis Tribune After a two-year stint on the copy desk, Rowan has won awards from many other organizations, including the Sidney Hillman Foundation, the Capital Press Club, and the National Conference of Christians and Jews. He has also been awarded honorary degrees from Simpson College and Hamline University.

After graduation from Bernard High School in McMinnville Tennessee, Mr. Rowan spend three years in the Navy during World War II. At the age of nineteen he won one of the first fifteen commissions granted to Negros. He studied at Tennessee State University; Washburn University; Oberlin College for a bachelor's degree in mathematics; and at the University of Minnesota for a master's degree in journalism.

Mr. Rowan lives in Minneapolis with his wife and three children

From Chapter One of WAIT TILL NEXT YEAR
The Lovely Mob

An atmosphere of uneasy excitement hung over Louisville's Parkway Field on September 28, 1946. The Louisville Cardinals and the Montreal Royals, two of the best teams that ever graced minor league parks, were about to square off in the Little World Series. But in the brooding tension arose not so much from sports loyalties and antagonisms as from the fact that the Royals lineup included Jackie Robinson at the climax of his first season as the first Negro in modern organized baseball.

Well before the game was about to start Robinson sat in the royals dressing room a towel draped over his shoulders and a pair of sweat socks in his hand, staring at his locker. He had stopped to think how much this series – these games in the South – meant to him and to millions of other people and this forced him to relive the other tense moments of his year as the most famous "guinea pig" in the world.

Jackie read the sports pages religiously so he knew that his coming to Louisville had aroused debate, but he would have known of the tension if not one word had been written. A man, he thought, especially a colored man, couldn't walk through a crowd like this, as he had just done on his way to the dressing room, without sensing its hostility.

Will it be any worse than those first games in Baltimore?, Jackie wondered. What could I face here that I couldn't face in Syracuse? He thought seeking to console himself.

Then Jackie thought back to that amazing day in August little more than a year ago when Branch Rickey president and general manager of the Brooklyn Dodgers had stunned him with the announcement that he was to be the Negro pioneer who would open up baseball to colored men. What an awesome, theatrical and unbelievably wise man Rickey had been on that day.

"Jackie . . . there's virtually nobody on our side, " he said. ...

To Rae, whose love and wise counsel sustained me through the most trying of these years, and to our children, who I hope will find fewer barriers blocking their paths to dignity and happiness.

.... JACKIE ROBINSON

WAIT TILL NEXT YEAR

1....The Lovely Mob

An atmosphere of uneasy excitement hung over Louisville's
Parkway Field on September 28, 1946. The Louisville Colonels
and the Montreal Royals, two of the best teams that ever
graced minor league parks, were about to square off in the
Little World Series. But the brooding tension arose not so
much from sports loyalties and antagonisms as from the fact
that the Royals' line-up included Jackie Robinson, at the climax of his first season as the first Negro in modern organized
baseball.

Well before the game was to start, Robinson sat in the Royals' dressing room, a towel draped over his shoulders and a
pair of sweat socks in his hand, staring at his locker. He had
stopped to think how much this series—these games in the
South—meant to him and to millions of other people, and

this forced him to relive the other tense moments of his year as the most famous "guinea pig" in the world.

Jackie read the sports pages religiously, so he knew that his coming to Louisville had aroused debate, but he would have known of the tension if not one word had been written. A man, he thought, especially a colored man, couldn't walk through a crowd like this one, as he had just done on his way to the dressing room, without sensing its hostility.

Will it be any worse than those first games in Baltimore? Jackie wondered. What could I face here that I didn't face in Syracuse? he thought, seeking to console himself.

Then Jackie thought back to that amazing day in August a little over a year earlier, when Branch Rickey, president and general manager of the Brooklyn Dodgers, had stunned him with the announcement that he was to be the Negro pioneer who would open up baseball to colored men. What an awesome, theatrical and unbelievably wise man Rickey had been that day.

"Jackie, . . . there's virtually nobody on our side," he said. "No owners, no umpires, very few newspapermen. And I'm afraid that many fans may be hostile. We'll be in a tough position, Jackie. We can win only if we can convince the world that I'm doing this because you're a great ball player, a fine gentleman. . . .

"I wish it meant only hits, runs and errors—only the things they put in the box score," Rickey had said in the grandiloquent style that was his trademark. "Because you know—yes, *you* would know, Jackie—that a baseball box score is a democratic thing. It doesn't tell how big you are, what church you attend, what color you are or how your father voted in the last election. It just tells what kind of baseball player you were on that particular day."

If nothing had counted but hits, runs and errors, Jackie Robinson would have had few worries that September day in Louisville, for a season full of box scores left no doubt as to his ability to play baseball. But as Rickey had said, more than baseball ability was involved in his case. Customs, passions, fears and jealousies had to be considered. This, Jackie knew, was why these games in Louisville would help Rickey to decide whether to promote him to the Brooklyn team in 1947. These Little World Series games in Kentucky would show just how perilous were the reefs of prejudice and fear that lay along the course Rickey had charted.

There were no Negroes in the American Association, which Louisville represented, and Montreal's promising second baseman would be the first ballplayer of his race to perform in organized interracial competition in Louisville, which was very definitely a southern city. Policies of racial separation were firmly established in public schools, recreational programs, hotels and public places—including Parkway Field. Compared with many cities in the South, Louisville was a citadel of democracy; still, the mores here were such that the top men in baseball were watching these first three games of the Little World Series for clues to how far and how soon they should move to erase baseball's racial barriers. They had reluctantly accepted the signing of Robinson, but most of them argued privately that Rickey had acted too soon and not too wisely in taking him on, even for the Dodgers' International League farm club, because most minor league clubs on which promising Negroes would have to start were either in the South or played against southern teams. Louisville would confirm or destroy their belief that the South—even the Upper South—was not ready for integrated baseball.

The racial element in this Little World Series was intensified by the fact that the Louisville club owners had limited the number of Negroes who could attend the games, on the grounds that the fewer Negroes who were admitted, the less likelihood there would be of racial conflict. The *Louisville Courier-Journal* opposed the "Negro quota" decision, contending that "This is the very thing that creates tensions and resentments," but on this first day of the series, scores of Negroes who had traveled hundreds of miles for a look at Robinson were turned away. Thousands of white spectators filed into the park past clusters of disappointed and resentful Negroes.

When the line-ups were announced, and a dissonant chorus of boos greeted his name, Robinson chatted with a teammate and pretended not to hear. But when he walked toward the batters' circle, then the plate, in the first inning, the boos grew to a roar that drowned out the fervid clapping and screaming of the little cluster of Negro fans.

"Hey, black boy, go on back to Canada—and stay!" shouted someone behind home plate.

"Yeah, and take all your nigger-loving friends with you," someone else hollered.

Jackie reached down to scoop up a handful of dust, consciously refusing to look toward the stands, but his sensitive ears plucked the epithets, the racial insults, the sarcastic laughter from the general howl, and he knew that he was in for three trying days in Louisville. In spite of his promise to Rickey, it was hard to "turn the other cheek" to insults, beanballs and sharp spikes.

So Jackie let the warm, dry dust trickle through his fingers and wiped his hands on his trousers as he tried to convince himself that there was really nothing different about Louisville. He had been insulted by experts in some International League cities. Still, he knew that neither he nor any other Negro could avoid that hot-pit-of-the-stomach feeling that operated almost as a conditioned reflex in times of racial provocation. When he stepped to the plate he realized how nervous he was. His hands still felt damp, the bat slippery in them.

Robinson batted miserably that day, and he was no sensation in the field, but in the end he had the consolation of seeing his team win, 7 to 5, to take the lead in the best-of-seven series. But the next night, spurred on by Robinson's poor first-day performance, the hecklers intensified their barrage—so much so that Louisville sports writers apologized to Robinson for their behavior. Yet if they began with the hope of getting Robinson's goat, they apparently succeeded. The highly touted Negro got one puny hit in eleven times at bat during the three games in Louisville, and the Colonels won the last two games, 3 to 0 and 15 to 6. As the teams moved to Montreal for four contests, Louisville was a solid favorite to take the pennant symbolizing the best team outside major league baseball.

Stories of his treatment in Louisville had been played up in Canada, where Robinson had become a national favorite, so when the Royals returned home, he was besieged by well-wishers. But he was not prepared for the boos that shook Delorimier Downs as the Louisville players were introduced in Montreal.

When the game got under way, each Louisville player to emerge from the dugout was met by an ear-splitting shriek of boos. "Is this the kind of treatment every visiting team gets here?" a Louisville newspaperman asked his press-box colleagues.

"Of course not," said a Montreal writer. "The fans are returning the welcome the Louisville fans gave Jackie Robinson."

Robinson sat in the dugout chuckling. He sympathized with the Colonels, who were somewhat innocent victims of the wrath of Montreal, but it made him feel good to see that the Royals' followers cared that much.

"In a situation like this it's hard to say exactly how you feel," he told a teammate, "but when fans go to bat for you like this you know you wouldn't mind playing for them the rest of your life."

The Royals took the field to a thunderous ovation—and then Louisville's special brand of lightning struck. The undaunted Colonels hopped off to a 2-0 lead in the first inning, added another tally in the third, then made the margin 4-0 in the fifth. The crowd was quiet now; it looked as if Louisville would walk away with the series.

The Royals came to life in the bottom of the fifth, scoring one run, and they added another in the sixth. The teams traded runs in the eighth, to leave Louisville with a 5 to 3 advantage, and with just three put-outs needed in the ninth to give them a third victory and an almost insurmountable lead in the series.

Robinson was saying a little prayer as he jogged back to the dugout. The Good Lord knew better than he how desperately he needed to get going, how much Montreal needed to win that game. It was as if he had suddenly become aware of the immense weight on his mind and heart and shoulders. He told himself that if he didn't make it to the majors people would call him a colossal flop; he would be used as proof that no Negro was qualified to play in the majors. But surely, he thought, Rickey would give more weight to his season-long performance than to his record in this series! Or would he? Writers could cite this series as proof that he folded under pressure, and say that this pressure was trifling compared with what he would face in the majors.

Montreal fans stamped and cheered desperately, crying for a rally, and Jackie repeated his prayer for the strength and courage to do what he knew he needed to do.

Montreal hopes rose as Louisville pitcher Otis Clark walked the lead-off batter, then soared as he threw four balls to Robinson. When Clark walked the next hitter and loaded the bases, Louisville called in Joe Ostrowski to put out the fire. Ostrowski couldn't find the plate either; he walked the first man he faced, forcing in a run for Montreal and moving Robinson to third.

As Ostrowski started to pitch to the next batter, Jackie took a daring lead, then rushed headlong toward the plate as if attempting to steal home. As the crowd gasped in excitement, Robinson skidded to a stop and raced back to third, with Louisville catcher Fred Walters eying him menacingly, his arm poised as if to throw the ball to third. But the Colonels noticed that the Montreal runners on second and first were also taking extra-long leads when Robinson dashed away from third, so they decided to cross up the Royals and try to pick off the man at second rather than throw for Robinson.

Ostrowski peered at Robinson cautiously as the Negro eased sideways away from the bag, his arms out from his sides to give him the delicate balance needed to move fast in either direction. The pitcher cranked up his pitching arm and once more Jackie started his threatening dash. Walters caught the fast ball and sprang from his crouch with catlike agility, snapping the ball toward second. Runner and fielder converged in a cloud of dust, but the ball bounded wildly into centerfield as Robinson trotted home with the tying run.

Louisville managed to preserve the deadlock, but it was obvious in the bottom of the tenth that the Colonels had lost their poise. The crowd cheered frantically as an error, a fielder's choice and a sacrifice put Montreal runners on second and third. The Royals tried a squeeze play, but the runner on third was out at the plate. The Colonels' strategy now was to walk the next batter intentionally, to load the bases and bring to the plate the man whose hitting had been so anemic in Louisville—Jackie Robinson.

The throng maintained an ear-shattering roar as Jackie left his kneeling position in the batters' circle, paused to squeeze the resin bag, then strode to the plate with an outward look of ice-cold calmness. Someone in the Louisville dugout was yelling a steady stream of taunts—that old baseball custom called jockeying—but over it Jackie could hear the fans begging for a hit, could hear a part of himself urging him to make up for that flop in Louisville.

Ostrowski leaned low to get the sign, straightened up to peek at the runner on third, kicked his foot high and hurled the ball. Strike one. Robinson had watched a knee-high curve bite the outside corner. Ostrowski fidgeted about, kicked dirt from the mound, then repeated his pitching routine. This time Jackie swung, and as his bat met the fast ball, Ostrowski seemed to take reflex steps toward the clubhouse. He knew, and so did the screaming crowd, that the ball game was over. Robinson had smashed a single—the kind ballplayers called a "blue darter." With the victories now tied at two each, Montreal was back in the series.

Robinson proceeded, the following night, to get the Royals off to a fast start when he doubled in the first inning and raced home on Tom Tatum's single. The Royals got single tallies in the first three innings, but Louisville fought back with a run in the fifth and two in the seventh, to tie the score.

Montreal fans stood briefly for the seventh-inning stretch, then began a rhythmic clapping and stamping as they exhorted the Royals to rally. Jackie responded by smashing a triple, later trotting home on Lew Riggs's two-base belt. Then, after Al Campanis walked in the last of the eighth, Robinson knocked in an insurance run and Montreal went on to win, 5 to 3.

Now, on an unusually mild October night, 19,171 fans flocked out to see if their stalwarts could end the series. Clay Hopper, the Montreal manager, had called on Curt Davis to pitch, while Louisville was going with Harry Dorish, who had blanked the Royals in the second game.

Dorish was strong again, giving up only six hits, but a second-inning lapse hurt him. He walked Riggs to start the inning, and Dixie Howell doubled to score Riggs, then raced home himself on a single by Campanis.

Davis yielded hits to the first Colonel batter in each of the first three innings, but the crafty old right-hander was too tough in clutch situations, so Louisville failed to score. The Colonels threatened again in the sixth, but a sparkling double play, Robinson to Campanis to Les Burge, snuffed out the rally.

Louisville battled back gamely in the ninth, when Walters led off with a double and Chunk Koney reached first on a slow grounder to Davis. Then Al Brancato hit a smash to Robinson, who flipped to Burge for a quick double play. Louisville pinch-hitter Otto Denning grounded out, Riggs to Burge, and it was all over. Montreal had won, 2 to 0, to climax a rousing comeback and win the series.

Screaming fans jumped over barriers and rushed past policemen onto the field, in one of the great demonstrations of baseball history.

They grabbed Curt Davis, hoisted him high, and raced across the outfield, shouting and cheering. When Hopper waved good-by, fans lifted him to their shoulders and paraded around the field. Robinson, who had optimistically made a tentative reservation on a night plane to Detroit, where he was to begin a barnstorming tour, scampered through the crowd like the halfback he had once been. He reached the clubhouse and tried to shower and dress hastily amid his cheering, celebrating teammates, unaware that some five thousand fans remained in the park, stamping their feet, singing, *"Il a gagne ses epaulettes,"* chanting, "We want Robinson, we want Robinson!"

Finally an usher was sent to ask Robinson if he would please come out to say good-by, or the people never would leave. As Jackie walked out, his teeth glistening in a broad smile, the crowd surged toward him. Men slapped him on the back and hugged him. Women threw their arms around him and kissed him. Little boys pulled at his clothes. A group of young men hoisted him to their shoulders and romped around the field, shouting and singing. As Robinson was bounced along in the air, amazed and moved, tears began to run down his face. He was laughing and crying simultaneously.

Finally he convinced the young men to run with him to the clubhouse, where he began to pack his gear.

As Manager Hopper was leaving the dressing room, he walked over to shake Robinson's hand. "Jackie, you're a real ballplayer and a gentleman," he said. "It's been wonderful having you on the team."

Jackie was silent a moment, then he said, "Thanks, Skipper. It's been great playing for this team. You'll never know how much I appreciate all the things you taught me, the confidence you showed in me right from the start."

As this white Mississippian left the dressing room, soon to go back to his Mississippi plantation, Robinson stood almost dumfounded, remembering that this was the man who had said, "Mr. Rickey, do you really think a nigger's a human being?" Rickey had told Jackie of that remark, explaining that he knew as well as Robinson himself that Hopper's attitude was part of his heritage. But that day in spring training Rickey had also said to Jackie, "Don't worry about Clay Hopper and his Mississippi background. Don't worry about the fact that he has some deep racial prejudices. Always remember this, Jackie: Prejudice is the world's biggest coward in the face of fact. Proximity—if we can get enough of it—can solve these problems of racial prejudice and bigotry. Perhaps six months of proximity will change Clay Hopper, and make it obvious to him if not to the world that racial prejudice is silly business; it's child stuff."

Jackie watched Hopper disappear through the door, thinking how right Rickey was; prejudice *did* run away from truth. He picked up his duffel bag and started out, the last player to leave the stadium. To his amazement, he found the passageway still blocked by about five hundred yelling, pushing fans. Robinson shouted that he had to catch a plane and yelled for help from the ushers and policemen, but the crowd was so thick they couldn't get through to him. Jackie lifted his bag over his shoulders and tossed it over the heads of some of the fans to a waiting friend, who began to work his way through the crowd. Then Robinson hunched his shoulders and plunged in. Once again the crowd began to hug and kiss him, to rip at his clothes, pat him on the head and shout words of appreciation, to ask questions whose only purpose was to elicit just any comment from the baseball player Montreal had adopted as its own.

Finally Jackie broke through the mob and galloped after the friend who was running with his duffel bag, the crowd in hot, noisy pursuit. Doors opened and windows flew up as townspeople peered out to see the wild commotion. For three blocks Robinson ran, steadily pulling away from the crowd. Then his friend yelled, "Over here," as he pointed to an automobile that cruised slowly along the curb. The automobile had four strangers in it, four fans who realized Jackie's plight. "Jump in, jump in," they shouted. Robinson leaped into the car and landed half in the lap of one of the occupants. Everyone roared with laughter.

"Quite a day, huh?" said the driver.

Robinson looked back at the crowd, most of whom had given up. Only a few youngsters were still trying to outdistance the automobile.

"Yes, quite a day," he said gently, his voice filled with emotion.

Back in the press box at Delorimier Downs, sportswriter

Sam Maltin had his own special description of the kind of day it was.

"It was probably the only day in history that a black man ran from a white mob with love instead of lynching on its mind," he wrote.

2....A Special Kind of Wealth

In his sleep on the plane that night and in his waking moments for days to come Jackie Robinson replayed that Little World Series, savored again those wildly triumphant moments after the final game. That demonstration by the fans—the whole year, in fact—seemed just too story-bookish to be true. As the letters and telegrams of congratulations, the invitations to speak and make public appearances, poured in, Jackie shook his head in amazement, saying to himself often and occasionally aloud, "If I'm not the luckiest guy in the world, I'd like to meet him." It seemed so incredible that he, who two years earlier was a frustrated ex-G.I. whose career seemed headed nowhere in particular, had been touched with the magic wand that brings fame and a life of excitement.

Jackie thought back over his twenty-seven years and was

reminded that in many ways his life had been filled with good fortune. Even during childhood, when he was hungry and dangerously near the web of delinquency, he had been blessed with a special kind of wealth—the limitless courage and deep affection of a mother who never allowed her children to lose faith in God and the belief that hard work is eventually rewarded. His mother, poorly educated but wise in the ways of human beings, had imbued him with pride, with a passionate will to win, and perhaps it was these things as much as his physical gifts that caused Branch Rickey to tap him with that wand.

2

Yes, long before Jackie Robinson entered baseball—long before he was born—the train of events began that led directly to what could now be called good luck: his triumph in organized baseball. Jackie was a pioneer, a crusader, the symbol of a changing order, in 1946, because his mother had been a crusader in her own way, an opponent of the status quo, in 1906. She didn't think of herself as a crusader, but as we listen to her relive those early days, it is obvious that, to retain her self-respect, she had to be.

It was at a Christmas party on the Jim Sasser plantation near Cairo, Georgia in 1903, that Mallie McGriff met Jerry Robinson and, at age fourteen, permitted him to become the first boy to walk her home. For what seemed like an eternity, this shy couple strolled silently across the fields, along a pathway girding the brown fields that in the summer were green with whippoorwill peas, turnip greens and striped watermelons. As they walked along the edge of a pine thicket, a rabbit skittered into the underbrush and Mallie chuckled. Finally Jerry Robinson broke the silence with a bashful declaration: "I sure like you!" and Mallie gave a blushing smile in return.

As Robinson walked her to the porch, Mallie's father stepped to the door and announced brusquely, "You can be on your way now, young man."

"I'll come by and walk you to church Sunday?" Robinson whispered hoarsely—so hoarsely, in fact, that Mallie's father had no difficulty hearing.

"He'll not be walking you to church," the father said sternly. "The very idea, walking home with a boy at your age! I ain't turned you out yet, and when I do everybody will know."

Mallie McGriff looked down at her dress, still high above her knees. How she hated the sight of her kneecaps showing. But it was tradition among the prouder Negro families in these parts that when a young girl was "turned out" her dress would drop below her knees and all the young men would know that she was free to date. Among the proud Negro families, none was prouder than the McGriffs.

Mallie's father had been a slave, and his memories of those days of servitude were vivid; now, even though he and his family still lived in approved peonage, he was trying zealously to prove that Negroes deserved the institution of freedom. Like many another Negro family of that period, the McGriffs established puritanical codes of conduct for their children.

But for all her parents' expressions of disapproval, Mallie knew that she loved Jerry Robinson, and six years later, on the third Sunday in November, 1909, she married him.

Early December was hog-killing time, a festive occasion, and Mallie, now living on the Sasser plantation with her husband, waited eagerly for Jerry and the other workers to come home from the kill. When they arrived, all they had were the liver, lights and "chitterlings," or intestines of the hogs.

"No tenderloin?" asked Mallie. "Not even a backbone or a neckbone?"

Her husband explained that for years Sasser had enforced a ruling that his hog slaughterers were not to take home anything other than the organs of the hog.

Mallie was outraged. "This is worse than slavery," she said, "and we're going to change things. You've practically been raised on this plantation, yet you're little better off than a slave. You're working for wages—twelve dollars a month— and out of that you've got to feed us both."

When Christmas came the young groom went to Sasser to borrow fifteen dollars on his next year's pay. He gave five dollars to his bride to prepare for Christmas. Mallie stared at the money. Her family had been far from wealthy, but five dollars to buy food and gifts for Christmas? Virtually nothing.

"Jerry," she said, "if God wills, I'll make do on five dollars this Christmas. But you're working for wages, and at the end of the year you have nothing to show. You're a good man— strong, intelligent. Stronger, more intelligent than the man you work for. This is not right. You must farm for yourself. Tell Sasser we'll half-crop or we'll leave. But no more of this laboring for twelve dollars a month and then having to beg Sasser before you can pick turnip greens in the field. I'm not used to this."

Prodded constantly by his wife, Robinson eventually rebelled and told the plantation owner that he would stay on the farm only as a half-cropper, and to his surprise, Sasser consented. Robinson was a hard worker, a good farmer, and his family—they soon had three sons—began to have plenty to eat and something to spare. But after nine years of marriage, Mallie faced the tragic realization that in freeing her husband from the shackles of the plantation system she had endangered the family's happiness. With spending money in his pocket, and clothes that put him a notch above most Negro men in the area, Jerry Robinson was drifting away from the farm to the "fast" life of Cairo.

Mallie argued and pleaded, to no avail, but she knew even then that she could not totally condemn her husband. For decades the South had given no real recognition to the Negro family, primarily because the Negro male was important only as a horse is important: he was labor, salable chattel. If a Negro man had a wife and children to support, that was beside the point. Let her get another man. The children belonged to the woman; the man belonged to the system—thus male irresponsibility had become a way of life.

Still, an understanding of what slavery and peonage had done to Negro men was little consolation to Mallie Robinson, who was faced with the unhappy choice of bringing up a family in a household filled with bickering and conflict, or bringing them up alone. Believing that her children, any children, needed a father around, she finally agreed to a reconciliation and it appeared that her marriage was saved. The Robinsons now had four living children—the last one had died in infancy—and when, the following year, Mallie told her husband she was pregnant again, Jerry expressed delight. Mallie knelt that spring night and thanked God for the new harmony and asked His blessing on her family and her unborn child.

At 6:30 P.M. on the last day of January, 1919, Mallie Robinson lay grimacing with pain in their little farm home near Cairo. Because of the terrible flu epidemic no midwives were to be had, and she was attended by a doctor, the first present at any of her deliveries. As she fought to convince him not to use ether, which she feared, and stifled her cries of pain, she pushed into the world a son, Jack Roosevelt Robinson.

When the doctor had gone she struggled weakly to tighten the waistbands about the baby and herself—("Must get that waistband tight or the baby will have an ugly navel,") she thought—as she watched her husband and his brother plodding about unfamiliar chores. Nature had not yet provided milk for the baby, so the men fixed "sugar teats"—sugar mixed with lard wrapped into a tiny piece of cheesecloth. Mallie looked at the lard the men were dropping all over the floor and smiled.

"Bless you, boy," she whispered to her infant. "For you to survive all this, God will have to keep His eye on you."

3

By crop-planting time in 1919, Mrs. Robinson knew that her marriage was hopelessly lost. Jerry wanted to quit farming, for, as he put it, Georgia summers were too hot for his children to be in the fields pulling grass, catching boll weevils and picking cotton and peanuts.

To Mallie the farm meant an abundance of food, adequate shelter, a wholesome atmosphere for the children; Cairo was a threat, not only to whatever was left of their marriage but to the economic security the family enjoyed. She opposed moving.

Six months after Jackie was born, Jerry Robinson told Mallie that he was going to visit a brother in Texas, and that after getting work there, he would send for the family. He asked if he might take their three-year-old daughter, Willa Mae, with him. Mallie was suspicious, having heard that Robinson planned to go to Florida with another woman—but in any case she was not about to let a toddler go along on a job-hunting trip, so she refused to let Willa Mae go. On July 28, 1919—and Mallie Robinson remembers it well— Jerry Robinson left his wife and children, supposedly to catch the eleven-o'clock train for Texas; instead he caught train number 230, north-bound on the Short Line, and went to Florida with another man's wife.

Mallie's parents asked her to return home with her children, but the proud mother refused. Her brother came by and offered to help her harvest the crops. "When you get your half, your family can manage," he said.

The plantation owner had other ideas. He asked angrily why Mallie had not warned him that Robinson planned to leave so he could get the sheriff to stop him.

"The sheriff?" said Mrs. Robinson. "Slavery's over, Mr. Sasser, and that man is free to go where he pleases."

Sasser replied that Mallie was "too uppity for your own good" and advised her that he was keeping all the crop.

Mallie was stunned, for she was counting so heavily on that crop, but she would not ask the plantation owner for mercy.

"Just remember, Mr. Sasser, that the Bible warns that 'Ye shall reap what ye sow,' " she warned.

"You and your damned Bible," said Sasser as he stalked away.

A few days later Mallie was notified that a new family was moving onto the plantation and that she and her children would have to give up their house. Sasser was offering them a rickety little cabin. Mallie wept privately, then scrubbed and dressed her children. With little Jackie in her arms and the other children around her, she walked with dignity off the Sasser farm and got work with a family whose domestic chores she had done before she was married.

Despite the kindness of her employers, Mrs. Robinson was far from happy, and she was full of doubt about the wisdom of trying to raise her family in Georgia. When her preacher, the schoolteacher and other Negroes got together to chat they said that something had "come over" Georgia and the South. Politicians were asking for ballots almost solely on the basis of who hated Negroes most. A revived Ku Klux Klan was terrorizing Negroes and building a political empire. In many places the traditional paternalistic attitude toward the Negro had been replaced by rancor and cruelty.

Even a poorly educated Negro woman could sense these things, although she might not understand them fully, and conclude that the future was not particularly bright for a proud, ambitious Negro in Georgia in 1919. That thousands of Negroes did sense this is borne out by the fact that the decade of 1920 to 1930 produced a wave of Negro exodus from the South.

One of Mallie's brothers had settled in California after serving in the First World War. When he returned to Georgia for a visit, wearing a double-breasted suit with pants that held a crease "sharp enough to cut your throat," Mallie questioned him at length about life in the Far West. She listened more intently than the rest as he boasted, "If you poor Georgia folks want to get a little closer to heaven, come on out to California." Mallie prayed fervently that night and got off her knees with a conviction that God wanted her and her children to go West. So on May 21, 1920, at the age of thirty, Mallie and her children went to the train station with a small army of relatives that her brother had talked into deserting Georgia. The excited travelers stood in the hot Georgia sun, their clothing in a weird assortment of suitcases, baskets, boxes, old trunks and makeshift bundles, staring impatiently up the tracks, waiting for the clatter of the locomotive that would carry them to New Orleans and onward to the West Coast.

Soon Mallie said excitedly, "I hear that freedom train awhistling 'round that bend out yonder!" The train belched its way down the tracks and halted noisily. The Negroes clambered aboard. Despite crying babies, bottle feedings, diaper changing, fights between children, and the like, Mallie found the trip a childhood dream come true. Just beyond the windows of this noisy, unbelievably speedy machine were many of the fabulous places that she had read about in an old geography book.

The group reached Los Angeles at night and Mallie was fascinated. She wrote her former teacher that this city with its great glittering lights was "the most beautiful sight of my whole life. Tell my girl friends that to get here I crossed a river that was so wide you couldn't see from one side to the other, climbed mountains so tall the tops were hidden in the clouds—and that our train was so long that on the sharpest curves you could lean out of the last car and light a cigarette by the fire in the engine."

In Pasadena, the clan from Georgia moved into a ramshackle apartment of three rooms and a kitchen. Mallie and her five children slept in one room—little Jackie in the bed with his mother; her sister and brother-in-law and their two children were in another; her brother, a nephew and her husband's cousin slept in the third room. There was no hot water, no kitchen sink, and the dishes were washed in the tin tub that was also used for baths.

Three days after their arrival, however, Mallie figured she had things organized well enough for her to go to work as a domestic. She arrived at 8:00 A.M. and was working diligently when, at 4:00 P.M., her employer advised her that it was time she went home. Mallie stood on the verge of tears. In Georgia she always had worked from sunup to sundown, and she knew that her work must be unsatisfactory for them to send her home while the sun was still high in the sky. She was overjoyed at the explanation that this was her regular quitting time, for it would enable her to get home in time to help prepare supper for the children and give them some motherly supervision.

Supper for the Robinsons was not much in those days, and would not be for many years to come. A meal of pinto beans and bacon skins, or white navy beans boiled with a slab of salt pork, was considered first class. The moments of greatest delight for the youngsters came when their mother returned from work with a piece of cake or some other goody left over from a party given by her employer.

Soon Mrs. Robinson's first employer left town and she was in desperate need of work. Someone told her about the advertisements domestics could place in the newspaper, so she left her children and set out to walk the several miles in search of the *Pasadena Star News*. When she had difficulty finding it, she stopped to ask directions in a building where she saw a huge sign saying, WELFARE. When she explained to the woman behind the desk what she sought to do, the woman smiled and said, "This is as far as you need go." She opened the door to a room with great piles of clothing and said to Mallie, "Go on in and dress yourself up and pick out some clothing for your children."

Mallie chose a fur-trimmed outfit for herself—the classy kind of outfit that she had never seen worn by a Negro, not even by many of the whites for whom she had worked in Georgia—and decided to wear it home. When she got there, her sister was flabbergasted. "Why, I started not to let you in the house. I looked out the window and saw you coming and I said who on earth is this colored lady and what's she coming up here for?" She was even more flabbergasted when Mallie opened the bundle of clothes for all the children and announced that the woman at the welfare had taken down a lot of information and promised to see that the Robinson family got two grocery orders a week, three quarts of milk a day and an allowance of thirty dollars a month for rent, fuel and other necessary items.

Mallie found herself another job and quickly decided that with her income and the help from the Welfare Department she could get her family out of that crowded apartment. She talked it over with her sister Mary Lou, who was ill and unable to work, and decided that they should buy a lot with two houses on it so her sister could baby-sit for all the children while Mallie worked. By some good fortune, they stumbled upon a Negro man who had purchased a house at 121 Pepper Street, with a lot big enough for a second house. He offered to sell to Mallie because, he said, he wanted someone to occupy the place, since he wouldn't be able to collect insurance on it if something happened to it while it was empty. Mallie moved in, only to learn that it was in an all-white neighborhood. The man had got hold of it by having it purchased by a niece from Texas who looked white, and his fear that something would happen to the house while it was empty was justified—the whites in the neighborhood had threatened to burn it down.

When Mallie and her children moved in, the white neighbors turned their bitterness toward them. When she asked her oldest son, Edgar, to go get a loaf of bread, Edgar strapped on his skates (he had a passion for wheels, and never went anywhere except on skates—later it was a bicycle and then a motorcycle), and sped to the store. A neighbor called the police, who came out to notify Mallie the noise of the skates on the sidewalk was disturbing the neighbors.

"I'm sorry they're so touchy that the noise of skates disturbs them," replied Mrs. Robinson. "But there's no law against skating on the sidewalk, is there?"

"No," said one policeman, "but the man who called us told us that his wife is afraid of colored people."

Mallie smiled and said that she would ask her son to skate around the block in the other direction when she sent him to the store.

A few days later the police were back, saying that this man had complained again that his wife was terrified and hadn't been able to go out of the house since the Negroes moved in.

"Well, I'm afraid that woman will be in her house a lifetime if we've got to give up our house," said Mallie.

Mallie lectured her children sternly on how to behave, for she did not want to give the neighbors just cause to complain. She made little kind gestures toward reaching peace with her neighbors, but their hostility was strong. Some neighbors had drawn up a petition, but upon being advised that they could not force the Negroes out, even if every white family in the area signed the petition, they decided to buy them out. But the petition-signers had no money. They hoped to convince a fairly wealthy widow who lived next door to the Robinsons that she should provide the money. The widow wanted no part of this, however. One day she called Mallie to the fence and said, "You must think I'm awfully mean. I'm not, really. If it wasn't for the other whites in the block I'd be happy to have you as a neighbor. No one ever kept that house so well, and I've watched the way your children behave themselves. Why, I wouldn't care if you lived in my home."

The plan to buy out the Robinsons collapsed when the widow got up at the protest meeting to announce that she wouldn't provide a nickel. But the harassment and abuse of Mallie Robinson and her children was to continue for several years. The biggest agitator was, ironically, the poorest man in the neighborhood. The actions and comments of his children were a graphic and pathetic illustration of the manner in which the poison of prejudice seeps down from generation to generation.

One day when Jackie was about eight his mother sent him out to sweep the sidewalk. The young daughter of this Negro-baiting man was sweeping the walk across the street. She spotted Jackie and began to shout, "Nigger, nigger, nigger boy."

Jackie shouted back that she was "nothing but a cracker."

The girl began to sing a little rhyme: "Soda cracker's good to eat, nigger's only good to beat."

Before this quarrel ended, the girl had shouted to her father, who became involved in a brief rock battle with Jackie. The stone-throwing ended when the man's wife rushed out to scold him for "engaging in a rock fight with a mere child."

Those who recall most intimately the childhood of Jackie Robinson express surprise that he did not end up in a reform school. The grinding poverty, a broken home, a mother away working most of the day, the racial conflict, provided a fertile ground for delinquency. Friends of the family say that it was Mallie's love that inculcated in Jackie and his brothers and sister a sense of dignity and pride that kept them out of severe trouble.

Jackie was still a toddler when Mrs. Robinson told Willa Mae that in order for her to keep her job Jackie would have to be taken to school. Her sister had died just as the second house was about to be built, and Mallie had no one to help look after the children.

"But, Mamma, he ain't big enough," Willa Mae protested. "They won't let him in."

"They've got to let him in," said Mallie. "It's the only way I can be sure he won't get into trouble with me gone. And I've got to be gone or we can't eat."

So Willa Mae went off to kindergarten at Grover Cleveland School with her brother toddling behind her. She came home that day with a note from the teacher advising Mrs. Robinson that little Jack was too young to come to school, especially since he couldn't talk. Mallie got busy that night teaching Jackie to say, "Good morning, Teacher," and sent him back to school the next day, although she was worried because he hadn't done too well at pronouncing the "T." The teacher sent another note complaining that the situation was most irregular, so Mallie went over to explain her plight: "If I have to stay home to watch Jackie, I can't work. If I can't work, we'll have to get more money from welfare. I'm too proud to go down and beg for more money, and there's no sense in putting that burden on the taxpayers as long as I can work. So would it be all right if Willa Mae just put Jackie in the sandbox every morning? He's a mighty good boy. He'll play there without bothering anyone."

The teacher agreed, so for a year Willa Mae brought Jack to school, deposited him in the sandbox and took him home with her—while the kindergarten teacher marveled at the motherly devotion of the six-year-old girl.

She might have marveled more had she seen the fights between Jackie and Willa Mae that took place almost daily at

121 Pepper Street. Mack couldn't stand to have anyone touch his sister, so when Jack battled Willa Mae he battled Jack, and when Mack battled Jack, older brother Frank battled Mack, because Frank thought nothing on earth was so delightful as his baby brother. Yet there was a strong bond of affection, born partly of mutual hardship, that tied all the children together.

The teacher was so impressed by Mallie's desire to work and her devotion to her children that she kept a close eye on Jackie, seeing that he was brought into the room when it rained, and inviting him in on other occasions to join the children when they were playing. One day she noticed that Jackie was frothing at the mouth and that Willa Mae seemed ill. She sent both of them home. Mallie took the children to the doctor, who gave Mallie some pills with the explanation that youngters should take them and that if they got worse he should be called. Mallie suspected that the youngsters were a lot sicker than the doctor indicated. She sent Edgar to the store for two bottles of strawberry pop, and when neither Jackie nor Willa Mae would drink it, she knew they were seriously ill, for there was nothing they considered a bigger treat then strawberry pop. Around midnight Jackie began to gag as if unable to breathe. Mallie went to the kitchen and got a bucket of lard into which she dipped her hand. Then she rammed her fingers into Jackie's mouth and down his throat. She pulled out a rope of phlegm. Mallie sat up all night, pulling phlegm out of the boy's throat. The next morning her sister's child began to froth at the mouth. Mallie had a medical book which she studied frantically, and concluded that the children had diphtheria. She sent for the doctor, who rushed out and agreed that the diagnosis was correct. "If you hadn't used that lard Jackie would be a dead boy by now," he said.

As each Robinson boy grew old enough, he went out to earn, in whatever way possible, money to help the family make ends meet. Mack tried to solve the family's financial problems by becoming a prize fighter. He was sure that he could become another Jack Johnson, but when he came home from the training session before his first fight with his eyes closed, his lips battered and his nose bloody, Mallie told him she preferred poverty to money earned that way.

"From the looks of your face, I can tell God never intended for you to make the kind of money that boxing promoter promised you," she said. So Mack gave up boxing and concentrated on running, for which he was already noted in neighborhood circles.

Meanwhile, Jackie was discovering the delightful life of a boy and a ball. His mother had unraveled some old woolen socks and rolled the strands into a ball which she covered with a rag. Day after day Jackie was out with a stick pounding this rag ball up and down the street.

Not long after Jackie left the sandbox and went to school on a legitimate basis, he announced proudly that his mother could save some money, for she wouldn't have to fix lunch for him any more. Mallie laughed, thinking how he ate like a horse.

"Going on a diet?" she asked.

"No, ma'am," said Jackie proudly. "We've got two baseball teams at school and the kids on one team said they'd split their lunches with me if I'd play on their side."

Later Jackie convinced his mother that he was old enough to handle a paper route, so he got up at four o'clock on Sunday mornings to sell the *Los Angeles Times* and the *Los Angeles Examiner*. He and his brothers did all manner of odd jobs, from shining shoes to selling hot dogs. Then Jackie's uncle agreed to give him a dollar a week for helping him water shrubbery in the evening. The neighbors on Pepper Street still chuckle about the way a pigeon-toed lad would rush home every Saturday shouting, "Mamma, come meet me. Come meet me, mamma. I've got a dollar for you!"

4

No one who knew the Jackie Robinson of 1946, tight-lipped and unflinching in the face of provocation, could doubt that his teen-age years in Pasadena had tempered him for his role as a guinea pig. In ways that the public and the baseball world had not yet seen, those boyhood days of poverty, of growing up in a town that he hated because it crushed the hopes and dreams of Negro youngsters, were making indelible impressions on his psychic makeup.

There were the unforgettable mornings when Mrs. Robinson got up in the winter darkness and left for work before the children had stirred, unable to get breakfast for her children because her employers were waiting for theirs. Jackie and Willa Mae dressed themselves, often to trudge off to school without breakfast. Those sandwiches his classmates gave him to play on their team were often the only food Jackie got all day. He and Willa Mae would rush home to ask in unison, "Mack, you didn't eat all the bread, did you?" As Mack would shake his head "no," Jackie and Willa Mae would race to the breadbox; then they would sweeten a glass of water and gorge themselves—if the bread and sugar lasted—on what had become a favorite and basic item in their diet.

Too often, however, there wasn't even bread and sweet water, so they sat hungry, hoping their mother would bring home some leftovers. When she did not, she would count her money carefully, allotting herself enough for carfare, and then send a child to the store to get day-old buns and, when possible, a nickel's worth of sugar.

Although Mallie did not receive much pay for her domestic work, her employers were generous in other ways. When they held a big party they would hire Willa Mae as extra help, and it was amazing what a difference a couple of dollars could make in the budget of a poor family. Mallie frequently came home with used clothing passed along by her employers, or friends of her employers who had children about the ages of Mallie's. The Robinsons—like many another Negro family—would have spent many days cold and hungry during the 1920's and 1930's had it not been for this kind of generosity.

Even the kindergarten teacher occasionally came to school with a bag of second-hand clothing for Jackie and Willa Mae, and the Robinson family rejoiced. Perhaps there never was a madder scramble than the Robinson boys tussling over a newly arrived pair of used trousers, each boy claiming that they fit him perfectly and thus should be his.

5

Out of this atmosphere of poverty, racial antagonism, broken homes and general resentment on the part of the have-nots for the haves, an atmosphere which has spawned the frightful youth gangs of today, there emerged a street gang in Jackie's youth—the Pepper Street gang. Not vicious and murderous like those which plague the nation's big-city slums today, but a mischievous group of youngsters expressing the general frustrations of youth as well as the specific frustrations of minority-group youngsters in a community beset by many forms of discrimination and segregation, some of them subtle, some far from subtle. A favorite prank of the Pepper Street gang was to go to the private golf course and hide behind some grapevines adjacent to a fairway where a reasonably good drive would come over the hill and out of sight of the golfer. One boy would dash into the fairway, pocket the ball, and then hide in the nearby fields with the gang, practically convulsed with laughter as a puzzled golfer would stand in the middle of the fairway screaming that it was a "perfect drive, right down the middle at least 225 yards," and that for the life of him he couldn't figure out what happened to that ball.

Later a gang member would go to the clubhouse and try to peddle one shiny golf ball at a bargain rate.

Chasing golf balls, illegally and legally, was just one of the methods Jackie had devised to help keep hunger away from his household. Members of the gang would perch outside the baseball park waiting for someone to hit a home run. Mack and other members recall that even in those days Jackie had an uncanny ability to "play the hitters"; he always seemed to be standing where the baseballs landed.

In his teen-age years, Jackie frequently found himself in trouble with the law. Another favorite stunt of the Pepper

Street gang was to perch on the curb just before going home, with the young men seeing who could hurl a clod of dirt most accurately at passing automobiles. This game would continue until a police car arrived, when members of the gang would fire their final salvo at it and then run helter-skelter toward their homes. Jackie was always too fast for the policemen, but some lead-footed member of the group inevitably got caught. The policeman would show up at Jackie's house with a list of the names of the offenders, and Jackie would be hauled off to the police station for a lecture by Captain Morgan, who was in charge of youth.

The Pepper Street gang included boys of Mexican, Japanese, Negro and Caucasian background, and Morgan would call each racial group in separately for his lecture. Afterwards the boys would compare notes with great laughter. Morgan would say to the Japanese: "If you keep associating with these Negroes they're going to get you into trouble"; and to the Negroes: "If you keep running around with these Japs you're going to wind up in the reformatory"; and to the Caucasians: "A white boy is just asking for trouble when he keeps running around with these colored fellows."

Morgan's references to race never bothered Jack particularly, because he felt that the captain was reasonably decent considering the number of times gang members were hauled before him, and the number of times that his mother was at the police station lecturing the captain on her expectations that policemen would treat her boys fairly. The policemen knew, too, that the Robinson boys would catch the devil from Mallie if anyone could convince her that her boys had done wrong.

On one occasion, members of the gang became fed up with the racial gibes and sarcasm of a man who still hadn't reconciled himself to the presence of Negroes in the neighborhood. So the boys spread his newly sodded lawn with tar. When Mallie came home the angry man was waiting to tell her that if she didn't do something he'd press the police to act. Mallie quizzed Jackie, who said that he wasn't the culprit, but that maybe Mack had helped spread the tar. Mack said he was present but that the actual tar-spreader was a Japanese lad, who passed the buck to a Mexican, and so forth. Mallie talked to the parents, who permitted her to round up all the youngsters and march them to the man's home, where they were ordered to get the tar off his lawn. There are people in the neighborhood who laugh to this day about the spectacle of a half-dozen teen-age boys sitting on a thickly tarred lawn with a pail of kerosene and several rags, some trying to swab up the tar, others trying to remove it by clipping the grass with scissors.

Recreational activities were virtually nonexistent for Negro youngsters in Pasadena in those days. They were permitted to swim only once a week at Brookside Park. In neighboring Monrovia, Negroes were allowed to use the pools only on Monday. As a result, the Pepper Street gang repeatedly violated the law by swimming in the city water reservoir. One day the gang stopped by the golf course to hound a few golf balls, but decided hastily that the hundred-degree temperature was too hot for this kind of activity. So they went to a nearby grove where they pilfered a few oranges, a dangerous activity in view of the fact that the groves were watched closely and that they were certain to go to jail if caught. With their bags of oranges they moved on to the reservoir for a swim. The gang splashed around for a while, then lounged in the sun for a delicious lunch of stolen oranges and grapes. Soon they plunged back into the reservoir.

Suddenly there was a frantic rush out of the water as they heard a voice boom out, "Looka there—niggers swimming in my drinking water!"

The sheriff and some deputies had surrounded the reservoir and now ran, guns drawn, to round up the youngsters.

As the policemen were about to haul their catch off to jail, a deputy aimed his gun at the hillside and said, "Come out or I'll shoot." For many years the Pepper Street gang would laugh about the sight of one of their members crawling stark naked from behind the bushes, where he might have escaped arrest had not this eagle-eyed policeman noticed a bush that trembled with the young man's fidgeting.

The roundup over, sixteen young men were crammed into one small room at the police station. When, after four hours, a Negro lad claimed he was "so hot and thirsty and hungry I'm gonna faint," the sheriff said sarcastically to a deputy, "The coon's hungry. Go buy a watermelon." When the deputy returned the sheriff passed out chunks of the melon and then took photographs of the Negroes eating it.

Just before sunset he opened the door and waved toward the distant hill with his gun. "Now, git toward that hill," he said angrily, "and when that sun goes down I don't wanta find a one of you in sight."

Thirty-two feet scampered down the hot road so speedily that, as the boys liked to tell it, the sun was higher in the sky when they went over the hill than when they left the jail.

3....Saturday's Hero

During those lean years of the early 1930's, Jackie Robinson and his family had one consolation: there was plenty of that company that misery loves. Those were unhappy years for millions of American families, black and white, urban and rural, rich and poor. So many white people were unemployed that Negroes with even sporadic employment were found largely in the domestic categories. There were no professional fields open to Negroes (other then teaching in Negro schools in the South and preaching in Negro churches) that could even partly assuage the growing thirst for recognition, for status, particularly among Negro youth. Luckily for Robinson, this need for a feeling of importance, for knowing that you belong to something and that you belong all the way, did not become a wading deeper and deeper into the morass of delinquency.

For many years, athletics had been the salvation of Negro youngsters who found the doors to Boy Scout, YMCA and other activities closed, sometimes politely, sometimes rudely. They were being driven by physical hunger, by psychological rejection, to dominate boxing; had begun to assert themselves in track; had made a beginning in football with the exploits of such great players as Bobby Marshall at Minnesota, Fritz Pollard at Brown, Paul Robeson at Rutgers and Duke Slater at Iowa. It soon became apparent that athletics would be the salvation of Jackie Robinson, would help him to burn off the anger that Pasadena built up in him every day.

Blessed with speed and marvelous coordination, Robinson became an athletic standout at Muir Technical High School, although the scouts did not single him out immediately as a potentially great college star. Coaches who considered Negro prospects clearly preferred those who played like demons but were meek enough to keep their mouths shut. Robinson obviously did not fit the latter requirement, for even in his high school days the word was quickly spread around the circuit that he was "too aggressive," "cocky," "arrogant," and "uppity."

Robinson's coaches were delighted with his competitive spirit, however, for it infected the entire squad. He made Muir Tech a high school terror in several sports, for he was the holler guy, the sparkplug, the kind of clutch performer extolled in the pulp magazines. As a result, every team on Muir Tech's athletic schedule walked onto the football field, the basketball court, the baseball diamond, with basically simple instructions: "Stop Robinson."

Many high school players figured (as supposedly mature men would later) that the safest and easiest way to "get Robinson" would be to get his goat, to make him so angry he would lose his coordination, his ability to concentrate on the game. In the tough games, some of the teams were not above making derogatory remarks about his color, his ancestry, his economic status. Usually, however, this had the effect of spurring him to superb performances.

But Glendale High School proved that there were ways to get Robinson. During his senior year, Muir Tech met Glendale in the Rose Bowl for the conference championship. On the opening kickoff, Robinson was tackled after a modest run-back. As he was getting to his feet, a Glendale player lunged into him, breaking two of Robinson's ribs and forcing him out of the game. Glendale went on to intercept three passes thrown by Robinson's substitute, and won 19 to 0.

Finding himself less than hounded by the ivory hunters of collegiate football's bigger leagues, Jackie made plans to go to Pasadena Junior College after graduation from Muir Tech.

The one person who was bitterly disappointed that Jack wasn't offered full scholarships and other assistance by one of the bigger universities was his brother Frank, who got a vicarious thrill out of Jackie's athletic exploits. Frank was sickly and unable to compete himself, so he had virtually made himself an extension of Jackie. He was a constant counsel to his younger brother, telling him which players to watch on the opposing team, shouting from the sidelines to Jackie to do this or that, to be careful here or there—so much so, in fact, that fans occasionally commented on the way "that colored fellow seems to think he's coaching the team." Frank made it clear in conversations with his colleagues that his brother Jackie was good enough to play anywhere if given the chance.

"Why, Jack can run circles around anybody in that Notre Dame backfield. It just burns me up that a Negro can't play football at places like Notre Dame. But we'll show 'em, you just wait till next fall and we'll show 'em."

So when Jack went out to practice that first fall at Pasadena, Frank was on the sidelines shouting encouragement. Frank was almost a father to Jackie, and much of the effort Jack expended was from a conscious desire to make Frank proud.

In an early practice session, Jackie tried a bit too hard. He tried to run around left end, but when the end forced him near the out-of-bounds line, he tried to cut back sharply on a slippery turf and caught his foot in a hole. As he twisted in pain two tacklers hit him. He limped about for a while, then finished the practice session. Later, the trainer found that he had broken his ankle.

So Jackie Robinson began his collegiate career on the bench, agonizing with a team that sputtered and stopped, that just couldn't get an offense going. Before the season was half over —and before his ankle had healed properly—Jackie was back in practice. He played first-string quarterback during the last six games of the season, all of which Pasadena won except for a scoreless tie with Compton. Scouts were deciding, a bit late, that the skinny kid from Muir Tech was more than just a flash in the pan.

In fact, the basketball season convinced them that Robinson was a potentially great all-around athlete, for he was the team's top scorer and led the team to one of its best seasons in years. The scouts liked the way Robinson fought back, the fact that he seemed at his best when the pressure was greatest.

Long Beach Junior College came to Pasadena in January, 1938, determined to box in the Negro star, and almost precipitated a major riot. This is the *Pasadena Chronicle's* report of that incident:

"With Jackie Robinson going to town in several different lines . . . Pasadena and Long Beach climaxed the renewal of their traditional rivalry last Saturday night by staging a riot in the local gym after Pasadena won, 54 to 47.

"Robinson, besides coming off with high point honors for the evening, also came off top man in his personal war with Sam Babich, substitute Viking forward.

"Babich, the stormy petrel of the Long Beach squad, started a one-man campaign against Robinson as soon as he was inserted in the game . . . The two continually fouled each other all through the last half and at the conclusion of the game, had it out.

"Babich walked over to Robinson, asked him if he wanted to make something of it, and when Jackie naturally said,

'Sure,' lashed out with a right hook that landed just over Robinson's eye. The next moment Babich was lying on the floor of the gym with Robinson on top of him and sporadic fighting had broken out all over the gym."

After policemen and coaches broke up the fracas, the student body president at Long Beach went to the Bulldogs' dressing room and apologized to Robinson. He asked if Jackie would shake hands with Babich for photographers so as to dispel any notion that deep bitterness existed between the schools.

"Sure," said Jackie. "I'm not angry at anyone."

He walked to the Long Beach dressing room only to find that Babich refused to shake hands. As several Long Beach players turned angrily on their teammate, Robinson strode away. The student body president followed, apologizing for "the poor sportsmanship of one member of our team. Please don't hold it against the entire Long Beach student body."

By the spring of 1938, sports writers in the Los Angeles area had begun to realize that at Pasadena, in the shadows of the Rose Bowl where so many grid greats had cavorted, there was a mighty fine athletic specimen. Robinson, the highly touted football and basketball star, was now pulling the iron-man stunt of serving as the sparkplug of both the track and baseball teams.

Late in the spring Robinson and his coaches were faced with what seemed an impossible dilemma. On the Saturday afternoon of the conference track meet at Pomona, the Pasadena baseball team was scheduled to play a championship game at Glendale. The coaches agreed that even Robinson couldn't be in two places at once. They asked Jackie if he wanted to make the choice. He didn't. He loved baseball, but he also loved to run. In fact, observers seemed to sense that the part of baseball he loved most was running the bases. Finally the Pasadena coaches worked out an arrangement whereby Robinson could almost be in two places at the same time. Officials at the track meet agreed that if he would come to Pomona early, they would supervise him in the broad jumps and then he could drive to Glendale for the baseball game.

Robinson got to Pomona about an hour before the track meet was scheduled to start. "Awfully nice of you to let me do this," he said to an official. "I just feel I couldn't miss that baseball game. Don't know that I'll hit a lick today, but I'd feel awfully bad if the team lost and I wasn't there."

Even as he expressed open and modest doubt, Robinson could feel steely determination building up inside himself. Sports writers talk of that intangible thing called *desire*, that great emotional surge that makes it possible for a mediocre team to be, on a certain crucial day, a great one; that fired-up urge that makes Davids slay Goliaths, inferior boxers lick champions, slow-armed castoffs hurl no-hitters. Robinson had it. The lean, sinewy boy toed the mark, then sped down the runway. As he approached the take-off board, the muscles in his legs rippled with tension and he sprang into the air, flailing his arms and legs.

"That, sir, was a fair-to-middling leap," said one official to the other.

"I'll say," was the reply as the official stretched the tape. "Twenty-three feet, six! Nobody will top that today."

There was a low gasp from a few early spectators who had gathered around to watch. Robinson was standing a few feet away, his sweating, muscular body gleaming in the bright sun, looking into the distance as if unaware of the spectators' admiration or even their presence.

The news that he had exceeded twenty-three feet filled Robinson with even greater desire. Once again he dashed down the track and leaped, his eyes shut tight, his teeth gritted, his limbs churning frantically. When he crunched down in the soft dirt the officials rushed up eagerly with the tape.

"My God," said one. "Twenty-four, six!"

Robinson trotted back to the mark and crouched like a sprinter, then he dashed toward the jump pit with blazing speed. When he felt his foot hit the jump board just right, he called upon every ounce of energy he possessed to propel himself through the air. It was a prodigious leap.

Robinson was putting on a sweater as the official stretched the tape.

"Twenty-five feet, six and a half inches," said the official.

Jackie had set a new world record for the broad jump by a junior college athlete.

He sprinted to the car for the drive to Glendale. His waiting friend, Jack Gordon, raced the motor noisily, then spun gravel behind him in the take-off. As they reached the highway, Robinson began to laugh, slapping himself on the thigh.

"That's the limit," he said. "The absolute limit. Wait till Frank and Mamma hear that I just beat Mack's broad-jump record!"

A few hours later the baseball team was sharing Robinson's joy. From the shortstop position where he fielded brilliantly, from the bases where he ran daringly, Jackie helped the Bulldogs to the baseball championship. It was a glorious climax to a season in which he had batted .417, stolen twenty-five bases in twenty-four games and was named the most valuable junior college player in Southern California. But college baseball did not attract large crowds or much newspaper publicity, so no one gave more than a passing thought to a newspaper item that quoted Jimmy Dykes, manager of the Chicago White Sox at the time, as saying to Robinson's coach: "That boy could play major league baseball at a moment's notice."

In the fall of 1938, with no broken bones to hobble him, Robinson became a football sensation as he led Pasadena to eleven straight victories and the junior college championship. He scored 131 points and gained over 1,000 yards from scrimmage. He was the fire, the strategist, the multiple threat on what old-timers still swear was the best football team ever assembled at a junior college.

In the season opener against Santa Ana, Jackie galloped 83 yards with a punt and kicked a field goal. Against San Bernadino he ran for three touchdowns and passed for three more.

He dashed for three tallies as the Bulldogs racked up Ventura, 27 to 6.

Jackie approached the game with Taft Junior College with misgivings, partly because Taft was always a tough opponent but primarily because the game was to be played at Taft. As far as Jackie was concerned, the town might as well have been in Mississippi, judging from the signs on business places announcing, WE DO NOT SOLICIT NEGRO TRADE, and even a general warning, NEGROES, DON'T LET THE SUN SET ON YOU HERE.

As Robinson feared, a few spectators hurled racial gibes at him, but he followed Frank's advice to forget the crowd and play football. Jack knew that Frank was worried about the Taft crowd, though, for he had seen him tuck under his topcoat the little jack hammer that he used for changing tires. The game was bitterly contested, but Pasadena had too much power and crushed Taft 27 to 0.

Against mighty Compton, Robinson set 40,000 fans to marveling as he ran for 15 yards to cap a 56-yard scoring drive, intercepted a pass and then threw for a score, and finally tallied again on a 45-yard romp.

Jackie Robinson was becoming a legend. In Los Angeles, people who claimed to know about football talked not about UCLA or Southern Cal, but about "that colored boy out at Pasadena that they say is better than Grange."

San Francisco sports writers figured that the advance buildup for Robinson was utterly ridiculous, so they went out with a "show me" attitude when the Bulldogs invaded Kezar Stadium on November 11 to play San Francisco Junior College. Robinson showed them. The first time he got his hands on the ball he swivel-hipped 75 yards to a touchdown without an opponent laying a hand on him. A few minutes later, on the play in which he used his dazzling speed to best advantage, Robinson sprinted to the outside, faked the defensive end so beautifully that the latter was left sliding empty-handed on his belly, then raced 55 yards to a touchdown. But a teammate was caught clipping, so the run was nullified. A few plays later, however, the dazzling tailback caught a punt at midfield and raced through the San Francisco Bears. After passing for a couple of touchdowns, Robinson ran from scrimmage 20 yards out, and as he drove with his knees churning high, as he twisted out of the grasp of practically every man on the San Francisco team, he was the perfect picture of an athlete who didn't know how to coast, to take it easy.

At the end of the third quarter, when Pasadena coach Tom Mallory took Robinson out of the game, the San Francisco fans and even those cynical newspapermen stood to give him a tumultuous ovation. But with San Francisco hopelessly behind, and no Jackie Robinson to watch, the game became unbearably dull, even for the officials. One sports writer claims that in the middle of the fourth quarter the head linesman strode over to Coach Mallory and said, "I know this is a most irregular request, but I sure wish you would put Robinson back in. I want to see that guy run some more."

One reason why many major colleges were not beating the bushes for Negro football stars in the early thirties was that coaches feared Negroes might be more trouble than help. They brought on worries about schedules, for dozens of border state and Deep South schools would not play teams with Negroes, and about hotel and restaurant facilities. There was also the problem of team morale, for many people had been thoroughly indoctrinated in the notion that under no circumstances was a Negro to be placed in a position of authority over a white man. Politicians, civil service agents, factory superintendents, union stewards and virtually every straw boss with any degree of "social acumen" knew that you did not violate this code unless you were willing to face "trouble." The same code was applied to athletics in the form of unwritten assumptions that in football, Negroes didn't play quarterback, and if they did, they didn't call signals; they didn't play first-string unless clearly superior to white players; they were not to hog the headlines, and they were to be "considerate" enough of the welfare of the team to "take it easy" where social functions were concerned—which usually meant trumping up a "previous engagement" as an excuse for not joining in the festivities.

Coach Mallory found out what these taboos, these racial pit-
falls meant when six white kids from Oklahoma joined the
Bulldogs. In those days Jim Crow was rigidly enforced in
Oklahoma (no Negroes were at the University of Oklahoma,
let alone playing on the Sooner football team), so these six
players had had almost no contact with Negroes. They decided not to challenge Robinson and Ray Bartlett, first-string
Negro end, but they were pretty rough on the Negro substi-
tutes, who took their troubles to Robinson and Bartlett.

"Coach, I hate to bring this issue up," Robinson said, "but
I think someone better tell the Oklahoma fellows that this is
California and we don't go for that racial mess out here."

"Racial mess?" said Mallory. "Why, those fellows have expressed nothing but the highest regard for you and Ray."

"I know," Bartlett said. "But they're making life miserable
for the Negro subs."

"And the point we want to make," Robinson added, "is
that they are decent to us because we're first string. But you
know it takes a lot more than first-stringers to make a winning football team. I think the law ought to be laid down
right now that there will be no racial bickering on this
squad."

"Oh, I don't know," Mallory said, obviously trying to figure
out how to handle the situation.

"Well," Robinson said impetuously, "if it isn't important
enough to get straight at the outset, about the only thing
Bartlett and I can do is transfer to Compton Junior College."

That did it. Compton was Pasadena's main rival, and Mallory was horror-struck at the notion of Robinson and Bartlett
playing against him. He said he would talk to the Oklahoma
six immediately.

Robinson remembers that experience as one of his first major lessons in the flimsy nature of bigotry—and in the subtle
art of good human relations.

Coach Mallory laid down the law and the Oklahoma fellows became more than decent. We saw that here was a case
where a bit of firmness prevented what could have grown
into an ugly situation. I learned that people tend to carry

old prejudices with them and put them into practice—un-less someone is strong enough to impose a new set of values. I concluded that whether it is a coach barking out the rules or a statute declaring a new standard for society, the vast majority will fall in line with the rules or the law, provided they are based on reason and justice.

I learned, however, that you have to do a lot of things to make change palatable to people. People *can* lose their prejudices when they get to know another group—provided that other group is not doing things to reinforce the prejudices. So I decided that Bartlett and I had a responsibility to do something to make the Oklahoma fellows feel that they had nothing to fear from Negroes—that they were just as valuable to the team as we were.

One Oklahoma boy was a big tackle who had never scored a point in all his years in football. In one game, after we worked up a lead to coast on, I made up a play. I shifted the end back and made the tackle eligible to receive a pass. We caught the opposition sleeping, and when that big tackle hugged in that pigskin for a touchdown he was happier than any kid you ever saw with his Christmas toys. That tackle was a terror the rest of the season, slashing open holes big enough to drive a Mack truck through.

That convinced me that it was smart to share the glory—that in the final analysis white people were no worse than Negroes, for we were all afflicted by much the same pride, jealousy, envy and ambition. So I got a real thrill out of making up plays to give the blocking back or a lineman a chance to score, to get his name in the papers. It paid off handsomely, too, for there were crucial moments when one of those teammates would come into the huddle saying, "If you call 41A I'll clear the path." And he would, too—sometimes he'd open up a hole so big I could practically walk for a touchdown.

Now recruiters for the major colleges descended upon Pepper Street, talking about pocket money of the sort a poor Negro boy from Georgia had never heard of. There was one recruiter, a wealthy businessman from Fresno, who offered not only to make things comfortable for Robinson, but to get a scholarship for any girl friend he chose and also to provide an apartment near his alma mater for Jackie's mother. Robinson turned him down. A recruiter from another big West Coast school made an even more fantastic offer. When Jackie explained that he had discussed the matter at length with his mother and his brother Frank, and had decided that a good education would be best for him in the long run and that he ought to get it at UCLA, in the area where he would probably be hunting a job, the recruiter said to Frank: "Well, let me make you another proposition. This may sound strange, but if Jackie won't play for us, the least we can hope for is that he won't play for UCLA or any other West Coast Conference team. I think I can make you a firm commitment to pay his tuition and all his living expenses at any school he wants to attend back East, or any school any place else, just so long as it's not a West Coast team." Frank laughed in the man's face.

Jackie was going to UCLA, not because he figured the education there was better than at some other institutions, but because he knew it would break Frank's heart if he attended a school so far away that Frank would not be able to see the games. As it turned out, Frank never got to see his brother play big-time football. On the morning of May 10, 1939, Frank rode his motorcycle to Pepper Street to tell his mother that he was going to sell it because it was more than he could afford, now that he had a wife and children to support. Before he left, however, he got a telephone call informing him that he had been accepted in a motorcycle club and became so elated that he decided not to sell his machine, but to trade it in on a newer one.

That afternoon Jackie was playing whist at the home of one of his buddies when another friend, Carl Anderson, rapped on the door to say that there was an important call for Jackie at his house. The caller had thought the whist game was at Anderson's.

Jackie went to the telephone to get a brief and somewhat cryptic report that "your brother just got hurt on a cycle so you'd better get down to the police station." Jack ran back to the whist game to tell them that he had to leave.

"My brother was in an accident; fell off a cycle."

"Is it serious, Jackie?" asked a young woman.

"No, I'm sure it isn't. It's got to be Edgar and his bicycle, and I don't think there's any way to kill him. That guy's been hurt nineteen hundred times. Bashed into a car not long ago and got his neck almost cut off. But he sailed through. Nothing could kill him."

Jackie went to the police station and was told to go to the hospital, where he found, to his great shock, that the injured brother was Frank. His mother was already there, weeping softly.

"Is he hurt real bad, Mamma?"

"I don't know, Jack, but it seems real bad. He seems to be in an awful lot of pain."

Jack went quietly into the room and saw his brother in agony.

"Mother, Mother!" Frank was crying, "can't stand it . . . Don't prolong my agony, Mother. Ask the doctor if you can just turn me over and let me die in peace."

Jackie dashed out of the hospital sobbing. He ran home and fell into bed, pulling the pillows over his head.

His brother, who had meant so much to him as advisor and inspirer, was dying. The thought of sports at UCLA—or anywhere—without Frank was almost unbearable.

The next morning Jackie sat quietly, stupefied, as his mother spoke again and again of how Frank had died in so much pain.

"Oh, if only I had turned him over and let him die like he wanted to," Mrs. Robinson would say.

Jackie Robinson had come to the first of those inevitable sadnesses of life.

Jackie's first days at UCLA were not happy ones, not only because he was without Frank's guidance, but because he had become involved in a public ruckus and been arrested. As a result, there were some at UCLA who cautiously regarded him as a troublemaker, a ne'er-do-well who just happened to know how to play football.

The trouble that produced this feeling sprang almost out of nowhere a few weeks before he entered college, when Jackie was driving home from a softball game with Bartlett and a few other buddies. Suddenly a car sped up behind them, careened between two cars and cut in front of Bartlett's, almost forcing them to collide head-on with another car.

"Jesus Christ, did you see that fool?" Bartlett asked rhetorically as he stepped on the accelerator and sped up to the stoplight, where he pulled alongside the man who had almost forced them into a collision. Before Jackie knew what was happening, Bartlett had jumped from behind the wheel and dashed over to the other car, driven by a white man, to shout, "What the hell are you trying to do, kill everybody in Pasadena?"

"Listen, boy, you drive your car and I'll drive mine."

"Buddy, don't I look pretty big to be a boy?" Wham! Bartlett had slapped the driver.

The white man jumped out of his car; Robinson and the other softball players jumped out of theirs. The man looked at Bartlett and his buddies and said, "Well, I'm the only white guy here, and I'm not foolish enough to try to fight all of you."

"What do you mean, all of us?" said Robinson. "This is between you and Bartlett and we're not in it."

"Naw, I won't fight in this area with all these colored people, but I'll fight him anywhere else."

People were gathering from all directions, for this was a busy street, and the argument was holding up traffic. A young police officer was moving through the crowd, his pistol in his hand, shouting to the youngsters who had gathered around to "Go on home, get out of here."

Woodrow Cunningham, who had been a member of the Pepper Street gang, was passing by. He ran up to see what was going on, and the policeman grabbed him and pushed him backwards. Cunningham shouted angrily, "What are you doing pushing me around? I haven't done anything."

Robinson knew that Cunningham had a sharp temper, and the policeman seemed extremely nervous for a man with a pistol in his hand, so Robinson jumped between Cunningham and the policeman saying. "Take it easy, Woodrow, take it easy." Robinson then felt a hand grasp him by the arm and a voice say: "You're under arrest."

The policeman waved his hand around the crowd, saying to others, "And you're under arrest, and you're under arrest." Robinson soon was on his way to jail.

His friends called John Thurman, baseball coach at Pasadena, who came down and posted a twenty-five-dollar bond for him; he was charged with blocking the sidewalk and resisting arrest.

The white man whom Bartlett had slapped told Thurman that Jackie was "guilty of nothing, so I'd be perfectly willing to testify in his behalf."

"That's mighty decent of you," said Thurman, "but I don't think that will be necessary."

The Pasadena coaches advised Robinson to forget the incident because they were sure the whole thing would be dropped.

"What do you mean, dropped?" asked Robinson. "Does that mean that nothing will be in the newspapers?"

He was assured that if the charges were dropped almost certainly there would be nothing in the papers, and he forgot the incident.

In the fall, when he was notified that his case would come up in Pasadena police court, he was advised not to show up in court because the whole dispute had been worked out. Robinson was shocked to pick up the *Los Angeles Times* of October 19, 1939, and read that his bond was forfeited when he failed to appear in police court to answer charges of obstructing the sidewalk. A charge of resisting officer John C. Hall was dismissed by Judge Herbert Farrell.

Robinson felt sick inside when he read this story. He was even sicker when he read the other newspapers and found that they not only carried stories about the incident, but were using sports gimmicks to make the story more sensational.

"GRIDIRON PHANTOM LIVES UP TO NAME," said one page-one headline. "City officials and UCLA's gridiron opponents were warming the same mourner's bench yesterday—and pondering the futility of trying to out-maneuver Jackie Robinson, the Bruins' pigskin-packing phantom," said the story, which went on to declare that police court officials had found Robinson so slippery they couldn't get him in to stand trial and therefore his bond had been forfeited.

These were stories that Robinson never could quite live down at UCLA, even though he was to become perhaps the most illustrious athlete in the history of that institution. These stories stamped him as a troublemaker even though his relations with everyone at the university were good. But because of this incident the newspapermen were always looking for similarly sensational stories. Some manufactured them when they didn't occur. For example, they spread as fact rumors that a bitter feud existed between Robinson and Kenny Washington, another great Negro backfield star on the 1939 football team. One newspaperman wrote that after one game Robinson and Washington engaged in a bitter, bloody, knock-down-drag-out battle in an alley. Robinson laughed at the stories, denying that there was any feud whatever. "At least you can give me credit for having common sense," he said to his friends. "And nobody with common sense is going to fight a big guy like Kenny Washington."

Even as he tried to shrug the rumors off, Jackie was beginning to understand how lives fall into a pattern, how yesteryear's mistake often must be paid for through the ages. A policeman arrests a boy of ten for stealing an apple and that boy becomes a prime suspect fifteen years later when someone ransacks a building; similarly no newspaperman was likely to give Jackie Robinson the benefit of the doubt at any time he might hear some rumor of misbehavior.

As the 1939 season opened, the spotlight was on Robinson, but he did little to meet his advance billing as the most dangerous backfield man on the West Coast when the Bruins squeaked through the opener with a 6 to 2 triumph over Texas Christian. The next week end, however, football fans and other West Coast coaches got an idea of what they were in for when Robinson dashed 65 yards for the winning touchdown as UCLA stopped Washington, 14 to 7.

Still, UCLA was something of a dark horse. It was generally conceded that the forward wall was not of championship caliber, and that UCLA would make trouble for the championship contenders like Southern Cal and Stanford only if Robinson, Washington and Company could control the ball with their offensive heroics.

The Stanford game was next, and the UCLA faithful waited eagerly, knowing that this game would give some real indication as to where their team was going. It was obvious from the outset that Stanford's Indians were unwilling to cooperate in the building of any black Horatio Algers. They trotted into Stanford's stadium four backfield men who, a year later, were to be recognized as one of the great offensive combinations of all time: quarterback Frankie Albert; a bone-crushing fullback named Norm Standlee, who ran in the tradition of Ernie Nevers and Bobby Gryson; and two speedy, shifty halfbacks named Pete Kmetovic and Hugh Gallarneau. This Stanford team was just getting the experience, the poise and confidence that would give it the conference championship and a Rose Bowl invitation the next year—and it outcharged, outsmarted and outfought the favorite Bruins from the opening kick-off.

With only five minutes left in the game, the Indians were leading, 14 to 7, and the Bruins' attack continued to sputter. UCLA coach Babe Horrell refused to discard his much-criticized strategy of using Robinson more as a decoy than as a ball carrier. Horrell argued that when the swift halfback went in motion toward the sidelines, he took two defending players with him—"and who've we got that can take out two defending players with one block?" Horrell also argued that with Robinson fading out as a decoy he opened up the opposition's defense for plunges by Kenny Washington and by Bruin fullback Leo Cantor. But Stanford's tricky, shifting defense upset this strategy time after time, with Washington carrying the ball twenty times for a net gain of a mere 25 yards. On the other hand, Robinson had carried it only four times for a net gain of 62.

So with five minutes left, Bruin fans sucked in their nostrils and forgot the scent of roses, for the team's Bowl hopes would be killed by a loss to Stanford. About all Stanford had to do now was stall out the time, and a great victory was theirs. But quarterback Albert neglected to play it safe, and Robinson— old never-say-die Number 28—set the stage for a Frank Merriwell finish.

When the Indians pushed the ball just inside Bruin territory, Albert got visions of another touchdown. He faded back to strike for a tally, flinging the ball downfield toward halfback Jim Groves. Groves and Robinson leaped high on the Bruin 30-yard line, but Robinson, the spring of a broad jumper and a basketball star in his sinewy legs, leaped higher. As he hit the turf with the pigskin, he squirmed out of the clutching hands of Groves and was off like a sprinter, bobbing and weaving, side-stepping and dashing, finally halted by Albert's shirttail tackle in the shadows of the Stanford goal.

Cantor and Washington ripped into the Indian line and a murmur of panic spread across the throng of Indian partisans as Washington blasted to the Stanford 5. It seemed that the Bruins' big chance had collapsed, however, when a 15-yard penalty pushed them back to the 20. Washington faded back and flipped the ball to Robinson, who twisted and squirmed to the 5. Washington then faked to Robinson— Horrell was right, for the whole Stanford team leaned left to try to fence in the dangerous halfback—and handed off to Cantor on a reverse. The big fullback crashed into the end zone, virtually untouched.

Then Robinson, who had galloped 51 yards the first time he handled the ball, only to find himself hamstrung for the rest of the day, stepped back grimly to try for that crucial tying point. The ball was snapped and placed to the ground as the thud of lineman-against-lineman was drowned out by the roar of the spectators. Two quick steps and the weary, perspiring Negro kicked. The ball split the uprights. UCLA had fought back gallantly for a 14-14 tie and preserved a chance for that trip to Pasadena. Nobody wanted a trip to Pasadena more than Jackie Robinson, who couldn't help but realize that for the ragged lad who once sold hot dogs there to come back to its athletic palace as a star of the West Coast champion team would be the most marvelous kind of "home-town boy makes good" story.

At the end of that Stanford contest, a lot of people were convinced that Robinson was just the guy to take the Bruins to Pasadena. Claude (Tiny) Thornhill, the Stanford coach, told newsmen that Robinson was "the greatest backfield runner I have seen in all my connection with football—and that's some twenty-five years." Every sports writer present had marveled at Robinson's performance, but more than a few raised their eyebrows when Thornhill went so far as to say that Robinson, before his football days were over, would be recognized as a greater ball carrier than the immortal Red Grange.

"That one run in the first quarter that carried the ball 51 yards on Robinson's reverse showed me enough so I wouldn't have to watch him any more to realize that he's the greatest piece of football running machinery this Coast Conference has ever seen," said Thornhill.

"Now, Tiny, you aren't forgetting that your own school had a great bone-crusher named Ernie Nevers, are you?" asked a newsman.

"Listen, boys, I've seen a lot of grid greats. Ernie Nevers, yes. Eddie Mahan, that great Harvard back and one of the best broken-field runners ever to put on a cleated shoe, but this kid Robinson can do it better than all of them."

Robinson made Thornhill look like a very wise man as the Bruins rolled over Montana, 20 to 6. Then Oregon's Webfeet came to town, with their admirers predicting boldly that Tex Oliver's boys would show the Bruins a thing or two. That they did. They passed Babe Horrell's gang dizzy and pushed them all over the field. Late in the game, the Webfeet were leading 6 to 3, and they seemed to be able to gain at will against the Bruins, who had trouble getting an offense going. Then came the explosion. Washington faded back and flipped the ball 43 yards to Robinson, who left two defenders sprawling foolishly as he dashed 23 yards to score. Then, to put the game on ice, Robinson grabbed the pigskin on a hand-off and swung wide around right end to pell-mell his way 83 yards up the sidelines to the promised land. Because of Robinson's explosiveness, the Bruins had won from a team that outplayed them completely.

Afterwards, disconsolate Tex Oliver shook his head and said, "I guess you've got to have a mechanized cavalry unit to stop this guy Robinson."

When someone asked Oliver for a comparison between Southern Cal and UCLA, the two teams now likely to battle it out for the roses, Oliver said he felt the Trojan line was stronger than that of the Bruins, but "Robinson leads all the backs. He may be the difference in the game when the two teams clash."

The Bruins found out, though, that there was still a lot of football between that victory over Oregon and the crucial clash with Southern Cal. They stayed "up" enough to dump California, 20 to 7, then Santa Clara caught them napping and stunned Bruin followers by stopping the Robinson-Washington combination cold for a scoreless tie.

Now fans began to see what football experts had known all along: that UCLA didn't have the linemen, the depth of material, to make the kind of team that can take good teams in stride and save the extra effort for the crucial games. For example, the Bruins obviously were looking ahead to Southern Cal, and to some extent, to the clash with Washington State, when Oregon State's Beavers invaded the Coliseum. The Beavers took advantage of every mistake the Bruins made, and they boomed into a 13 to 7 lead in the third quarter. They fought doggedly to hold this lead, and when, with only a few minutes remaining, Oregon State's mighty fullback, Jim Kissellburgh, punted out of bounds on the Bruin 18-yard line, thousands of UCLA fans got up to go home.

But Kenny Washington, a great all-American, refused to

give up. He rifled a 15-yard pass to Woodrow Strode. Some of the departing throng paused in the aisles, defying the cries of "Sit down, sit down." Kenny dropped back again and hurled a bullet to Macpherson for 20 more yards. Now, with the Beavers expecting the Bruins to fill the air with footballs, Washington crossed them up by handing off to Cantor, who slammed viciously through a hole for 14 yards and then lateraled to Robinson, who went 11 more before he was hauled down. With the crowd in a tumultuous roar, Washington raced to his right and turned Oregon State's left end, gaining 16 yards to the Beavers' 6-yard line.

Three cracks into the Beaver forward wall gained only four yards, and now, with 68 seconds remaining, with last down coming up and two yards to go, nervous, frenzied UCLA fans were jumping like fleas on a stove. The signal was called for fullback Cantor, who a few minutes earlier had made a fumble that allowed the Beavers to take the lead. This time he hit Oregon State's right tackle with the fury of a maddened bull and plunged into the end zone for the score. The Bruins missed the extra point and had to settle for their third deadlock of the season.

Bitterly disappointed over two straight ties, but with a wide eye still cocked on the Rose Bowl, the Bruins celebrated Thanksgiving by meeting Washington State's Cougars in the Los Angeles Coliseum. The Bruins got more fight than they expected, approaching the final quarter on the short end of a 7-to-6 score.

But in the dying moments of the third quarter, with the ball on the UCLA 19, Robinson began to run like a demon. When the opposition put two, then three men on him, Kenny Washington ripped through the gaping defense. Finally, with the ball on the Washington State 26, Kenny drifted back to pass. He spotted "old Number 28" in the flat and Jackie clutched the pigskin to his chest and ambled down the sideline, finally cutting back across the field to leave a host of Cougars sprawling in his wake.

A few minutes later the Bruins' twosome was on the march

again. At the Bruins' 34-yard line, Washington faked a run to the right and handed off on a reverse to Robinson, who scampered 66 yards.

UCLA held the Cougars after the kickoff, taking the ball on downs. Before Washington State could get its breath, Robinson was off again, sprinting all the way to the Cougar 18-yard line before being pushed out of bounds. By this time Coach Horrell figured the Cougars were a beaten team. He pulled his two Negro stars out of the game. As Robinson and Washington trotted off the field arm in arm, 30,000 fans gave them a standing ovation.

Now the stage was set for the big one—the battle against the Trojans from Southern California.

All the Bruins needed was a victory over once-tied Southern California, those bitter rivals from across town, in what sports writers all over the country called one of the truly big games of the year.

A 7-7 tie with Oregon was the only blemish on the record of the Trojans, who boasted a 33-to-0 shellacking of Stanford, as well as victories over Illinois and Notre Dame. The game obviously was a match between UCLA backfield punch and Trojan all-around strength and depth.

The bitter contest was scoreless for three quarters. Late in the fourth quarter a Bruin drive, highlighted by Robinson's running and Washington's passing, stalled on the Trojan 2 when Washington fumbled. Then, in the last seconds of the game, Washington hurled a spectacular, last-gasp pass toward the Trojan end zone. As Number 28 raced down the field, 103,303 spectators strained on tiptoe, only to see the ball fall incomplete a few inches beyond Robinson's desperate lunge.

With painful disappointment written all over his face, Robinson trudged off the field, unable to hear the deafening applause from that mammoth throng; he was too busy chastising himself for not having run faster or lunged farther to pull in Washington's desperate pass. The game had ended in a tie, and that meant conference members would have to vote that night on whether USC or UCLA would get the Rose Bowl bid. Robinson knew that the nod would go to USC, which now had only two ties to three for UCLA, not counting the latter's non-conference deadlock with Santa Clara.

It was no consolation to Robinson that for the season he had led the nation's ball carriers with an average of more than 12 yards per try, or that he had averaged a phenomenal 21 yards on punt returns. He was almost sick with disappointment as he lingered in the shower, thankful that, with the water splashing off him, no one would know that a big, tough Bruin halfback had cried after failing to win the big one.

At the close of the football season Robinson went out for basketball, where he was no less a star than in football. He led the southern division of the Pacific Coast Conference in scoring and was such a star that Nibs Price, University of California coach, labeled him the best basketball player in the United States.

When sports writers called Price's attention to the fact that the University of Southern California had a forward named Ralph Vaughn who was generally considered to be the nation's best basketballer, Price declared, "Robinson has more natural talent, speed and spring than any man in the conference, including Ralph Vaughn. Furthermore, if Robinson had played as much basketball as Vaughn has, Robinson would outscore the Southern California forward twofold."

A few weeks later Robinson scored 18 points to lead UCLA's Bruins to a 35-33 victory over Price's Bears.

Autumn of 1940 was long and dull on the UCLA campus. The school had lost a lot of key men, including Kenny Washington, from that undefeated 1939 squad, so football didn't amount to much. Robinson was still there, but without good linemen to open holes, without other good backfield threats to keep the opposition from loading the defense against him, Jackie was held to a less-than-scintillating running average of 3.64 yards per carry. When football was discussed at Kerckhoff Hall, the favorite campus hangout, Jackie usually got around to telling friends how this frustrating season was turning out to be his greatest lesson in humbleness. The Bruins wound up winning one game out of ten—a 34-to-26 triumph over Washington State, with Robinson scoring on jaunts of 60 and 75 yards.

But the boredom involved more than football miseries; 1940 just seemed dull, period. You could discuss Hitler, but there was no real sense of personal involvement. Campuses were not yet filled with idealistic talk of war as the destroyer of the best of mankind, or war as a brutal but necessary means of maintaining a population balance. Young American males were not yet fired up with a desire to dash abroad, sword in hand, to save for humanity all that was good. Indeed, if it had not been for the fact that someone occasionally hummed "Body and Soul" or "I Want Some Sea Food, Mamma" (songs whose lyrics were banned by many radio stations in those tamer days) or declared melodically, "I'm gonna move . . . way out on the outskirts of town, 'cause I don't want no iceman always hanging 'round"—but for these symbols of decadence, one might have wondered why, even in 1940, adults were speculating that the younger generation was going straight to hell.

On the afternoon of one of the duller of these days, a group of pledges of Alpha Kappa Alpha, a Negro sorority, sat in Kerckhoff chatting about the social affairs and other functions that the sorority sponsored, when Robinson walked by.

"There's Jackie Robinson, Rae. Would you like to meet him?" said one of the pledges.

Pretty, dimple-cheeked Rachel Isum looked up and said casually, "Yes . . . of course."

The "of course" was an almost instinctive bit of politeness, added because Rae knew that a couple of her friends had reason to assume that she did not care to meet Robinson. They had heard her comment in an uncomplimentary way that Robinson looked so cocky, so arrogant, as he stood in the backfield with his hands on his hips.

The introductory scene was hardly one of love at first sight. To Rae's polite greeting Jackie responded with "Hi" in a tone that could hardly be described as warm. Fortunately for both, the awkward scene was broken when someone shouted, "Pop! Pop! Here comes Pop!" Jackie dashed away at the head of a pack of muscular young men who hopped out the window and disappeared behind the shrubbery.

"Who on earth is Pop?" demanded a startled freshman girl.

An upper-classman explained that certain athletes received small sums of money as a token of appreciation of their athletic prowess, but that to satisfy the purists the lads had to swing a mop or drag a rake at certain times of the week.

"You'll find that most of their mopping-up operations take place right here, where the shovel-leaners congregate until Pop makes his rounds," she added sarcastically.

As was expected, when Pop walked out of sight the athletes began their pilgrimage back to Kerckhoff. Just as he had led the pack away, Jackie Robinson was the first to return. No one was more surprised than Rachel Isum that she was still there, and she was bothered a trifle by her awareness that she really had hoped he would come back, that she wanted to talk to him. But when she saw him coming she grabbed her books and walked out of the building, meeting him on the lawn.

"Leaving so soon?" Robinson asked.

"I'm a working girl," said Rae. "I can't spend all my time in Kerckhoff Hall."

Robinson smiled as he said, "Well, we're all working people. Didn't you just see how eager we all were to get to our jobs when Pop walked in?"

Rae laughed with Jackie as the initial coolness wore off.

"How do you get home—do you drive?" he asked.

"A group of us arranged a car pool. I'm the driver."

"Your car?" said Robinson. "Don't tell me you're one of those rich little girls from the other side of the tracks?"

"Didn't you just hear me say I'm a working girl?"

Robinson offered to walk her to the parking lot. As they strolled across campus he asked her about herself, learning that she came from a middle-class family and lived in a comfortable section of Los Angeles. Her father had heart trouble, which, she explained, was one reason she felt obligated to work and help buy her own books and clothes.

"Of course I've always liked to work," Rae said. "I had an NYA job in high school, although I had to tell a little white lie to get it. I'm sure they thought my family would starve if I didn't get that job.

"But what about you?" she continued. "All I know about is Jackie Robinson the athlete. Tell me more."

"There's nothing to tell particularly that you don't already know," Jack replied modestly.

"Well, I've got to go," said Rae as she opened the door of a black Ford V-8. "Maybe we'll have a chance to chat again."

She really hadn't planned to leave campus for an hour, but she had committed herself by saying that she was in a rush to get to work, so Rae drove away. She thought about how shy Jackie seemed, and she was pleased. It was such a relief to find that he was not the cocky, man-of-the-world type she had suspected him to be. Rachel Isum realized that she was consciously hoping that they would chat again.

In the days that followed, Rae saw that Jack was shy to the point of being stand-offish, was so introverted that those who could not reconcile such characteristics with being a campus hero were quick to label him a snob. Young women who had found him difficult to talk to, impossible to interest, spoke of him as an "odd one." Jackie knew all this and he liked it that way, for he deliberately sought to avoid entanglements with girls. What his classmates did not understand was that the circumstances of his youth had created in him some insecurities, a lack of confidence, in situations involving young women. In the first place he did not trust them; he found it difficult to believe that they were interested in him as a human being—not just as a campus football hero. He had been involved in one minor romance, when a cute young thing was eager to be his steady during football season, but became less than steady when the season and its social affairs were over.

So when his teammates and friends urged him to join them in their strivings to build reputations as Romeos, Robinson would say scornfully, "No girl's gonna make a fool outa me."

The truth was that, even at the point of greatest collegiate glory, Jackie could not forget the teen-age parties in Pasadena, the games of post office, of spin-the-bottle. It was here that he saw the extent to which race consciousness and color snobbery had rubbed off on Negroes; how, in their frantic search for status, for self-respect, Negroes were resorting to the same caste-system thinking that dominated the white world. He noted that almost always the better-looking girls would send their "special deliveries" to the lighter-skinned boys, or the ones whose parents could afford to buy them a sport coat, a pair of slacks that would hold a crease, the young men most likely to have the money to treat them to a movie, or a hamburger and a Coke. And they would always spend more time in the "post office" accepting or delivering the messages of these young men. And a poor boy, dressed in his second-hand, ill-fitting clothes, dark-skinned beyond question, could tell when he had spun his bottle to the wrong girl: the reward was a giggle and reluctant peck, but none of the ego-building sounds of rapture as she emerged from the back room where the game's rewards were given and received.

You built up a defense against this sort of thing by saying that you really didn't want to waste your kisses on girls whose thinking was so shallow, on girls unable to see the worth of an individual beyond his complexion, his dress, the economic status of his family. And you developed a preference for post office over spin-the-bottle, because you could remember not to send letters to the wrong girl, whereas that bottle would make no allowances for the prejudices, the insecurities, of the participants.

Yet, Robinson knew, there was a point beyond which he could not blame the girls, for to a degree they were unwitting creatures of their society and generation. He sensed in a way that he could not articulate then that it had become a universal part of our language of symbolism that "black" connotes bad, undesirable things. Filthy little boys get "dirt-black" but white is the symbol of cleanliness, purity, virginity; evil men are black-hearted, but those who show magnanimity —well, it's mighty "white" of them; black clouds are ominous, white clouds but puffs of meringue against a blue sky;

black symbolizes despair, mourning, hopelessness, but white is hope, light, gaiety. Small wonder, then, that children not yet aware of race sometimes speak with aversion of someone who is black!

By what intellectual armor, then, could a Negro fend off the subtle prejudices that had become so much a part of the mass of daily thought association that they had permeated Negro society? Oh, Negroes laughingly declared that "the blacker the berry the sweeter the juice," but the truth was that even the declarer was expressing awareness that Negro society had succumbed to the prejudices, the connotations of color consciousness. So it was that, no whites being present, a Negro man might speak of a dark-skinned woman as "a stovepipe blonde." Or Negroes would speak, sometimes mockingly sometimes sardonically, of our society as one in which, "If she's white, she's right; if she's yellow, she's mellow; if she's brown, she can stick around—but if she's black, she can get back."

It seemed apparent to Robinson that the society-minded females in his circle (and by some disgusting coincidence, these always tended to be the ones with the long hair, trim figures, paler complexions, and thus the more attractive by the standard of the day) were so imbued with these notions of caste and color that he didn't stand much chance of sweeping them off their feet. So he became a lone wolf, a serious guy who cared little for parties and who made it clear that he was a one-woman man looking for a one-man woman.

During his first football season at UCLA, Robinson found two white girls waiting at his jalopy after practice every day. These girls—obviously full of the campus hero worship that knows no bounds of race—got some polite conversation, but no further encouragement.

"Why do you keep running away from those ofay chicks, man?" asked a Negro acquaintance.

"I guess I just don't trust them," said Jackie. "I still remember how, when Negroes sued to use the public swimming pool in Pasadena, city authorities set out to penalize Negroes leading the campaign for integration. If you had a job at city

hall, you were in trouble. When they couldn't find a legitimate excuse for firing some Negroes, they got white girls to
tempt them, to give them the old come-on. First thing these
Negroes knew they were out on their fannies, accused of making insulting passes at white girls."

"Aw, come on, Jack," said the friend. "These are two nice
kids who're just excited to be near the campus hero—just
like any other girl. Don't tell me you think they're part of a
plot."

"I don't really, but I can't see anything but trouble ahead
if I start fooling around with them."

Rachel Isum decided quickly that she could penetrate Jackie's wall of suspicion, his ingrained aloofness toward girls.
So she would park her Ford and say good-by to her school-
mates. Then she would sit in the car doing her homework,
lifting an eye every so often to watch for Robinson's jalopy.
She knew that if she waited she almost certainly would see
him, because Robinson could be counted on to get to school
late. Since he was about the last person to reach this parking
lot, there was no problem of picking his car out from among
the hundreds arriving during the rush period.

Just when Rae had begun to despair at Robinson's distrust
of girls, had begun to believe that he was serious in his declaration that he wouldn't go steady with any girl while on
campus, he surprised her one morning by saying: "It seems I
never see you except for a few minutes here where we really
never have a chance to talk about anything. Would you go out
with me sometime?"

"Like where?" said Rae.

"The Homecoming game and dance are coming up soon,"
said Jackie. "Would you like to go?"

"Homecoming dance?" Rae said, hoping that Jackie would
not detect her pleasure and excitement. "Where is it being
held?"

"The Biltmore Hotel—it's a real swell affair."

"Biltmore, h-m-m? Oh, I'd be delighted to go."

Rachel almost asked Jackie if he had ever been to the Bilt-

more, but then she thought better of it. She had never been
there or to any of the other big white hotels, and she doubted
that any of the other Negro girls on campus had. In Los
Angeles, as in most cities across the nation, white hotels were
still reluctant to accept Negroes as guests, though some did
permit Negroes to participate in functions with groups that
were predominantly white. But she did not want to mention
that she had never been to the Biltmore for fear Jackie would
consider her unsophisticated and a potential embarrassment at
the dance.

Rae's eyes sparkled with excitement as she told her parents
about her invitation. Her father did not share her enthusiasm,
for he too imagined that the campus football hero must be a
conceited wolf who would mean no good for a nice freshman
girl. Mrs. Isum helped to ease her husband's misgivings and
Rae set about preparing for the dance. Her first declaration
was that she hadn't a thing to wear, so she purchased her first
"dressy black dress" and a little black hat with fox trimming.

"Mother, I'm sure all the other girls will have fur pieces,
and I'd hate for the bit of fox on this hat to be all I wear,"
Rae complained.

Mrs. Isum laughed. "You know the only fur coat in our
whole family is your grandmother's old black Alaska seal."

Rae remembered that she had always considered this coat
beautiful. She got it out and rubbed her hand up and down
it, watching the fur change color.

"My Lord, it must weigh a hundred pounds—but I'm going to wear it."

On the night of the Homecoming dance Jackie Robinson
arrived to pick up a coed who was dressed to the teeth in her
black dress, her black hat with the fox fur and a huge Alaska
fur seal that all but swallowed her.

Later Rachel was to look back on that night and say: "It
was wonderful, I was thoroughly excited over going to a dance
at the Biltmore. Although I tried to hide this at the time, I
also was very proud to go with Jackie Robinson. I'm sure I
must have been quite a comical character in that huge fur.

We danced to 'Star Dust,' 'Mood Indigo,' 'I'll Never Smile Again,' and all those tunes that were popular at the time, and we chattered and jabbered away, but half the time I was hardly aware of what my dancing partners were saying. I was too busy scolding myself for having made up my mind before meeting him that Jackie was an arrogant show-off. I told my mother when I got home that he was one of the nicest boys I'd ever met. I didn't tell her, but I was saying to myself that he was a little too nice! Like most girls, I presume, I guess I was hoping that there would be just a little bit of the Romeo in him, as my father seemed to fear."

After the Homecoming dance, practically the same old pattern prevailed, with Robinson and Rae seeing each other only as he strolled into the parking lot, late for some class. They did have an occasional date, however, and Robinson visited her house a few times—but never frequently enough for her father to become convinced that his intentions were wholly honorable.

In the spring of 1941, less than four months after their first date, Robinson went to Rae's home and told her he was quitting school without waiting to graduate in June. His mother needed financial help. In addition, he had a job offer at a youth camp at Itascadera run by the National Youth Administration, and he had been promised that if he got in on the ground floor he was almost certain to be named athletic director when a new camp was opened.

Rae was stunned. "Jack, you must be joking."

"Joking? Coming from a poor family and having a mother who has to work her fingers to the bone to keep you eating and in school is no joke," Robinson said.

"But, Jack, you're a senior. You've made good grades, and in a few months you'll get your degree. That degree can make all the difference in the world when you look for a job. You'll regret it a million times if you quit school now."

"I've thought about all that, but I've come to the conclusion that somebody has to help my mother. She has worked herself almost to the point of collapse. Don't forget she's been at this practically since the day I was born. I just can't feel right inside, knowing that she needs help and not giving it when I can."

"What does she say, Jackie? I'll bet she wants you to stay in school."

"Well, she would. I've never yet heard her complain or suggest that anyone ought to give her some help. That's probably one reason why she hasn't gotten more help than she has from some of my brothers. But this is something I've got to do."

Jackie and Rae looked away from each other, thinking thoughts they were reluctant to share.

"Is it my education, my college degree, that you're mostly concerned about?" asked Robinson.

Rachel pretended not to get the full implications of that question. "What is there more important than your getting an education, a college degree?" she countered.

"I didn't say there was anything more important. All I asked was whether that was the only reason you were trying to talk me into staying on campus."

Rachel took his hand and squeezed it. "You know as well as I do that there are other reasons," she said, "and I never like for anyone to ask a question when they know what the answer is."

Robinson reached over so quickly that she was startled, and pulled her into his arms. He kissed her for what seemed like an eternity. Then he arose as swiftly as he had embraced her and took his football jacket off the chair.

"I'd better go," he said. "I know I'd better go, because there's so much to do before I leave for Itascadera."

Robinson's departure from UCLA provoked some of the most glowing eulogies ever printed in newspaper sports pages. Columnists seemed engaged in a contest to see who could write the most convincing argument that Robinson was (1) the best all-around athlete ever to play on the West Coast; (2) the best all-around athlete in America; or (3) the best Negro athlete of all time.

For example, George T. Davis, sports editor of the *Los Angeles Evening Herald and Express*, wrote: "It may sound like heresy to say he'll overshadow such heroes of the past as Morton Kerr and Jesse Mortensen of the Trojans, Brick Muller of California and Ernie Nevers of Stanford, but it's my honest opinion that Jackie Robinson will go down in history as the greatest all-around athlete in Pacific Coast history."

Another sports writer, Al Wolfe, wrote: "This is a good time to reflect upon who might be termed the Mr. Big of intercollegiate athletics . . . Well sir, you can plow through the 48 states and the District of Columbia, through Coney Island and Catalina too, without discovering a youngster so adept in the various exercises as the baby right in our own back yard. The laurel wreath herewith is dispatched to Mr. Jackie Robinson, UCLA. There may have been better footballers, better basketeers, better baseballers and better track men, but cudgel our memory as we will we can think of nobody more able in the four put together."

The operators of the All-Star football game recognized Robinson's talents by inviting him to participate in this annual Chicago event. But as far as the cynical sports writers in the East were concerned, Robinson was small fry, out of his class in the presence of big names of the year like Tom Harmon of Michigan, Norm Standlee of Stanford, George Franck of Minnesota—athletes who had gotten more headlines because their teams had won more games, and who were obviously the "people's choice" among the All-Stars. In August of 1941, however, when Robinson went to Chicago to practice, United Press reported that "It took one scrimmage to establish the Negro boy's rightful place among the All-Stars."

Orin (Babe) Hollingberry, Washington State coach and a member of the All-Star staff, told the U.P. reporter that Robinson was "the best athlete I ever saw. Why, he could play shortstop on a major league team right now, and he's plenty uncanny on a basketball court."

Although the Chicago Bears whipped the All-Stars soundly, Robinson lived up to his laurels by dashing downfield to take a spectacular pass from Boston College's Charlie O'Rourke and score one of the All-Stars' two touchdowns. After the game, Vincent X. Flaherty of Los Angeles wrote: "In the general uproar about Joe Louis and his universal appeal, the colored race has lost sight of Jack Robinson, the UCLA phenomenon whom seasoned observers consider the greatest colored athlete of all time." Flaherty went on to talk about the merits of Jesse Owens, Duke Slater, Paul Robeson, Henry Armstrong, Jack Johnson, Fritz Pollard, Joe Louis and many more, and to say that when it came to versatility not one of them "could hope to compete with Robinson."

"Just before boarding a plane for Los Angeles," Flaherty continued, "I met Robinson for the first time. He is a soft-spoken, dark-skinned kid with a flash of illuminating white teeth which attract your attention the minute he grins, and he says the reason he's good in practically every avenue of sports is because he loves them all and has been taking part in them all ever since he can remember.

"And where the less talented Joe Louis has reaped a financial harvest out of boxing, the future holds no such riches for Robinson, who studied physical education at UCLA and who intends to make his mark in coaching . . .

"So it is a shame, then, in this day when Joe Louis monopolizes the affection of the Negro sports public, that Robinson isn't equally appreciated, or more universally known. He has everything Joe Louis has and more as regards personality, intelligence and native talent. And although there may be another Joe Louis in boxing, the thought of another athlete such as Jack Robinson appearing upon the scene seems utterly fantastic. He is the Jim Thorpe of his race."

4....The Lone Star Mutiny

The decade between 1930 and 1940 produced a growing number of Negro sports heroes in American colleges. Unlike many white athletes, however, they found their achievements very little help in job hunting. The wealthy businessmen who had lavished attention upon them as high school seniors were too busy to see them as college seniors. A colored star became "just another Negro" once his playing days were over, and Jackie Robinson was no exception.

He liked his job at Itascadera, for he was helping underprivileged youngsters to stay off the streets, to learn a trade, to shape a future not yet warped and distorted by delinquency and bitterness. Still, he had quit college because his family needed money, and the Itascadera job paid very poorly. Jackie decided to try to grab some of the quick money supposedly available in professional football.

The major pro football teams of the United States were not much interested in Negro players in 1941, so Robinson joined the Honolulu Bears. He was a tremendous drawing card in Hawaii, and his earnings enabled him to give his mother the financial help she needed. However, the football season was much too brief, so by late fall he was working as a laborer with a firm building ammunition shelters near Pearl Harbor. Now, with the season over, here he was in a job that gave him no intellectual satisfaction whatsoever. Robinson decided to go back to the States and resume his efforts to keep boys in surroundings like those in which he had grown up from getting into the deep trouble that he had avoided almost miraculously.

On December 5, 1941, Robinson left Hawaii on the *Lurline*. Two days out, he was playing cards when crew members began racing about the ship painting windows black. In the wake of the painters came rumors that the ship was in various kinds of difficulty. Some passengers were on the verge of hysteria when the captain finally announced that the Japanese had attacked Pearl Harbor and the United States was at war. All vessels flying the American flag in the Pacific were in jeopardy.

"We expect to reach the United States safely, of course," the captain said. "However, in the event of trouble, we want all of you to be prepared. We are passing out life jackets which we will ask every passenger to wear at all times."

The captain explained that the windows had been painted as a nighttime precaution and that passengers must not expose any light whatsoever, for to do so would make the *Lurline* an easy target for a submarine.

Robinson took his life jacket with the realization that his hand was trembling a bit. He was seized by something close to a superstition, something akin to the feeling of many air passengers that to take out special insurance for a plane trip is an invitation to trouble. So Jackie refused to wear his life jacket. He was, however, a most uneasy man during the rest of that zigzag blackout trip home.

Jack had a joyful reunion with Rachel, who again chided him for leaving UCLA before getting his degree, and for staying in Hawaii so long.

He told her sadly that chances were good that he would be away even longer because the draft board had raised some questions about his civilian status.

"Some questions?"

"Yes, for one thing about my being the chief means of support of my mother. I guess that could be cited to keep them from drafting me."

"You aren't pressing that point, though, are you?"

"No—in fact, that's not the big issue. It's that old business of an athlete being in a touchy spot where the draft is concerned. I'm still bothered by a broken ankle I got in junior college. The doctors say there are bone chips in it and that they doubt that I'm qualified for military service."

"Well, just remember how the public feels about these things, Jack. If anybody gets the notion you're using that ankle injury to avoid service there'll be a huge blow-up about how a big strong halfback is shirking his duty to his country."

"Don't worry. I'm not eager to go, but I'm not foolish enough to ask any special favors on the basis of that ankle."

Robinson guessed correctly that some newspapermen would not understand how a man could dash like a whirlwind through eleven big bruisers, all striving to knock his brains out, and not be able to serve in the armed forces. Under this kind of pressure, and to Jackie's relief, the draft board, inducted him for "limited service."

Jackie's first assignment was to Fort Riley, Kansas. When he and five other recruits appeared for duty they were assigned to cavalry units. Asked who in the group had had experience with horses, three men raised their hands. In standard army fashion, those three were assigned to a mechanized unit, and Robinson and the two other soldiers were assigned to horse units. Thus Robinson's first big role in the task of crushing the forces of Naziism was to hold horses while a veterinarian vaccinated them. A good many people at Fort Riley were treated to the sight of a frantic horse snapping its head up and down, waving Jackie helplessly through the air. Once this ceased to be entertainment, a veteran soldier tipped Robinson off to the fact that if he twisted the ears of the horses they would remain fairly calm for the vaccination.

At Fort Riley, for the first time in his life, Jackie saw a really rigid pattern of discrimination. After his three months of basic training, Robinson applied for Officers Candidate School only to be advised unofficially that Negroes were not permitted in OCS at Fort Riley. Luckily, Joe Louis, world's heavyweight boxing champion but then in the army, was transferred to Fort Riley a few days later and played several rounds of golf with Robinson. Robinson told Louis how angry he was that Jim Crow apparently was going to prevent Negroes from attending OCS. Louis had heard the same thing from other Negroes. He investigated and found that they had all been rejected for OCS, always with the stock disqualifier, "He is not a leader of men." Joe's response was as direct as one of his left jabs: he telephoned Truman Gibson, a Negro civic leader who was then a civilian adviser to the Secretary of Defense, and invited him to come to Fort Riley. Gibson flew out immediately, and heard the complaints of Negro GI's at a meeting arranged by Louis. A few days later Robinson and several other Negroes were in OCS.

In January, 1943, Robinson received his commission and, in celebration purchased an engagement ring for Rae. He remained at Fort Riley as acting morale officer for a Negro company in which morale was probably the thing most sorely needed. The soldiers complained constantly about injustices heaped upon them because of Jim Crow regulations. Jackie was particularly irked to find Negro soldiers at the post exchange standing ten-deep in a waiting line behind the few seats set aside for Negro soldiers.

One night he walked into the company barracks to hear a bitter discussion under way. "You know, it just doesn't make sense for any of us to beat our brains out to fight a war that doesn't mean a damn thing to us," said a corporal.

"I disagree," said a sergeant. "It's just like Joe Louis said: Sure there are a lot of things wrong with this country, but there ain't a damn thing wrong with it that Mr. Hitler can fix."

"That's a bunch of crap. They want to send me ten thousand miles away to fight for democracy when a hundred feet away they've got stools I can't put my black butt on and drink a bottle of beer."

"You're right," said another soldier, "but what good does it do to gripe and say we don't intend to fight? Nobody here ready to move to Japan or Germany."

"Nobody said a damn thing about moving to Japan or Germany. I say it's stupid to think you can treat a man like a pack horse and have him go out in a feverish rage to die happily for his country. If they want to Jim Crow me, that's one thing, but they don't have to insult me by asking me to appear to be so dumb and naïve that I'm going around shouting platitudes about how we're going to win because God is on our side. Man, they're gonna have to talk a long time to convince me that God's any more on the side of Senator Bilbo than He's on the side of Hitler."

Negroes in the company stared at the soldier with uneasiness and suspicion. Finally the corporal cracked: "Nobody here gonna deny you got a mighty good point, but take a tip from me: don't go spreading that stuff around too far, or you gonna find yourself locked up on charges of working for the enemy or something."

Lieutenant Robinson now made known his presence.

"Well—the company morale officer!" shouted one soldier. "Lieutenant, what you gonna do? The morale is low!" The men laughed loudly at what they all recognized as an attempt to razz the lieutenant. Robinson recognized it as something else—as a sociological fact of life that affected Negroes as much in civilian life as in the military. What that corporal actually wanted to say, but would not dare say, was that sports celebrity Jackie Robinson sported a gold bar on his uniform, but that when it came to the showdown with Jim Crow, Lieutenant Robinson and the greenest, dumbest Negro recruit at the fort were lumped into the same category: they were just a couple of Negroes.

"I'll tell you what I'm going to do, Corporal," said Robinson. "Tomorrow I'm going to see what can be done to change that situation at the PX."

The next day Robinson telephoned the provost marshal, a Major Hafner.

"Major, this is Lieutenant Robinson of the Provisional Trucking Battalion. I want to get some information about facilities at the post exchange."

"What do you want to know, Lieutenant?"

"Is there an official policy of racial segregation at the post exchange, or is it just custom?"

"Well, it's both custom and policy."

"Then who made the seating arrangements, Major? My men protest this setup where white troops can come in and get service without delay but Negro troops have to stand in line even to buy a bottle of Coke or a candy bar."

"Lieutenant, we've done the best we can to provide service to our colored troops," said the major. "But I think you can understand that if you started taking facilities away from whites and giving them to colored soldiers this would become a real problem and might adversely affect the morale of our white troops."

"Well, what do you think this does to the morale of the Negro troops? I'm their morale officer, and I've heard them griping and bitching about the Jim Crow setup. You've got fellows here preparing to go abroad and defend their country just like anybody else and they aren't going to understand why they can't be allowed to go to the PX or anywhere else they want to and use the services just like any of the other boys."

"Lieutenant Robinson, are you suggesting that we ought to mix the races at the post exchange and let these Negro troops sit where they please?"

"That's exactly what I'm suggesting. When they get over into those battle areas nobody's going to separate any bullets and label them 'for white troops' and 'for colored troops.' "

"Well, let's be reasonable, Lieutenant Robinson. Let me put it this way: how would you like to have your wife sitting next to a nigger?"

Robinson was stunned—then rage surged through him. "Major, I happen to be a Negro," he said, "and I don't know that to have someone's wife sitting next to a Negro is any worse than to have her sitting next to some of these white soldiers I see around here. But it's obvious to me that guys who think like you do are the reason why conditions are so bad in this camp."

"Well, I just want you to know that I don't want my wife sitting close to any colored guy," interrupted the major.

"How the hell do you know that your wife hasn't already been close to one?" snapped Robinson in anger. "Well, just you let me tell you this. You're the kind of guy who has no conception of what democracy is all about, and you've got no business enjoying it . . ."

The provost marshal had hung up. Robinson realized that his battalion headquarters was as silent as a tomb. Not a typewriter was moving. Everyone had stopped to listen to the angry words of a young Negro lieutenant who seemed oblivious of the fact that only a thin partition separated his office from that of the colonel.

Robinson sat for several seconds squeezing his fists so tightly that all the blood ran out of the knuckles, leaving his skin a grayish color. He strode out to Warrant Officer Chambers, a veteran of more than twenty years' service.

"Say, I just had a somewhat lively discussion with the provost marshal . . ."

"You don't need to tell me, I heard it. So did everyone else," replied the warrant officer. "I wouldn't worry about it too much, but if I were you I would tell Colonel Longley, the battalion commander, what the provost said to you and why you said what you did."

Robinson told his story to the battalion commander, whom

he regarded as a decent man as well as a first-rate soldier.

"I don't like this segregated setup at all, Robinson, because I don't think it's good for my battalion or for the country," the colonel said. "And I don't think there's any excuse whatsoever for the provost to say what he said to you. I'm going to write the general and give him my opinions of this thing."

Robinson doubted that the colonel would be allowed to make any changes. Nobody had even been able to shake the system enough to permit him to play baseball with the camp team. During basic training, when he applied for membership on the baseball squad, the captain in charge had told a white officer in Robinson's battalion that "I'll break up the team before I'll have a nigger on it."

Some members of the squad expressed disgust at the captain's stand and demanded a meeting to discuss Robinson's application. Several players who knew of Robinson's college record argued that he would be an asset to the team and that they personally would enjoy playing with him, but the captain was adamant, and Robinson was denied the right to play.

Robinson learned, however, that the powers that be were not completely against Negroes participating with white athletes. Football was a big sport at Fort Riley during those wartime days, with the team playing such highly regarded foes as Missouri, which was the opening opponent that year. One colonel at the fort had a son on the squad, so as a matter of pride he wanted the team to be a winner, and he lost no time spreading the word that the team needed a good runner like Robinson.

When Robinson was advised that the colonel wanted him to play football, he replied with delightful devilishness: "I couldn't play baseball when we had no opponents that would object; now you don't mean to tell me that you're asking me to play football when the opening game is against Missouri, which doesn't play against teams with Negroes unless the Negroes are left off the squad?"

Robinson found, however, that someone had already thought of this. They were offering him a two weeks' leave of absence just before the Missouri game, so as to be able to say that Robinson would not appear in it because he had not practiced long enough to get into condition. The colonel was convinced that they could take Missouri without Robinson, but that they would need him later on.

Not one to pass up a two-week leave of absence, Robinson said that of course he'd be delighted to go home for two weeks. When he returned he was asked to pick up his football equipment and join the team. He replied that, in view of the fact that he was not permitted to play baseball because of his race, he had decided not to play football, where there was considerable danger of being injured. Very promptly he received an order to report to the colonel whose son was on the football squad.

"You are aware, Robinson, that we could order you out to play football?"

"Yes, sir. I am sure that you are aware, though, that no one can make me play inspired football. I don't think anyone will want me on the team so long as I have the feeling that I could never put out for a football team at a camp where I was denied the right to participate in other activities because I am a Negro."

The colonel was angry, but he saw that it was useless to try to force Robinson to play. However, the decision did not make Jackie the best liked man at Fort Riley. His gunnery instructor, one of the men who had supported his bid to play baseball, said, "Jackie, your refusal to play football hasn't made you very popular around here."

"I know," said Robinson, "but I'm not looking for popularity. I just want to be sure everybody knows how I feel—that if I'm good enough to play football I'm good enough to play baseball."

Whether this refusal and the ruckus over the PX had anything to do with it or not, Robinson was soon transferred to Camp Hood, Texas, where he was assigned to the 761st Tank Battalion. Jackie was startled to find himself in a tank battalion, for he had never had the slightest contact with a tank. Yet here he was with orders to help prepare a tank unit to go overseas.

"Sergeant," he confided at the earliest possible moment, "I've been given command of this group, but I know little if anything about a tank battalion. I'll have to count heavily on you and the men under my command, and I'll ask a lot of questions and seek a lot of help."

This confession of ignorance so surprised the sergeant, who thought every young officer was a ninety-day wonder not yet dry behind the ears, but just green enough to pretend he knew everything, that he really pulled the men behind Robinson, whose unit wound up with one of the best records in the battalion for speedy, efficient preparation for embarkation.

Robinson's commanding officer, Colonel Bates, whom he had come to regard as a wonderful officer who understood the special problems faced by Negro troops, and who insisted upon fair treatment of all the people under his command, called Robinson in.

"Lieutenant," he said, "you have one of the best records of all the platoons in the unit. I'm singling you out for special commendation."

Robinson shifted his weight uneasily as he replied: "Thank you, sir. But I must tell you that I am merely an officer transferred from a horse outfit to a mechanized group, and I arrived here knowing nothing about my duties. Any commendation must go to the sergeant and the men, who did a magnificent job not only of preparing themselves but of helping me to learn."

"I don't care how you accomplished what you did, Lieutenant. I'm interested only in the results. I understand that you're on limited service, Robinson, is that correct?"

"Yes, sir, because of bone chips in my ankle."

"Robinson, because we're about to go overseas, we're going to need officers with leadership ability. I would count it a special favor to me if you would go overseas with this battalion. You know of course that because of that ankle, in order to do so you will have to sign a waiver relieving the Army of all responsibility in the event you are injured. I want to be honest with you; you would run the risk of losing some benefits that normally come to a soldier injured on overseas duty if you sign that waiver."

"I appreciate the confidence you express in me, sir, and I'd like very much to go overseas with you. Let me think about it."

Robinson thought it over for a couple of days and decided to sign the waiver. But camp medical authorities wanted to give his ankle another thorough check, so they asked him to enter a military hospital thirty miles away.

Robinson was in the hospital for several days—still there was no decision as to whether he could go overseas. After some time he tired of cursing Army bureaucracy and red tape and left the hospital for a visit with some of his buddies. After traveling the thirty miles back to the camp he discovered that his friends were on an overnight trip, so he decided to head back to the hospital. The wife of a Negro officer saw Robinson at the Officers Club and told him she would ride part way with him, since she lived halfway between the post and the hospital. Robinson and the young woman, who was light-skinned enough to pass for white, got on the bus chattering amiably. Soon the young woman noticed that the driver was glaring into the rear-view mirror, apparently assuming that Robinson had sat beside a white woman. He yelled back, "Hey, you, sittin' beside that woman. Get to the back of the bus."

"I believe the driver is yelling at you," said the woman, obviously afraid a disturbance was about to take place.

"He's not talking to me," Jackie said angrily.

The driver stopped the bus and walked to where Robinson and the woman sat.

"Listen, you, I said get to the back of the bus where colored people belong."

"Now you listen to me, buddy; you just drive the bus and I'll sit where I please. The Army recently issued orders that there is to be no more racial segregation on any Army post. This is an Army bus operating on an Army post."

"You just let me tell you, buddy," said the driver 'if you

ain't off this bus by the time we get to the last stop, I'm going to cause you a lot of trouble."

"I don't care what kind of trouble you plan to cause me," snapped Robinson. "You can't cause me any trouble that I haven't already faced. I know what the regulations are and I don't intend to go to the back of this bus. So get out of my face and go drive the bus because I don't intend to be pestered by you any more."

The driver mumbled angrily as he stalked back to his seat. When they reached the last stop on the post, where Robinson and his acquaintance would normally have changed to a city bus, the driver got off ahead of the passengers and came back with three white men, one a dispatcher, the other two apparently drivers. Robinson was stepping off the bus when a white passenger whom Robinson recognized as the saleswoman at the post exchange, from whom he often had bought candy and toilet articles, began shouting to him: "I heard you. I heard that driver tell you several times to get back there where niggers belong. But you sat up there just as smart as if you didn't hear that driver. So if they prosecute you for violating our segregation laws, I'll testify against you."

"Listen, lady," he said angrily, "your segregation laws don't have a blooming thing to do with this. And in the second place it's none of your business, so why do you want to get involved?"

"Is this the nigger who's causing all the trouble?" asked the dispatcher.

Robinson bristled, then he looked at the people standing near him. He, this colored woman and two civilians were the only Negroes present in a crowd of white people. This was obviously no place to slug a dispatcher. Yet Robinson figured it would be a big mistake to give ground in a case like this, so he became bold. He put his finger in the dispatcher's face and said, "Listen, buddy, let's get a couple of things straight: you're a civilian, and your job is to run this bus system. The Army decides policies on this post, and a ruling just came down from Washington that there will be no more bus segregation on army posts. The second thing we want to get straight is this: I haven't bothered you, never saw you before in my life, so when you make a remark like that, you're asking for trouble."

As Robinson started to walk away, two military policemen, a corporal and a private, walked up with a driver, who had run to get them.

"I understand there's been some trouble here, Lieutenant," the corporal said. "Would you mind coming over to talk to the duty officer?"

"Of course I don't mind. Where is he?"

"Lieutenant Robinson, would you like me to go with you?" asked the woman who had sat with him. "You might want a witness. These things can get twisted around so badly."

"No, I don't see any reason to delay you. I'm within my rights, so I'm not worried about what's going to take place."

Robinson was taken before Captain Gerald M. Bear of the Military Police, who had already heard the driver's version of what took place aboard the bus.

"What are you trying to do, Lieutenant, start a race riot around here or something?" asked Bear.

"What am I trying to do? I'm simply trying to get from the Officers Club to the hospital."

Bear's secretary, a civilian woman and apparently a Texan, chimed in with the remark that "To sit up there where you know no colored people are supposed to sit, seems to me you were trying to start some trouble."

"I'm simply trying to enjoy my rights."

"Well you know you've got no right sitting up there in the white part of that bus," she replied.

"Just a minute," said Robinson, "who are you and who's questioning me here, an Army captain or a Texas civilian?"

"Now just a minute, Lieutenant," snapped the captain, "you do seem rather uppity and out to make trouble."

"Tell me, Captain, where are you from?" asked Robinson.

"That has nothing whatever to do with the situation. Don't accuse me of prejudice," replied the captain.

"Lieutenant, did you not deliberately pick that seat although there were others in the back?" asked the civilian secretary.

"Obviously I picked that seat or I wouldn't have been sitting in it," said Robinson.

The woman jumped up as if insulted and said, "I don't have to take that sassy kind of talk from you," and she stalked out of the room.

The captain pounded the desk angrily, telling Robinson there was no place in the Army for troublemakers. He told Robinson to return to the hospital and that the proper charges would be filed against him.

When Robinson reached the hospital an officer was there to meet him.

"What's the trouble, Lieutenant? We received a report that you've been involved in quite a disturbance."

"It wasn't much of a disturbance. I just exercised my right to sit where I please on the camp bus and the driver figured it was his duty to impose Texas segregation laws."

"Well, I sort of expected to find a drunken man," said the officer. "The report I got said a drunken Negro officer had tried to start a fight aboard a bus. Just for everybody's protection I think what I'd better do is ask people in the hospital to give you a test to determine whether or not there is alcohol in your blood."

"That's all right with me," said Robinson. "I've never had a drink of whiskey in my life, so if there's any alcohol in my blood we've got a medical miracle." The test, of course, showed no trace of alcohol.

About two weeks later Robinson was told that he had been accused of insubordination, disturbing the peace, conduct unbecoming an officer, insulting a civilian woman (meaning the captain's secretary) and refusing to obey the lawful orders of a superior officer.

When the charges were presented to Colonel Bates, however, he refused to sign them, arguing that if the charges were true, that if Robinson had acted so disrespectfully toward Captain Bear, and that if he had insulted Captain Bear's secretary in the manner set forth in these charges, then Captain Bear himself should be court-martialed for being so incompetent an officer as to allow a second lieutenant to do what Robinson had allegedly done.

There were some people in authority at the camp, however, who would not be outdone. The commanding general transferred Robinson from Colonel Bates' battalion to the 758th Tank Battalion, whose commander promptly signed the charges. Robinson was told to prepare for a court-martial.

Word that court-martial proceedings were scheduled spread rapidly about Camp Hood and through the surrounding community. Negro officers and enlisted men began to grumble openly that here was another case in which a Negro soldier was about to be offered up on the altar of segregation. Several Negro officers insisted that there must be a way to block the court-martial, but they found Robinson so angry over the situation that he could barely discuss it, except to say adamantly, "They'll never get away with it."

Knowing that unless someone did something they *would* get away with it, as they had in so many other instances, a group of Negro officers wrote to the National Association for the Advancement of Colored People, and two of the larger Negro newspapers, the *Chicago Defender* and the *Pittsburgh Courier*, urging that they inquire into the facts of the case. The officers were convinced that camp officials would press the case against Robinson only if they could do so under a cloak of secrecy.

The *Courier* immediately wired the post commandant asking for information about the case, and this caused a major stir. What happened at headquarters as a result of the inquiry is not known, but a few days later Robinson was advised that the grave charges against him, including the one of drunkenness, had been dropped. He was to be prosecuted on two charges:

Charge I: Violation of the 63rd Article of War.

Specifications: in that Second Lieutenant Jack R. Robinson . . . did . . . behave himself with disrespect toward Captain Gerald M. Bear . . . his superior officer, by contemptuously bowing to him and giving him several sloppy salutes, repeating several times "OK Sir", "OK Sir" or words to that effect, and by acting in an insolent, impertinent and rude manner toward the said Captain Gerald M. Bear.

Charge II: Violation of the 64th Article of War.

Specifications: Lieutenant Robinson . . . having received a lawful command from Captain Gerald M. Bear . . . to remain in a receiving room and be seated on a chair on the far side of the receiving room, did . . . wilfully disobey the same.

Robinson was assigned a young southern lawyer as his defense counsel. He was about to express his misgivings about the kind of defense a southern-bred man might give him in a case involving segregation, when the officer approached him.

"In all honesty and fairness to you I don't think I can do a fair job of defending you in this court-martial," the lawyer said.

"Well, I certainly admire you for being honest enough to say so," replied Robinson.

"It isn't so much that I hold any deep prejudices against Negroes, or that I have a great love for bus segregation," replied the southerner. "It's just that, having grown up in a segregated society, I haven't developed arguments against segregation that I feel I would need as a background to defend you adequately. So in justice to you, I thought I'd suggest to you that we bring in another young lawyer here from the Midwest who is very interested in defending you."

Robinson agreed. When the court-martial got under way, on August 2, 1944, Robinson and his lawyers sized up the board, which was headed by a colonel who was strictly a military man, but showed every sign of being fair and honest. There was one Army officer who was obviously a southerner but who was not challenged by the defense because of the belief that he, too, was fair and honest. Robinson was pleased to see that a major who had attended UCLA and a Negro captain who was a lawyer in civilian life were also on the board.

This is how Robinson remembers those fateful hours of testimony:

Colonel Bates came to that court-martial and confirmed every conviction I had held that not only was he a decent man with a keen sense of justice, but he had courage to speak out even at the risk of personal loss. The colonel gave such a high personal recommendation of me that the colonel heading the court-martial board reprimanded him with a suggestion that the colonel must be prejudiced in my behalf. Colonel Bates indicated that he had to be prejudiced in favor of an officer whom he knew to be honest and competent as against one who was either incompetent or a liar.

Captain Bear and the two M.P.'s came in with what was obviously well-rehearsed testimony. But in each instance where they were lying, my lawyer put the same questions to them in different ways. He fouled up Captain Bear completely. The two M.P.'s wound up giving conflicting testimonies. Some members of the board were openly hostile toward Bear. When he indicated that I was disrespectful to him because I cupped my chin in my hand while talking to him, a member of the board asked, "You gave the officer 'at ease,' did you not?" and he admitted that he had.

"Then you consider it disrespectful for a man to be at ease when you have given the order to be so?" The captain indicated that in this case he did.

My lawyer summed up the case beautifully by telling the board that this was not a case involving any violation of the Articles of War, or even of military tradition, but simply a situation in which a few individuals sought to vent their bigotry on a Negro they considered "uppity" because he had the audacity to seek to exercise rights that belonged to him as an American and as a soldier.

The Board quickly found me not guilty of any of the charges and specifications.

Without the court-martial to arouse his anger, to challenge him to prove that Captain Bear was a liar, if not a bigot,

Jackie Robinson might have died of boredom, for neither at Fort Riley nor at Camp Hood was he able to feel that he was making a meaningful contribution to the war. As had often been true in civilian life, there was always that implication that Negroes were dead weight, that there was a limit to how much they could do in defense of their country. It was as if someone were saying: You Negroes are in the Army because the white citizens of Pottsville never would tolerate our sending their sons to war and leaving you bucks to loiter on street corners, so you have been drafted, too. But don't get any notions that you're warriors, for we can win without you. Just load that ammunition, drive those trucks, cook that chow and stay out of the way of the fighting men.

No, no responsible American would ever have said that publicly. Few would have admitted that such were their conscious thoughts. But the pattern of Jim Crow—firmly entrenched in the Army, extremely rigid in the Navy, absolutely unbending in the Marine Corps—was such as to give any Negro the notion that he was merely marking time, serving out his sentence, adding to the numbers because in war, like football, numbers are impressive.

What made things even worse was the Army habit of building its training camps in the South, which brought many Negroes face to face with complete Jim Crow for the first time. It was bad enough being told that the white USO was off limits, or even that certain white residential areas were not to be entered after sundown, but many a G.I. was utterly confused in trying to make sense of Jim Crow laws and customs that varied so widely from one little town to another.

Many white G.I.'s also knew the boredom of camp life around these little southern towns, but for Robinson and other educated Negroes this life was doubly miserable. And if racial rebuffs and humiliations were not enough to make them reluctant to leave posts like Fort Riley, Camp Hood, and Camp Forrest, what they saw when they entered these small towns was enough to demoralize them completely. The pattern was always the same: jeeps and trucks beating a dusty path to the town's major honky-tonk, where local girls watched lust-filled G.I.'s pump quarters into a garish juke box that poured forth a loud, endless stream of Charlie Barnet's "Cherokee," Erskine Hawkins' "Tuxedo Junction" and Glenn Miller over and over with "In the Mood," "String of Pearls" and "Pennsylvania 6-5000."

Jackie would sit watching these honky-tonk scenes with a heart full of sympathy for these small-town girls, many not yet out of their teens and most only an hour or two away from their domestic chores, all dolled up in their cotton blouses and skirts and a splash of dime-store perfume, hungrily seeking entertainment, recreation, emotional outlet in the only place a Negro youngster could find it in most of these towns. How pitifully limited were the horizons of these youngsters. How saddening that one girl might find it her greatest thrill to have "a handsome corporal from New York" treat her to a greasy hamburger and a bottle of pop and lead her onto the sawdust-strewn dance floor. Often the honky-tonk manager would obligingly turn off the lights as Lil Green burst into the lyrics of "In the Dark" and Jackie, like other sensitive, educated Negroes, would listen to the raucous shouts of "Turn out the lights and call the law!" and sense the far-reaching tragedy of it all. Here was the beginning of that morbid parade of statistics about illegitimacy, divorce and venereal disease that men of ill will would continue to cite as proof that Negroes deserve little in the way of freedom.

Robinson found this social dilemma so frustrating that he often preferred staying on the base to going into town with the knowledge that he would come back morose, indignant at the thought that for the Negro G.I.—as for the girls they sought out—there was so little to do that was culturally or morally rewarding. Yet when he stayed at camp the mere environment reminded him that his military life was a mockery. He was heading a tank unit, but his most dangerous engagement had been with a civilian bus driver.

"I ought to get at least a battle star if I can capture three stools from the enemy at the post exchange," he once cracked, referring to his futile effort to halt segregation there.

Robinson was grateful to the volunteer citizens who provided USO facilities, for they did provide some opportunity to find recreation without resorting to the honky-tonks and dives, but he found it doubly irritating that so few Negro G.I.'s wanted to discuss their situation with the thoroughness of individuals planning to do something about it. A sudden vulgar comment about the PX or some other segregated aspect of camp life was supposed to make it clear how they felt; beyond that, most were too busy looking forward to another foray to another honky-tonk to consider any plan to erase their problems.

Jackie's "escape" was his knowledge that no matter how depressing the day might be, there would be one chore he would enjoy: writing to Rae, who was now studying nursing in San Francisco. So each night he would sit for long periods, writing tender letters that served not so much as a chronicle of current events in his life as a rose-colored memory book of Rachel's and his past. Funny what tricks a lonesome heart can play on the memory. A good-night peck becomes rapturous; a tight embrace while dancing to a slow tune conjures up visions of stars and clouds and paradises found; a bashful, cautious kiss on the beach is recalled as a moment of ecstasy to be remembered with a blush.

Yes, the mind plays tricks upon the man, and in his dream the vision, the memory, become real; yet the dream is not the flesh, the memory no caress, so thirty letters a month could not atone for the fact that during four years of courtship he and Rachel had actually been in each other's company no more than six months. The all-too-brief reunions only quickened the loneliness, the longings, and plunged him back into acute and helpless desire. And as sure as there was someone to console, "Absence makes the heart grow fonder," there was a wiseacre to add, "of somebody else."

Smiling grimly, Jackie Robinson said, "War is hell."

And who knew, during those hot summer days of 1944, the hellishness of war better than Rachel Isum. Her brother, a pilot, had been shot down in the European theater. Her brother, whom she loved so much, dead—dead, she was sure, despite her mother's trip to a fortuneteller who gazed into a grimy crystal ball and saw a gentle Yugoslav family befriending a "dark, handsome fallen airman."

Her brother probably dead, but what had she done for her country? Well, she had worked as a riveter at night and gone to school during the day, during her last year at UCLA, but what after that? Nothing. Just going about her nursing chores, studying, engaging in chit-chat with fellow students and corresponding with Jackie.

Rachel convinced herself that she had let her country and her brother down. Perhaps if she joined the Women's Army Corps she could make amends. No matter what, it didn't make sense for her to sit around on the shelf with her heart on her sleeve, waiting for a man who might never come back to her. "Don't sit under the apple tree with anyone else but me." Poppycock. How much could anyone ask of a girl?

After a hasty, anxious exchange of letters, it seemed inevitable that Rae was going to join the WAC's. Jackie suggested that, under the circumstances, it was ridiculous for them to consider themselves engaged.

For two days he watched mail call in agony. His memory had not tricked his mind to the extent that he had forgotten that Rae was proud and strong-willed. On the third day the mailman brought what he had feared was coming: a tiny, cotton-lined package, tightly wrapped, insured and registered, containing the engagement ring and the charm bracelet he had given her.

Jack stared at the sparkling ring, the brightly polished footballs and basketballs on the bracelet, and as the full import of their return hit him, the blood rushed to his head as a sickening feeling of shock surged through him. He walked to his room in the bachelor officers' quarters and lay on his bunk. He dropped the box with the ring and bracelet on his chest and stared at the ceiling. Then he turned the box on its side so he could look at the contents. He recalled the occasion on which he had received each medal on that bracelet, recalled with vivid memory the few times he and Rae had seen each other since she accepted his bracelet. He lifted the box to hurl it across the room. Instead he gripped it tightly in one hand, crushing it; quickly he looked at the ring to see whether he had bent it; noting that he had not, he dropped the ring, bracelet and crumpled box in a chair beside his bunk.

"Four years," he said aloud, as if someone had asked him what was wrong, "four whole years of my life thrown away—just like that."

During the brutally hot Texas nights that followed, Jackie Robinson lay awake, tossing and turning, mentally and emotionally at the edge of a bottomless chasm, gazing into the darkness below at the remnants of a million shattered dreams. Suddenly this girl he loved had become more than a soft mass of human flesh to embrace, to caress, to dream of one day having and holding; she was an innocent freshman girl for whom he had waited in the rain, happy to serve as a protector (even as he laughed at the fact that her father figured every college football hero was an incurable wolf). She was the girl he admired because she was "different," because she was not a social butterfly out chasing a football player because of the glamor of being seen with a campus hero. Now he realized that he appreciated her because she was no giggler, but a mature young woman who quickly understood his shyness, his brusqueness, his outspokenness, his tendency to quarrel with the world, who accepted and allowed for all these things because she had a deep understanding of him and the things that made him what he was.

Jackie told himself over and over that Rae was the girl he had wanted more than any girl in the world. He had wanted her not just for her keen intellect, for the advice she gave him on the problems he faced, not for her good looks (although no man ever lived who thought less of a woman because she was beautiful), but also because Rae was a dreamer, a woman who talked about the future and the good things she wanted her children to get out of life. Jackie wanted these things too, and he realized now that for four years he had been confident that he would have a much better chance of producing these things for his children with Rae at his side—Rae, a young woman from a middle-class family, but a girl with an infinite knowledge of the finest things in life.

At this thought, Robinson chuckled, but there was pain too, for he was remembering the day when Rae and he became engaged. He had told her that as a wedding gift he wanted to give her "something real nice," something she'd wanted all her life, but that since he was broke she would have to select it and let him buy it later. By paying on it gradually, he would be able to get it by the time they were married. So they had gone to the swankiest fur salon in Los Angeles, where Rae told the salesman without a blink that she wanted to look at a sable coat. The salesman just stared at her.

"This is to be my wedding gift—just what I've always dreamed of having," she explained confidently. "You must have a sable coat to fit me."

The salesman smiled. "Young lady," he said, "we don't even have a sable coat in the house. As far as we know, Mrs. Bing Crosby is the only one around here who owns one."

Robinson remembered how he had tried to hold the laughter inside, but finally was forced to chuckle openly, adding to Rae's embarrassment. She had regained her composure quickly, however, and asked the man to bring out Russian ermine. So for months now, he had been making payments on this ermine coat, hoping for the day when he would go back to that store and make the last payment and wrap it around the woman he would call his wife. Now it seemed inevitable that this day never would be.

What Jackie did not know, but hoped passionately, was that Rae also was miserable. She spent hours trying to rationalize her action, fishing for mental support from her fellow nursing students, whose chief reaction seemed to be unhappiness over the fact that Rae wouldn't be getting that weekly box of candy from Jack any more. How ironic, Rae thought, that before she sent back that ring she was sure she wanted to break the shackles of engagement, to live it up a bit and enjoy the gaiety of San Francisco, but now that the shackles were broken she had never in her life felt less like going on a date.

Jackie turned to a pretty, peach-skinned girl in a nearby town, hoping that she would be the magic balm needed by a heart on the rebound, but she failed to fill the void—a fact that became apparent to him only after he had given her the bracelet.

Soon Rae and Jackie found themselves involved in one of those romantic stalemates which, if unbroken, can seriously warp two people's lives. In this case it might very well have had even broader effects, for Rachel was to be a tremendous factor in Robinson's pioneering efforts in the years ahead. Robinson sensed this as he sat at Camp Hood, listening to a friend play melancholy records. As the strains of these melodies, the lyrics that told tormenting stories of foolishly separated lovers, played over and over, Jackie Robinson wondered how he could renew his romance and still maintain the pride that had buoyed him through life. He found a way, as men usually do:

"Dear Rae, Just thought I'd write a friendly note to assure you that there is no bitterness on my part. I want you to know that I still respect you and think you are a wonderful person."

"Dear Jack, I write simply to assure you that I hold no hatred toward you. I sent the ring back because I felt you wanted me to and that in that case it would be the best thing for both of us. Obviously I think you're a fine person too or I would never have accepted your ring."

"Dear Rae, I hope you are not trying to put all the blame on me for a foolish breakup that never should have occurred. I never asked for that ring back. All I said was . . ."

"Dear Jack, Well, I'm happy to know that you think i was foolish for us to break our engagement. But I still main tain that it never would have happened if you hadn't writ ten me that . . ."

Jackie still had the ring, but he and Rae now knew that the engagement was not really broken. All that had really changed were their letters, which became longer, and filled with the explanations and little concessions through which two lovers effect a reconciliation without either one's feeling that he or she has given up too much pride or self-respect.

At this point Jackie had become so involved in the court-martial proceedings that reconciliation efforts reached a low point. He told Rae very little about the impending trial—almost the only information of substance he could provide was a confession that "during a lonely, unhappy moment I gave your bracelet to another girl."

Rachel was momentarily stunned, for she recalled her great joy (and disgust with Jackie's carelessness) on the day the postman arrived with a little paper envelope, mailed from the Youth Camp at Itascadera, with medals dangling through the tattered envelope. Jackie had simply dropped it in this envelope and mailed it, with no insurance or other protection, knowing that she would receive it as a symbol of their going steady, which she had. Now it was gone. She wept briefly, then told herself philosophically that there is always a price for the mistakes people make, and that loss of the bracelet was the price she had paid for helping to break their engagement.

Then came the court-martial to fill Robinson's mind with worry that he might wind up on the army's rock pile, but even this could not prevent an occasional thought about Rae, about how desperately he wanted to get back to California and to her. Upon acquittal, Jackie returned to the hospital, where a decision on his ankle was still pending. Colonel Bates' division had already pulled out, however, and Jackie decided that he would not waive his rights in order to go overseas if he could not go with Bates.

"I sent an air-mail, special-delivery letter to the Adjutant General in Washington," he recalls, "requesting my release from military service. I figured that my letter and the results of that court-martial would probably hit his desk about the same time, and this would enhance my chances of getting a discharge. I wasn't sure what was happening when I received orders transferring me to Camp Breckinridge, Kentucky, but I didn't really care after I learned that I could have leave and visit California en route from Texas to Kentucky."

Jackie went from Texas to Pasadena, where he fretted nervously until his mother said, "Jackie, you know what you want to do is call Rachel. So why don't you go ahead and do it." He telephoned Rae and began with the matter-of-fact comment that he was on the West Coast and didn't want to leave without calling to say hello.

"You mean you're in Los Angeles and don't plan to come up to see me?" Rae asked.

"Well, considering all the trouble we've been through in the last few weeks, and the way things haven't been going right, I thought maybe you'd feel better if I didn't come up."

"Oh, Jack . . ."

The sweet, pleading tone of those two words did it. He grabbed his coat as he slammed the receiver down, forgetting completely to say good-by. He rushed out the front door to his old jalopy and spun the wheels with a screech as he drove away frantically, zooming up the highway in an automobile that roared as if the engine were about to explode, and rattled as if the fenders were about to fall off.

He and Rae had a joyous reunion—doubly joyous because Rae's worry about her brother had been lifted. Much as the fortuneteller had said, a gentle Yugoslav family had befriended him after his plane was shot down. Later he was captured and held in prison camp for eight months. Just liberated, he was now on his way home.

Jack couldn't offer Rae much in the way of out-on-the-town entertainment, for he had dashed up to San Francisco with almost no money. He didn't even have enough to stay in a hotel. He drove over to Oakland to visit his brother Frank's widow, hoping to stay at her apartment, but left when he saw there wasn't even enough room for his sister-in-law and her four children. So Jackie slept in the car every night and frittered away the days, waiting for Rae to get off duty at the hospital.

Jackie mentioned casually that the engagement ring was in the glove compartment of his car and that all Rae had to do to resume their engagement was to reach in and get it. Neither the technique nor the circumstances seemed satisfactory for a re-engagement, so Jackie left San Francisco with the ring still in his glove compartment. He was happy, though, for he was convinced that one day Rae would marry him.

At Camp Breckinridge, Robinson did very little other than wait for word from the Adjutant General. About two months after the court-martial, papers finally reached camp ordering a medical discharge for him.

While he was at Breckinridge, however, a puff of wind and an errant baseball provided a break that changed his life:

> I was walking across the camp recreation field when a baseball arched high into the sky and was carried toward me by a strong breeze. As it hit the ground and bounced toward me I leaned over and scooped it up with one hand. I saw a player running in my direction so I pegged a perfect strike to him. As it plopped into his glove he shouted, "Nice throw!"

> I strolled over to where this group was practicing and saw that the fellow to whom I had thrown the ball was breaking off a beautiful curve.

> "That's a dilly of a curve," I said. "Let me see that baseball again."

> He tossed it to me and I thought that it was lighter than the regulation baseball, yet it was no small feat to break off that kind of curve even with this ball.

> "You seem to know a bit about baseball," he said. "Are you a ballplayer?"

> I said that I had played baseball at UCLA. He said he had heard of me as a football player and a track man, but not as a baseball player. Then he explained that he pitched for the Kansas City Monarchs in the Negro American League and

that the team needed good players. He suggested that I write if I thought I could make the grade. I wrote.

Meanwhile, the president of Sam Houston College, a small Negro institution in Texas, wired asking me to become basketball coach. I accepted this job.

I was sitting on top of the world. It seemed unbelievable that a man who had just had so many troubles could be so happy--out of the Army, a job, and a girl waiting for me in California.

Jackie wasted no time getting to Los Angeles, where Rae was working, having completed her studies. This reunion was the happiest ever. That evening they went to the beach, where they sat in the sand and dangled their bare feet in the surf as it broke in jewel-like beads on this beautiful moonlit night. Then they would race barefoot at the water's edge. She and Jackie reminisced about the past and talked about the future. He took her into his arms and both sensed that a few moments together on a moonlit beach could wipe away more misunderstanding than a thousand carefully written letters.

As she moved out of his arms, Rae noticed that Jackie had pulled the engagement ring out of his pocket. "Oh, Jack," she said, "you've picked a beautiful moonlit night, and I'm trapped again." As she slipped the ring on her finger, both gave a sigh of relief; it was good to put an end to misunderstanding.

"Shall we get married tonight?" Jackie asked.

"No," Rae replied. "Let's wait a little longer. I don't think it would be fair to either my mother or yours for us to elope. That sounds like child's play anyhow."

"Well, let's get married in a few days. I don't see much point in waiting. I'm out of the Army, so you don't have to worry about me going overseas to make a quick widow out of you. And I've got a job."

"I know," Rae said, "but can't we postpone it for just a little while? You've accepted this job as a coach, but you're still talking about baseball with that Kansas City team. Why don't we get married after I go to New York? I've wanted to go for so long. My family has given me a hundred dollars as a graduation present and I intend to go to New York on that. I've written the Visiting Nurse Service in New York and my mother has made arrangements with a friend of hers for one of my girl friends and me to stay in an apartment. Can you please wait, Jack?"

Robinson hated the delay, yet deep inside he felt relieved, for his future seemed so much in doubt. He hadn't the remotest idea what the coaching job would be like—or what the Monarchs would do. He agreed to the delay and left for Sam Houston College, only to find that of the three hundred students, about thirty-five were boys, only seven of whom came out for basketball. Robinson whipped together a fair team, however, sending the campus into a frenzy when it whipped the team that had won the league championship the year before.

The coaching job did not last long, for the Monarchs finally wrote offering Robinson three hundred dollars a month to play for them. He demanded four hundred and the owners agreed, so in April, 1945, Jackie Robinson became a professional baseball player.

5....The Un-American Pastime

Jackie had been in the Monarchs' training camp in Houston only a few days when he received a telephone call from Wendell Smith, sports editor of the *Pittsburgh Courier,* the Negro weekly which had probably saved his neck at Camp Hood just by asking a few questions.

"Jackie, the Boston Red Sox have agreed to give some Negroes a tryout, and we need a couple or three good men. Can you come up?" Smith said.

"Aw, quit kidding," said Robinson. "What's up, Wendell?"

"I'm not joking. A city councilman and some other people have put so much heat on the Red Sox that they've consented to a tryout. Now we've got to put up or shut up."

"But I just got here, Wendell. Haven't even been here long

enough to prove I belong on the squad, and I can't afford to give up the job."

"You can work it out with the owners. We really need you, boy. You know how important it is to the whole race for us to put our best foot forward. We've got to have some players of your background and ability."

"You got anybody else?"

"I'm pretty sure Sam Jethroe of the Cleveland Buckeyes and Marvin Williams of the Philadelphia Stars will go. You could really fix us up pretty."

Robinson promised to see what he could work out, but just as he feared, the Monarch management opposed his leaving the team. When he informed Smith, the latter telephoned one of the owners and said, in effect, How would you white fellows who're making money off Jim Crow baseball like to have the *Courier* tell the public that you're blocking efforts to get Negroes into organized baseball? The owners decided that Robinson had better go to the tryout.

The three players met Smith in New York on April 12, and as they traveled to Boston, the newsman explained how the tryout had been arranged.

Dave Egan of the *Boston Record* had stirred up citizens of that area with his courageous attacks on Jim Crow baseball. "We are fighting, as I understand it, for the rights of under-privileged peoples everywhere," Egan wrote. "We weep for the teeming masses of India. Down the years, we must have contributed millions to the suffering Armenians. We have room in our souls to pity the Chinese, and the Arabs, and the brave Greeks. Could we, by any chance, spare a thought for the Negro in the United States? Do we, by any chance, feel disgust at the thought that Negro athletes, solely because of their color, are barred from playing baseball?"

One of the angriest sources of support came from a white city councilman named Isadore Muchnick, who represented a largely Negro neighborhood. When he could get no consideration from the Red Sox and Braves managements through normal requests, he startled them one day with the threat

that he would support recurring demands by religious groups
to ban Sunday baseball in Boston. Smith, who for years had
conducted a crusade against Jim Crow baseball, had read of
Muchnick's threat and had deliberated for several days as to
whether he ought to try to collaborate with Muchnick and use
this threat of a Sunday ban as a lever against stubborn baseball magnates. Smith knew, however, that a strange psychology, a perverse kind of logic, operated among many white
Americans where racial injustice was concerned. It made
them view as a "troublemaker" any Negro who deliberately
provoked a situation out of which he might secure equal
rights, even if those rights were clearly set forth in the Constitution, or even local statutes and ordinances. It is the kind
of logic that makes whites of supposedly good will turn
against a Negro denied service at a restaurant if there is some
indication that he went there with the deliberate purpose of
provoking a case so as to get the law enforced. It is the kind
of logic that says anyone working in behalf of the Negro must
use only to the most circumspect tactics, must never do anything that might be construed as a "plot" to outmanipulate a
perpetrator of injustice.

Smith knew that the baseball owners would win a lot of
sympathy from people who would consider it less than
cricket to pressure them with the threat of the Sunday ban.
Yet he also knew that Negroes had to be seen by baseball
managers, coaches and other top officials, else these officials
would go on forever hiding behind the myth that there were
no Negroes around who could make good in organized baseball; that not only were the Negro leagues virtually a racket,
but the caliber of baseball they played was no more than
semipro. Smith was confident that in those Negro leagues
there were more than a dozen men who, with a minimum of
polishing, could hold their own with the best, not just during
wartime major leagues, but in the majors of the best days.

Smith finally called Muchnick and told him that if the
councilman really wanted to put some pressure on the Boston
teams he could provide players of major league quality.
Muchnick told Smith to bring his players.

"So that's how we got this tryout," Smith concluded, "so don't expect them to roll out the velvet carpet for you. Just play the best ball you know how."

The group got an icy reception in Boston, with the Red Sox management offering what the Negroes considered a lame excuse why the tryout could not be held as scheduled.

Robinson was angry. "Listen, Smith," he said. "This is why I hesitated to come. It burns me up to come fifteen hundred miles to have them give me the runaround."

"It burns me up too," Smith said, "but I know they're hoping we'll get discouraged and go home. Let's stick around long enough to let them know we aren't going to be brushed off just like that"—he snapped his finger—"that if we do stay around long enough for them to run out of excuses, somebody's going to hear about it."

The next day the Red Sox had another excuse, and Muchnick got angrier. When he put more pressure on, the Red Sox announced that the tryouts would be conducted on April 16.

When Robinson, Williams and Jethroe got to Fenway Park, a tryout for about a dozen young white players already was under way. The Negroes ran onto the field and began to shag fly balls. Muchnick and Smith looked around uneasily to see what kind of tryout the Negroes were about to get. Various club officials watched from the stands as Jethroe loped across the green pasture like a gazelle, raising his gloved hand at that last split second to snag balls that, when hit, had seemed beyond the reach of any outfielder. Robinson roamed over what seemed an unbelievable amount of territory for a man whose gait was so awkward and unimpressive.

"I laughed a bit every time I caught a ball," Robinson recalls. "I felt that we were merely going through the motions, especially after being given the runaround for about four days."

An official whistled and waved at the Negroes, asking them to come in and hit. Williams, a right-handed batter like Robinson, was the first to bat, and he found Fenway Park's short left-field fence a delightful target. The pitcher fired a fast ball and Williams banged it high off the wall. Now Robinson stepped in, his feet spread wide apart, his bat held high and cocked a bit behind his head. The pitcher came in with a curve. Jackie lunged. A Red Sox coach mentioned the unorthodox way that Jackie's right foot left the ground completely, yet the bat smashed into the ball and sent it winging against that left-field fence. Robinson smashed pitch after pitch into the outfield, and the white players stood around the batting cage and watched, obviously impressed by the Negroes' ability.

When the coach waved to a bat boy to bring out a new box of baseballs so the Negroes could hit some more, Robinson chuckled again. "Boy, now that we're out here these people are going all the way to make it appear that we got a fairer than fair tryout. But they aren't fooling anyone."

When the tryouts were over the coach told the three players that they had made a good showing. He handed them application cards to fill out and said that they would hear from the Red Sox.

That night the Negroes met for dinner and to laugh about events of the last few days.

Jethroe: "Did you get that last line, boys—that 'don't call me, I'll call you' line?"

Williams: "I can hear them now, arguing about how quickly the world will come to an end if a Negro joins that Red Sox organization. Can't you hear somebody asking, 'Would you want your daughter to marry a Negro baseball player?' "

Robinson: "You know, fellas, it's against baseball regulations for a pitcher to have a marked or spotted ball. Maybe they figure every time we touch that ball a little black will rub off on it." The players fell out with laughter.

Smith sat brooding in disappointment, not so much because of the Boston reception, but because the Negroes and their tryout would not get the publicity he had hoped for— and for the saddest possible reason: the newspapers were full of stories about the death of Franklin Delano Roosevelt.

As the four men engaged in serious discussion of the situation, there was agreement that they should not despair. The

truth was that the future had never looked brighter for the
Negro athlete—or for the Negro in general, for that matter.
The economic crisis of the thirties and the great national
struggle to end it, the New Deal's intrusion into economic
and social relationships, and more than all else, the war
against Hitler and Tojo, had profoundly changed American
racial attitudes. All too often the Negro was still the shoeshine
boy, the Pullman porter, the janitor, the yard boy, but more
and more Americans had become unwilling to accept this as
the proper and inevitable pattern of life.

"Boston isn't the only place where the heat is on, and Egan
and Muchnick aren't the only people on our side," said Smith.
"They're giving Branch Rickey and the Dodgers so much heat
right now that Rickey's called a press conference for tomorrow. I'll be there.

"Ed Sullivan, Damon Runyon and a lot of people of that
caliber are giving baseball's bosses holy hell, so sooner or later
something's got to give."

"Well, it won't be easy," said Robinson.

"No," said Smith, "because a lot of Negroes and white lib-
erals are still talking out of both sides of their mouths." He
mentioned specifically a column written by Stanley Frank of
the *New York Post* in 1942 in which Frank said he didn't
want to see Negroes in the Big Leagues "under present conditions" because southern players would "brandish sharp
spikes with intent to cut and maim Negro infielders" and
pitchers would throw "murderous bean-balls" at colored
players.

"It galls the hell out of me to have some white guy tell me
that Negroes have to stay Jim Crowed 'cause it's safer. I'll
take my chances," said Jethroe.

The *Sporting News*, baseball's "bible," not only argued, in
a 1942 editorial, that separate leagues were best for Negroes,
but to support the contention that Negroes were not ready or
willing to mingle with white athletes, it told a story attrib-
uted to John Carmichael of the *Chicago Daily News:* " 'There's
still the story of Joe Louis, one of our favorite guys of all
time, being interviewed in his Chicago home the morning

after he whipped Jim Braddock for the heavyweight championship of the world,' wrote Carmichael. 'As the talk progressed,
the fumes of pork chops on the fire assailed the nostrils of both
men. Each allowed as how he could do with some. Quick as a
flash, Louis set up a card table. Arranged for one lunch to be
spread thereon.

" 'If you'll excuse me,' he told the reporter, 'I'm going to
have lunch with some friends in the kitchen. When we get
through we'll talk some more.' "

This, of course, was a subtle way of saying that Joe Louis
preferred segregation when it came to eating, and that most
Negroes preferred to keep to themselves. Louis says the only
trouble with the story is that neither Carmichael nor any
other newspaperman came to his house the morning after the
Braddock fight, and even if they had they wouldn't have
found him at home. And even had he been there, says Joe,
Carmichael wouldn't have smelled pork chops because Joe
never ate a bit of pork in all his years as a fighter.

Nobody knew better than Smith that organized baseball
faced a lot of pressures in 1945 that did not exist in 1942—
pressures that were too great to be diverted by propaganda
about the nature of Negroes.

For one thing, New York State now had a fair employment
practices law, and for a lot of people New York City's three
big league teams were obvious targets of that law. It was no
secret, either, that both Governor Thomas Dewey and Mayor
Fiorello La Guardia were eager to influence the huge Negro
vote, and a campaign was under way to convince them that
the one who could say he destroyed Jim Crow in baseball
would win it.

Major league magnates had begun to feel the pressure of the
Ives-Quinn (FEP) law only a few days after it was enacted.
Chick Solomon, a former ballplayer and a well-known Negro
sports photographer, was in Albany to photograph Dewey
signing the bill. Solomon returned to the Hotel Theresa, in
Harlem, where Negro National League club owners were in
session. Clutching a copy of the bill in his hand, Solomon said
to some of his friends, "The law is on our side now. Doesn't

mean it's going to make Christians out of these bastards who run the major leagues, but at least there's nothing to prevent any qualified Negro player from walking into a major league training camp and demanding a tryout. All we need is a good man and we can really put the pressure on, and I'm thinking that the man we need is a catcher named Roy Campanella, who can slug that ball a country mile."

Someone mentioned that, because of wartime travel restrictions, the Brooklyn Dodgers were in training at Bear Mountain, about fifty miles from New York City, and that it ought to be a simple matter to get one of the Negro players in New York to go there. Campanella was in Baltimore, so Solomon dropped the idea temporarily. Meanwhile, Joe Bostic, sports editor of the *People's Voice,* a Negro newspaper in New York, decided he'd put Solomon's idea into action. He contacted a pitcher named Terris McDuffie and a first baseman for the New York Cubans named Showboat Thomas and, accompanied by a sports writer from the *Daily Worker,* the Communist newspaper, showed up unannounced at Bear Mountain to demand a tryout from Branch Rickey. Rickey agreed to a token tryout and then announced that he was not interested in either player.

But pressure continued. Negroes picketed Yankee Stadium on opening day with signs reading: "If we can pay, why can't we play?" and "No ifs, ands or buts, black men are not allowed to play."

Benjamin Davis, at the time a New York City councilman and one of the top figures in the Communist party, issued a lurid pamphlet showing two Negroes on the cover. One was a dead soldier lying on a European battlefield, the other a Negro baseball player. The caption read, "Good enough to die for his country, but not good enough for organized baseball!"

Now Negro writers had pressured Rickey to explain why he was not interested in McDuffie and Thomas, so Rickey had called the press conference. But Rickey could not tell these writers what he really thought: that McDuffie and Thomas were inferior players who could not carry, either on or off the field, the load that would be on the first Negro in organized baseball; that Bostic had brought them to Bear Mountain primarily to get a story, which would have been justified if there had been any chance that the story would do any good. Rickey knew that to discuss the kind of Negro needed to break baseball's color bar would be to indicate prematurely that he had been thinking about it, so he devoted the press conference primarily to an attack on the Negro leagues as "rackets" and to announcing his plans to form the United States League, "a well-organized, legitimate Negro league," which might eventually take its place in organized baseball. He blasted the Communists for trying to "use" this issue and the Negro and said they were hurting whatever opportunity Negroes had of getting into organized baseball. When the meeting was over most of the Negro writers stalked out thoroughly dissatisfied, some of them quite angry.

Ludlow W. Werner of the *New York Age,* another Negro weekly, turned to a colleague: "My aching back! Did you ever hear such double talk from a big pompous ass in your life? I predict that it'll be a cold day in hell when that big windbag puts a Negro into a Brooklyn uniform."

Not one of these writers was aware of Branch Rickey's actions toward bringing Negroes into organized baseball, actions that had begun some two years before New York had an FEPC. In fact, in 1943, a few days after Rickey signed a five-year contract as general manager of the Dodgers, he told key men in the Dodger organization that the whole future of the Brooklyn team depended on whether or not its owners were willing to gamble on signing up good young talent so as to have a lead on the other teams at the end of the Second World War. Rickey told George McLaughlin, president of the Brooklyn Trust Company, which represented the Dodgers' chief financial support, that he intended to "beat the bushes and take whatever comes out." Rickey mentioned then that "this might include a Negro player or two." McLaughlin, a highly respected civic leader in Brooklyn, said, "Why not? You might come up with something."

As Rickey now tells it, he took this step with many motives, the desire to build the best baseball team being not the least one. But certainly a significant reason was the deep hatred of racial injustice that he had carried with him from childhood. This is how Rickey tells that story:

"As a boy in Ohio I grew up knowing Negroes. The two smartest kids in my room in grammar school were Negroes, and they were fine human beings whom I respected and admired. Later, I was baseball coach and director of athletics at Ohio Wesleyan University in Ohio. There was a Negro on that team named Charles Thomas who was not only an athlete of great skill but a real gentleman, a sensitive human being. He was a great outfielder. He covered a lot of territory, and his strong arm was one that base runners had to respect. I quickly figured, however, that that arm would be more valuable to the team behind the plate, where he could throw out runners trying to steal. I was deeply impressed by his ability to switch from the outfield to the more difficult, heavily responsible job of a catcher. In the spring of 1904 we went to South Bend, Indiana, to play a game. When we walked into the hotel the desk clerk looked up to announce that no Negroes were permitted to stay there. I bridled at first, and a lump came into my throat—a lump that I now know must have been extremely small compared with the one that formed in Thomas's throat. I turned to our student manager and asked him to go to the YMCA to see if the team could stay there. As the student manager walked away, Thomas turned to me and said that he didn't want to be a handicap to the team, that perhaps everyone would be happier if he went back to Ohio Wesleyan. I told him that under no circumstances would we do that, and I went to the manager of the hotel and said to him that I'd be happy to have Thomas stay in my room. I made this proposition simply to make the manager understand that I had no feelings of superiority about a Negro being in the same hotel, that indeed I'd be honored to have a man like Thomas as my roommate. I later realized that in many cases a Negro could stay in a white hotel if he were a servant traveling with a white man and that so long as this relationship of master and servant was obvious, then it was perfectly all right with whites who otherwise would object to a Negro's staying in the hotel. Apparently this sort of arrangement was satisfactory, so the manager permitted Thomas to go to my room with me. Thomas sat on the bed and wept. He rubbed his hands and said to me: 'Black skin. If only I could make them white!'

"That scene haunted me for many years, and I vowed that I would always do whatever I could to see that other Americans did not have to face the bitter humiliation that was heaped upon Charles Thomas."

The Negro writers who stalked away from that press conference could only assume that creation of the "Brooklyn Brown Dodgers" and another Negro league was Rickey's misguided idea of the way to fight injustice in athletics, for none of them knew (as no one in baseball knew) that Rickey had spent more than $35,000 to scout Negro players and that organized baseball was where he hoped to use them.

"I never mentioned to anybody, anywhere in all of this world, what I really had in mind," Rickey continues. "The baseball people were the very last ones that I wished to know anything about it. If the United States League succeeded on a permanent basis, well and good. That result, however, was incidental to my main purpose. I confess without any embarrassment whatever that the fundamental objective in my effort to organize this league was to enable me to do open scouting, with experienced men, in the Negro field. I was able to place my entire scouting staff, if I wished, into the Negro leagues, in Cuba, Puerto Rico and particularly Mexico. Within a year or so I found out that the best Negro players were right at home—in the United States."

If the Boston experience had saddened Wendell Smith, Rickey's performance made him sick at heart. But rather than stalk out in anger, Smith waited to talk to him, hopeful that he could get it across to the Brooklyn magnate that Negroes would not consider it a favor if he built the most efficient all-Negro league imaginable.

Rickey surprised him, however, by asking how the Boston tryout went. Before Smith could reply, Rickey continued:

"Were there any players in your group really good enough to make the majors?"

"There was one player who could make good in any league —Jackie Robinson."

Rickey leaned back in his chair, lifting his bushy eyebrows as he dragged on a cigar and sent a puff of smoke toward the ceiling. "Robinson, eh? Jackie Robinson. I must remember that name."

Rickey knew that he had the backing of the Dodgers' directors and stockholders, who had given him a blank check not only for wartime scouting but to bring into the Dodger organization the best talent he could find without regard for the customary though unwritten restriction of race. Now the most crucial task before him was to find a Negro who would be a virtual cinch to succeed on the field. To select the wrong Negro would be calamitous, Rickey knew, because baseball leaders would quickly do what was done so often in industry: point to one Negro's flop as an excuse for never giving another an opportunity to succeed. At the same time, Rickey knew that the advent of a Negro into organized baseball would be a matter of such great public interest, a matter reported and discussed by so many newspapermen with so many different kinds of prejudice, that a lot more than the man's baseball ability would be a factor in his success or failure. Rickey realized that baseball players become great public heroes, and that many baseball people were afraid a Negro baseball star would find himself besieged by white women eager to give him their affections. The image of Jack Johnson and his three white wives was always before them. Rickey wanted to make sure that the Negro selected to end Jim Crow in baseball would be the right man *off* the field—a clean-living family man whose character was above reproach. These two things, he felt, were utterly necessary in order to get a good reaction from the press, and from the public, which would ultimately decide the outcome of his project.

Beyond that, Rickey felt that he would have to have the cooperation and understanding of Negro leaders who, doubting his motives, might act rashly and wreck the project; or who, on the other hand, over-elated and enthusiastic, might antagonize white players and the white public. In the long run, he knew, nothing would be more crucial than this question of whether white players would accept a Negro.

Rickey thoroughly distrusted several baseball club owners and officials, and he was confident that if they got advance word of what he planned, they would prevent the Dodgers from taking on a Negro. Also, Rickey remembered, several of his scouts were southerners with ingrained prejudices. If he told them they were scouting players for an all-Negro team they would bring him accurate and honest reports on the ability of various players, but some of them would be handicapped by prejudice if told that they were looking for a Negro who eventually would play with white boys. This was particularly true in the case of Wid Matthews, a Mississippian whom Rickey considered very prejudiced against Negroes, but one of the ablest scouts in the country. Matthews was the first scout he sent out on this project.

Along with Matthews, Rickey sent out Tom Greenwade, George Sisler and Clyde Sukeforth, with instructions that they were to pay their own way into Negro games and talk very little about what they were doing, then send him their reports on players they thought had better than average baseball ability. His men scoured the field. On one occasion, Rickey found Sukeforth waiting to give him an unusual in-person report about a Negro pitcher that Sukeforth thought was "out of this world."

Sukeforth reared back and flung his arms through the air, as if to imitate the pitcher's style. "That's the way this big guy fogs that ball into the plate. We've just got to get this man, Mr. Rickey," Sukeforth said.

"What's his name?" Rickey asked.

"Don Newcombe, and he's a real pip," said Sukeforth.

Rickey checked Newcombe further and decided that he was a good prospect but not the "pioneer" he wanted.

Rickey's scouts also watched Campanella, both in Mexico and later in the United States. Some scouts raved; others were not overimpressed. Rickey took a personal look and thought

Campanella had great potential, despite the fact that he seemed to take his eye off the ball at the last second—what ballplayers call a blind swing—causing him to strike out a great deal. He also decided that Campanella was no pioneer. Eventually, Rickey agreed that the most likely prospect was that young fellow Wendell Smith had recommended to him, Jackie Robinson, whose name showed up most frequently and most favorably in scouting reports. Rickey asked his scouts to cover every detail of Robinson's strengths and weaknesses. Reports came back that he was a classy fielder, but that his arm wasn't strong enough for shortstop. Rickey again sent out Sukeforth, who sent word back that Robinson's arm probably wasn't good enough for shortstop, "but he could play second base in any league."

Convinced of the young Negro's ability, Rickey assumed personally the task of determining whether or not Robinson would be the right man *off* the field. He went to California, where he talked to people who had known Robinson in high school, junior college and UCLA. He got glowing reports of Robinson's athletic ability. He learned that Robinson neither drank nor smoked, that he was a "clean-living young man who didn't run around with girls." But there was one bit of derogatory information that kept popping up: Jackie Robinson was labeled a "smart guy whose major fault is that he likes to argue with white folks." Someone else said that, in basketball, "Robinson's number one trouble was that he would argue with and talk back to white officials and players." Someone else told Rickey that as a youth Robinson was often in trouble with policemen because he was always "shootin' off his mouth about his constitutional rights." Rickey came to the conclusion that there was nothing wrong with Robinson's background. "I appreciate your information," Rickey told one of the people he talked to, "but from what you have said to me, and what I have learned elsewhere, Robinson's biggest crime so far was being born a Negro. If he had done the things people are criticizing him for as a white player he would have been praised to the skies as a fighter, a holler guy, a real competitor, a ballplayer's ballplayer. But because he's

black his aggressiveness is offensive to some white people.
Well that doesn't militate against him with me. From what
I've learned, the boy's background is clean, and I think he's
the man I want. I've got to have a boy with some aggressiveness, with some guts, because he's got to be bold and gritty
enough to stand up unflinchingly, and he's got to be sensible
enough to live with the glorification that comes to a baseball
star."

Rickey's friend must have sensed that these were not the
words of a man looking for just another Negro to add to just
another Negro baseball team.

6....The Courageous One

Branch Rickey knew that it was time for him to talk directly
to Robinson, and to make his personal, man-to-man assess-
ment of Robinson's qualifications to lead a revolution that
Rickey felt would be crucial in both their lives. He sat in
his office one day in early August, 1945 thinking about the
way in which this issue had divided his family. His son, Branch,
Jr., was completely in favor of the Dodgers' bringing a Negro
into organized baseball, but he feared other owners would
make life miserable for his father. Mrs. Rickey, Sr., also
feared reaction.

"Branch," she had pleaded, "you're too old to go through
this ordeal, too old to take the abuse they'll heap on you."

"A man is never too old to do what he knows is right and
what his conscience tells him he must do," Rickey replied.

Then there were the daughters. "Lord," Rickey said to his wife, "that Jane"—a daughter in Elmira, N.Y.—"how she's supporting me. What a leaning post she has become, because she believes I ought to do it on the basis of principle. And Alice—she's got her oar in the water and she's pulling for me to beat the band. Mary and Sue—they're neutral, but I think they know that I've got to do this thing because it's right."

In late August, Rickey called in his most trusted aide, Sukeforth, and asked him to find Robinson and bring him to Brooklyn if he was convinced on this final viewing that the Negro really could make good as a baseball player. Sukeforth had trouble locating the Monarchs, who were playing a notoriously unreliable schedule, as Negro teams usually did, but finally he caught them at Comiskey Park in Chicago. Someone told him that Robinson would be wearing Number 8. Sukeforth bought a box seat ticket and waited. Finally he saw Number 8, the husky, muscular, pigeon-toed player who kept chattering in a high-pitched voice as he pounded his fist into his glove. Sukeforth stepped to the railing and motioned to Robinson, who walked over with a clearly suspicious look on his face.

"You're Jackie Robinson, right?"

"That's right."

"I'm Clyde Sukeforth of the Brooklyn Dodger organization."

Robinson gave a look of disbelief.

"Seriously, I represent the Brooklyn Dodgers. You might have heard that Branch Rickey, our general manager, is organizing another Negro league and a team of Brown Dodgers. He's eager to get some topnotch ball players. We've heard a lot of glowing reports about you and he asked me to come out tonight and look you over. He wants me to see you throw a few from the hole at shortstop."

Robinson thought of the runaround in Boston, but he was convinced that Sukeforth really represented the Dodgers. He had heard rumors of the Brown Dodgers.

"You won't see me throw any from the hole tonight," Robinson said. "I've got a bum shoulder. Fell on it a couple of days ago, and the trainer says I'll be out for a week."

"I see," said Sukeforth. "But I sure would like to talk to you after the game. Any chance of your meeting me?"

Robinson was silent as he pounded the pocket of his glove a couple times more with his fist. "What did you say your name was?"

Sukeforth spelled it out for him and told Robinson that he was staying at the Stevens, where he would be waiting in the lobby near the cigar stand.

"Sure, I'll drop by to talk to you. Ought to get there before midnight."

Waiting for Robinson, Sukeforth sat in the cocktail lounge, mulling over the instructions Rickey had given him. Rickey was still concerned about Robinson's ability to go to his right from the shortstop position and make that long throw to first. Sukeforth was unsure what to do, since he could not see Robinson play. Yet the boss seemed to want very much to talk to this player, so Sukeforth decided to ask Robinson to go to Brooklyn with him.

On the morning of August 28, 1945, Sukeforth led a bewildered young ballplayer into the office of a man who had an awesome reputation even among experienced players who had never been burdened by insecurities imposed by race. That morning, during three extraordinary hours in the walnut-paneled office of perhaps the smartest baseball man of his time, the mark of history was stamped on twenty-six-year-old Jackie Robinson.

As he and Sukeforth strode into this finely furnished office, decorated with a lighted fish tank, the man with the round belly and bushy brows got out of his leather swivel chair, shifted his cigar from the pudgy fingers on his right hand to those of his left and shook hands with Robinson. The formal pleasantries were brief, for Rickey quickly asked Jackie: "You got a girl?"

Embarrassed to face such a personal question so soon, Jackie replied hesitantly, "I don't know."

"What do you mean, you don't know?"

"I mean that I had a girl, one to whom I'm engaged, but the way I've been traveling around with the Monarchs, never seeing her or anything, a fellow can't be sure if he's got a girl or not."

"Is she a fine girl, good family background, educated girl?"

"They don't come finer, Mr. Rickey."

"Then you know doggone well you've got a girl! When we get through today you may want to call her up, 'cause there are times when a man needs a woman by his side. By the way, are you under contract to the Monarchs?"

"No, sir."

"Do you have any agreement with them, written or oral, to play with them either the rest of this year, next year or any length of time?"

"No, sir. No agreement whatsoever except that they pay me a certain amount every payday. But we just play from payday to payday. Either one of us could break it off at the end of the month if necessary."

"Tell me, Jackie, do you have any idea why I want to talk to you?"

"All I know is what Mr. Sukeforth told me, and the rumors I've been hearing about you starting a new Negro league and a team called the Brown Dodgers."

"No, Jackie, that isn't really it. You were brought here to play for the Brooklyn organization—perhaps, as a start, for Montreal."

Robinson was stunned. Was this another in that long string of situations in which he, like other Negroes, was encouraged to build mountains of hopes and dreams, only to see them tumble at the last minute?

"Me? Me play with Montreal . . . ?"

"If you can make it. If you make the grade."

Rickey turned to Sukeforth and asked him whether he thought Robinson could make the grade.

"He's a good ballplayer, Mr. Rickey," Sukeforth replied. "Probably the best bunter you ever laid eyes on, and can he run those bases!"

Rickey's voice rose into a stentorian roar. This man, who was an orator even if only asking someone to pass the salt and pepper, flailed his arms and cried out: "I know he's a ball-player. I've watched him. We scouted you for weeks, Jackie. We know what you can do on the baseball field. But this means more than being able to play baseball. I mean, have you got the guts?"

"I'll make it if I get the opportunity . . ." said Robinson in a comparative whisper.

Now Rickey was thundering again. "I want to be honest with you, Jackie. I want to level with you here today. I heard all the stories of racial resentment toward you. They told me out in Pasadena that you're a racial agitator. They told me at UCLA that in basketball you had trouble with coaches, players and officials. I just want to tell you that my thorough investigation convinced me that the criticisms are unjustified, that if you'd been white it would have been nothing. So I'm dismissing these rumors as not amounting to a hill of beans. But the thing I want to convince you of," he fairly bellowed as he pounded his desk, "is that we can't fight our way through this. Jackie, we've got no army . . ." and his voice was trailing off into a murmur ". . . there's virtually nobody on our side. No owners, no umpires, very few newspapermen. And I'm afraid that many fans may be hostile. We'll be in a tough position, Jackie. We can win only if we can convince the world that I'm doing this because you're a great ballplayer, a fine gentleman.

"So there's more than just playing," Rickey continued, his voice rising rapidly again, "I wish it meant only hits, runs and errors—only the things they put in the box score. Because you know—yes, *you* would know, Jackie—that a baseball box score is a democratic thing. It doesn't tell how big you are, what church you attend, what color you are or how your father voted in the last election. It just tells what kind of baseball player you were on that particular day."

"Mr. Rickey, when the chips are down, isn't what they put in the box score what really counts?" said Jackie, warming up to the man now, realizing that Rickey's loud bark was a lot worse than his bite, feeling that there was something he too could contribute to this startling discussion.

"Yes, it's all that *ought* to count, but it isn't. Maybe one of these days it *will* be all that counts. That's one of the reasons why I've got you here, Jackie. If you're a good enough ball-player, and a big enough man, we can make this a start in the right direction. But let me tell you it's going to take an awful lot of courage."

Rickey strode over and put his face close to Robinson's, which was now gleaming with tiny beads of perspiration; there were wrinkles etched deeply in his forehead, a sign of intense concentration. "Have you got the guts to play the game no matter what happens? That's what I want to know!" Rickey exclaimed.

"I think I can play the game, Mr. Rickey," said Robinson without flinching.

"All right. You're standing in the batter's box in a tense situation. I'm a notorious bean-baller. I wing a fast one at you that grazes your cap and sends you sprawling back on your butt. What do you do?"

"It won't be the first time a pitcher threw one at me, Mr. Rickey," Robinson said matter-of-factly.

Rickey leaned back and studied Robinson's features for a few seconds. "All right," he said. "All right. So I'm an opposing player, and we're in the heat of a crucial game. I slap the ball out into the field and I'm rounding first and I charge into second and we have a close play and I collide with you. As we untangle I lunge toward you"—he lunged toward Robinson—"and I shout, 'Get out of my way, you dirty black son of a bitch!' What do you do?"

Robinson was silent, remembering those days in Pasadena when anyone who hurled that kind of epithet at him, in a football game or out of one, was likely to get his nose punched in. He looked at Rickey, waiting for the answer, and he licked his lips and swallowed. He knew the answer Rickey wanted. That he would grin and bear it. But before he could get the answer out, Rickey was unfolding another situation.

"You're playing shortstop and I come down from first, stealing, flying in with my spikes high, and I cut you in the leg. As the blood trickles down your shin I grin at you and say, 'Now how do you like that, nigger boy?' What do you do?"

Robinson was burning hot inside. Here stood a black man with a tremendous self-respect born out of adversity, a man with a burning sense of pride. His whole life had been an effort to convince the white people around him that even though the Negro was outnumbered, even though he might be fettered by new shackles imposed by society, even though he carried the burdens of poor education, poor economic background— that no matter what had ever been said, the Negro was not a coward—not a coward against any odds. "Mr. Rickey," he said, "do you want a ballplayer who's afraid to fight back?"

Rickey's face wrinkled in mock rage as he shouted, "I want a ballplayer with guts enough not to fight back!"

Rickey turned his back on Robinson and walked across the floor. Momentarily he was back again in front of Jackie, his hands out and his palms skyward as if pleading with the young Negro. "Remember what I said, Jackie. This is one battle we can't *fight* our way through. Remember what I said, Jackie: no army, no owners, no umpires, virtually nobody on our side. This is a battle in which you'll have to swallow an awful lot of pride and count on base hits and stolen bases to do the job. That's what'll do it, Jackie. Nothing else."

But Branch Rickey was not through. He was removing his jacket and rolling up his sleeves so he could act out all the hostile personalities that baseball's first Negro was likely to face. He posed as a hotel clerk telling Robinson that "no niggers can sleep here"; as a restaurant manager telling Robinson that he couldn't eat out front with the rest of the team, but that they would prepare sandwiches for him to eat in the bus, or fix him a meal in the kitchen; as an umpire calling Robinson out on a bum decision and then barking out angry words reflecting on the color of Robinson's face.

Now, his shirt wet at the collarbone and under the armpits, his face gleaming with perspiration, Rickey had projected Robinson from the Montreal Royals to the Brooklyn Dodgers and into the World Series. "So we play for keeps, there, Jackie; we play it there to win, and almost everything under the sun goes. I want to win in the most desperate way, so I'm coming into second with my spikes flying. But you don't give ground. You're tricky. You feint, and as I hurl myself you ease out of the way and jam that ball hard into my ribs. As I lie there in the swirling dust, my rib aching, I hear that umpire crying, 'You're out,' and I jump up, and all I can see is that black face of yours shining in front of my eyes. So I yell, 'Don't hit me with a ball like that, you tarbaby son of a bitch.' So I haul off and I sock you right in the cheek." Rickey waved his massive fist in Robinson's face, missing it only by a whisper. Robinson's nose twitched and his lips moved a bit. But his head was steady.

"I get it, Mr. Rickey, I get it," the Negro said. "What you want me to say is that I've got another cheek."

Rickey smiled with satisfaction. He pulled out a white handkerchief and wiped the sweat off his face. Then he strode back to his desk and pulled out a copy of Papini's *Life of Christ.*

Rickey began to read from the philosophy of Papini, who went into seclusion to write a derogatory report on the life of Christ and ended up by writing a laudation. Then Rickey handed the book to Jackie. "Read these passages of Papini's philosophy," he ordered. Robinson took the book and began to read silently:

NONRESISTANCE

But Jesus has not yet arrived at the most stupefying of His revolutionary teachings. "Ye have heard that it hath been said, An eye for an eye, and a tooth for a tooth: But I say unto you, That ye resist not evil: But whosoever shall smite thee on they right cheek, turn to him the other also. And if any man will sue thee at the law, and take away thy coat, let him have thy cloak also. And whosoever shall compell thee to go a mile, go with him twain."

There could be no more definite repudiation of the old law of retaliation. The greater part of those who call themselves Christians not only have never observed this new

Commandment, but have never been willing to pretend to approve of it. For an infinite number of believers this principle of not resisting evil has been the unendurable and inacceptable scandal of Christianity . . .

When Robinson handed the book back to Rickey the old baseball wizard was smiling. He offered a few more sentences to Robinson as what he later called "the glue to hold his resolution firm": "Jackie, I just want to beg two things of you: that as a baseball player you give it your utmost; and as a man you give continuing fidelity to your race and to this crucial cause that you symbolize."

When this almost unbelievable three hours was over, Branch Rickey held no doubt that Jackie Robinson was the man he wanted. Robinson agreed to accept a bonus of $3,500 and a salary of $600 a month as part of what was, in effect, a contract to play baseball with the Montreal Royals.

Rickey explained to Robinson the need to keep their agreement secret because he did not want to announce it publicly until December.

Jackie telephoned his mother and Rachel to tell them about this fantastic development, and went back to his job with the Monarchs.

2

As the November elections drew near in New York City, the question of Jim Crow baseball became a hotter and hotter issue. The Fair Employment Practices Commission was pressuring the three New York teams to sign a no-discrimination pledge. Mayor La Guardia's committee on antidiscrimination was pressing for a similar pledge. La Guardia asked Rickey and other baseball men if he could report by radio that baseball would shortly begin signing Negro players, largely as a result of the work of his committee. Rickey felt that this would be a serious mistake. He did not want the public or anyone connected with baseball to believe that he had signed Robinson for any reason other than his belief that Robinson was an excellent baseball player who would help the Brooklyn team. He contacted Robinson by telephone and asked him to fly to Montreal immediately. On October 23, 1945, Branch Rickey, Jr., Hector Racine, president of the Royals, and other officials met with Robinson and he signed a contract to play for the Montreal Royals.

The brief announcement that Robinson was in organized baseball broke like a thunderclap over the sports world that October day. Here was sports news of great magnitude, and even beyond the area of sports this was a story with deep implications, for some Americans would see the signing of Robinson as another challenge to the supremacy of the white man. Not many people wrote about it, but there was a lot of talk about the way Negroes dominated boxing. You could watch a movie of a boxing match between a Negro and a white fighter, or go to the fight itself, and see the not-so-subtle way in which racism would come to the fore, with many white fans crying passionately for the white fighter to beat the brains out of the Negro—and Negroes hoping for the opposite. In the sports pages, this fighter or that was called the "white hope" of boxing, and there was talk about the way Negroes dominated the sprints and the broad jumps in track. Some rationalized it away with chatter about the "natural African rhythm" of the Negro athlete, or about some special construction of the heel bone in the Negro that made him especially suited for running the sprints, but rarely would they concede that the Negro's success in these fields showed one simple thing: that no area of American life had been fully opened up to the Negroes without their acquitting themselves meritoriously.

All this made the signing of Jackie Robinson the big news story of the day and the top sports story of the year. Newspapers, wire services, radio networks sent their representatives out to beat the bushes, to dredge up comments—and the more provocative the better!—about the signing of Robinson, and then to speculate—responsibly or irresponsibly—about the outcome of Rickey's celebrated action.

Judge William Bramham, the minor league baseball commissioner, said at Durham, N.C., that his office would approve Robinson's contract because there was no legal basis for disapproval, but he lashed out at Rickey's action, predicting that it would inevitably prove harmful to organized baseball. Bramham said sarcastically: "Father Divine will have to look to his laurels, for we can expect a Rickey Temple to be in the course of construction in Harlem soon."

Then, as if to impugn the motives of Rickey, Bramham declared: "Whenever I hear a white man, whether he be from the North, South, East or West, protesting what a friend he is to the Negro race, right then I know the Negro needs a bodyguard. It is those of the carpetbagger stripe of the white race, under the guise of helping but in truth using the Negro for their own selfish interests, who retard the race."

The Brooklyn organization had foreseen comments like Bramham's. In fact, Branch Rickey, Jr., had anticipated more trouble than had his father—a great deal more trouble than there was. At the press conference at which Robinson's signing was announced, young Rickey said: "Mr. Racine and my father undoubtedly will be criticized in some sections of the United States where racial prejudice is rampant. They are not inviting trouble, but they won't avoid it if it comes. Jack Robinson is a fine type of young man, intelligent and college-bred, and I think he can take it, too. It may cost the Brooklyn organization a number of ballplayers. Some of them, particularly if they come from certain sections of the South, will steer away from a club with Negro players on its roster. Some players now with us may even quit, but they'll be back in baseball after they work a year or two in a cotton mill."

Young Rickey's remarks stirred a storm of protest. Bill Werber, of Washington, D.C., a former third baseman with three American League teams and a Duke University graduate, complained to the elder Rickey: "A large segment of the ballplayers who have in the past and who are presently contributing to the continued success of major league baseball are of southern ancestry or actually live in the South. To attempt to force them to accept socially and to play with a Negro, or Negroes, is highly distasteful. You are, in fact, for some unaccountable reason, discriminating against the majority. The attitude that your son has assumed is certainly not conducive to the morale of your own organization or baseball in general. His reference to ballplayers from the South is a definite insult to every southern boy."

A group of cotton mill owners, irked by young Rickey's remarks, threatened to sue the Brooklyn organization.

Branch Rickey was less interested in the reaction of the cotton mill owners and retired ballplayers, however, than he was in the comments of newspapermen, baseball fans and, most important of all, players active in the sport. The great Rogers Hornsby, a Texan, declared: "Ballplayers on the road live close together . . . it won't work." Alabama's Dixie Walker, the National League's batting champion and the sweetheart of the Brooklyn fans, told a newspaperman: "As long as he's not with the Dodgers, I'm not worried." But not all southerners were hostile. Rudy York, the great Detroit first baseman from Cartersville, Georgia, said in Atlanta: "I wish Robinson all the luck in the world, and I hope he makes good."

One of the most amusing aspects of the signing of Robinson—certainly amusing when viewed in retrospect—was the number of writers and players willing to pose as experts on the baseball ability of Negroes in general and Robinson in particular. Jimmy Powers of the *New York Daily News* stated flatly that Robinson would flop. "Jackie Robinson, the Negro signed by Brooklyn, will not make the grade in the big leagues next year or the next if percentages mean anything," he wrote. "Every major league ball club has a backlog of young talent, proven stars, returning from the war. Some big league clubs, like the Cards and Brooklyn, really have material for two teams. All clubs under the GI Bill of Rights must pay their returning big leaguers one year's salary at the same scale they received before they went to war.

"Robinson would have to be a super player to 'bump' a returning veteran. We would like to see him make good, but

it is unfair to build high hopes and then dash them down . . .
Robinson is a 1000-to-1 shot to make the grade.

"If the Negro player couldn't muscle into the major league
line-ups when 43-year-old outfielders patrolled the grass for
pennant winners and one-armed men and callow 4F's were
stumbling around, he won't make it in 1946 when the rosters
will be bursting with returned headliners, or competent big-
leaguers of proven ability."

Bob Feller, an Iowan who had never been accused of racial
prejudice, and one of the great pitchers of all time, told a San
Francisco newspaperman that he "couldn't foresee any future
for Robinson in big league baseball." He said that Robinson
was "tied up in the shoulders and couldn't hit an inside pitch
to save his neck. If he were a white man I doubt if they would
even consider him as big league material." Commenting that
Robinson had "football shoulders," which would handicap
him as a batter, Feller remarked that of all the Negro players
he had seen, only the legendary Negro pitcher, Satchel Paige,
and Josh Gibson, a Negro catcher who could knock a baseball
a mile, could make their way in the big show.

Old Satchel Paige chuckled a bit when he was told of Feller's comment. "They didn't make a mistake in signing Robinson," said the aging pitcher, who admitted wistfully that he
would have liked nothing better than to be able to play in organized baseball. "Jackie Robinson is a number one professional player. They couldn't have picked a better man."

Someone mentioned Feller's remark that Robinson
couldn't hit, and Paige pointed out that just a month earlier
he and a group of Negro stars had played against Bob Feller
and a group of hand-picked major league stars. Paige had
struck out ten major-leaguers in five innings. Bob Feller
fanned four Negroes over the same span.

Asked about Feller's comment, Robinson said: "Frankly, I
am more worried about my fielding than my hitting. I have
faced Feller a couple of times and he is a very good pitcher. In
the two times I batted against him in off-season exhibitions,
I got one hit, a double."

Robinson knew, however, that it was not fair to condemn players like Feller for derogatory remarks about the caliber of Negro baseball, because many of them were merely parroting the disparaging remarks of Negro sports writers. For example, when Larry MacPhail, the president of the New York Yankees, surveyed the problem of nonemployment of Negroes in organized baseball for Mayor La Guardia, he concluded that "there are few if any Negro players who could qualify for play in the majors at this time." To support this contention, MacPhail quoted none other than Sam Lacy, sports editor of the *Baltimore Afro-American* chain of Negro newspapers. Lacy had written: "I am reluctant to say that we haven't a single man in the ranks of colored baseball who could step into a major league uniform and disport himself in the fashion of a big leaguer. Some quite possibly excel in hitting, running or fielding, but for the most part fellows who could hold their own in more than one of these phases are few and far between—perhaps nil."

Two days after the announcement that Robinson had signed to play for Montreal, it appeared that baseball was in for the kind of wild donnybrook that every racist in the country could hope for. Tom Y. Baird, one of the white owners of the Kansas City Monarchs, implied that attempts to integrate Negroes into organized baseball would cause a dog-eat-dog fight in which owners of Negro clubs would try to keep Negroes out of organized baseball.

"We won't take it lying down," Baird told the press. "Robinson signed a contract with us last year and I feel that he is our property. If [Baseball Commissioner A. B.] Chandler lets Montreal and Brooklyn get by with this, he's really starting a mess."

Sports pages blared forth headlines declaring, in effect, that the signing of a Negro represented a peril to baseball. The *New York Post* declared: "Fight for Robinson's services may split baseball wide open." Milton Gross, the *Post*'s sports writer, went on to say that if Baird made good his threat to demand that Chandler declare Robinson's Montreal contract void, then the contractual status of organized baseball would face one of its most serious challenges in history.

Clark Griffith, owner of the Washington Senators, and Larry MacPhail issued strong statements in defense of the "property rights" of the Negro leagues—but their remarks were discounted when newsmen disclosed that both the Washington and Yankee organizations had profited handsomely from renting their parks for Negro league games.

The threatened legal blowup over Robinson's "obligation" to the Monarchs never occurred, largely because some unsubtle threats from the Negro press convinced Baird and J. L. Wilkinson, co-owner of the Monarchs, that it would cost them dearly if they sought to reverse an action that Negro baseball fans had sought for decades. Baird notified Rickey that he had been misquoted and had no intention of preventing Robinson from playing with Montreal.

3

Rachel Isum waited nervously and eagerly for the day of her marriage, and beyond that for the day when her husband would be involved in the biggest challenge of his life. She encouraged him to join a barnstorming tour to Venezuela, promising that they would get married when he returned.

While Jackie was in South America, Rachel worked in New York. The public-health nursing job she had wanted required a promise to work for a year, and she couldn't in good conscience commit herself for that long, so she went to work as a hostess in an expensive Park Avenue restaurant. She noted with interest that no Negroes ever patronized this place except for a turbaned man with a long beard. She chuckled often about this "foreigner," a man she was sure was an American Negro laughing himself to death on the inside at the fact that a colored man could be anything but a native-born American and receive courteous treatment in even the ritziest corner of the United States.

Rae visited the shops on Fifth Avenue, making selections

for her trousseau. She had an inherent taste and appreciation for things of fine quality, even though she could not always afford them. Finally she found the wedding dress she wanted at Saks Fifth Avenue—a prewar sample dress made of fabric that was no longer available. She explained that she didn't have all the money for the dress, but that she would make a down payment and would make her final payment after the last fitting. The store called in a bridal consultant, who helped Rae choose a veil to be tinted ivory to match the dress. Totaling up the bill in her mind, Rachel reminded herself that she had almost no money. She quit her relatively low-paying job at the restaurant and took a job as a nurse at the Joint Diseases Hospital. By the time Jack returned from Venezuela she had paid for the wedding dress, the veil and two suits, and was ready to go to California.

Jack had heard that diamonds were cheap in South America, so he and Rachel had agreed that he would have her wedding ring made while he was there. She had drawn a design of what she wanted and was delighted at the thought that he would bring it back.

When he returned and showed her the ring she knew that, as was often the case with men, her instructions had been quickly forgotten. Jack had brought back just the kind of ring she did not want. He was so proud of his selection (he had had their names engraved on it) that Rae quickly decided not to show any sign of disappointment. Then Jack unwrapped a gift to Rae from other members of the team: a large alligator bag that was so out of style then that many women would have scorned it as a "suitcase." Rae spoke with forced delight about "the marvelous piece of alligator used to make it." Jackie then revealed a third gift, a hand-carved jewelry chest. This was genuinely beautiful and Rae could admire it whole-heartedly. Jack had gone one-for-three, which is not a bad average, even in the matrimonial league.

The next day they left for California and the big church wedding to which they had agreed to please Mrs. Isum. After tedious rehearsals, the day came—February 10, 1946. Nerv-

ous and uncomfortable in the fancy attire he had rented,
Jack stood waiting at the altar for his bride, who looked regal
and lovely in her satin dress. They got through the marriage
vows as rehearsed (except for the usual bad moment when his
old friend Jack Gordon, the best man, almost never found the
ring), but as they started up the aisle and got nearly to the
door, Jack noticed a few old cronies from the Pepper Street
gang winking at him, giving him the chin-up sign. He paused
to shake hands with his old buddies and to chat with them a
bit about how he had just lost his freedom. Rachel marched
on outside the church, distressed that Jack had not realized
that he was to walk all the way out with her and that they
were supposed to hop into the car and drive away to the music
of rice bouncing off the windshield. Now here she was alone,
outside the church, the crowd surrounding her as she waited
for her groom to complete his bull session with the boys so
they could go on with the business at hand. Finally Jack
emerged and they got into the car and rode away to the reception.

One of Jack's friends figured that it would be a good joke
if he eased the young couple's car away while the reception
was in progress. When Rae decided that the propitious moment had arrived for the bride and groom to dash away to the
site of their honeymoon, just the way she had seen it done
a hundred times in the movies, she discovered that this joker
had eloped with their automobile. She changed to her traveling suit and sat with Jackie watching the guests leave one by
one.

"These characters," Rae said helplessly. She knew they considered Jack's wedding day their day to have fun, so there
would be no stopping them. In fact, she assumed—correctly
—that these members of Jack's gang would follow them
throughout the honeymoon. Just when Rae's patience and
good humor had reached a point of strain, the prankster returned the car, permitting bride and groom to dash away ro-
mantically to the Clark Hotel, a Negro place on the east side of
Los Angeles. Their first unhappy discovery was that Jack had
forgotten to make a reservation. No room was available in

the main part of the hotel, so the honeymooners were put in the annex. Rachel had hoped to find a little bouquet of flowers in the room when they arrived, but none was there.

A less understanding bride might have staged a woeful scene, declaring tearfully that such thoughtlessness indicated a lack of true love for the bride. But Rae knew (and there were scores of guests to remind her) that it really had been a very beautiful wedding—and that the little boners of the day were no indication whatsoever of a lack of affection. Jackie Robinson loved his bride truly because she did understand, understand more than she ever mentioned to him. Rae knew that the ordering of flowers at the proper time and similar genteel gestures are products of family tradition of the sort that many men like Jackie, growing up as he had in poverty and without a father's example, simply do not know. Their marriage might have gotten off to a tragically unhappy beginning, but as Rae thought about the entire day, she and Jack looked at each other and burst into laughter. They laughed their way into each other's arms. It was like the man said: love conquers all.

Rachel's aunt from San Jose had come to Los Angeles for the wedding and offered the couple her house for a week's honeymoon. They accepted happily, sight-unseen, and arrived in San Jose the day after the wedding to find that the aunt had a wood-burning cookstove. Rachel had never made a wood fire in her life and hadn't the remotest idea how to cook with one. The first night in San Jose she opened a can of pork and beans, and they had a struggle just getting it heated. The wood would smoke and sizzle, but it wouldn't burn. As it turned out Rachel spent the week washing and ironing, doing up all her aunt's linens and Jack's shirts.

She looks back on that week and recalls: "I had something less than a gay, exciting time, for Jack's cronies showed up and reminded him that the Harlem Globetrotters were in town. We spent two nights watching them; as I look back, I realize that they weren't as bad as I imagined. It's just that I'd have appreciated them more at another time. Then we got bored with the small town of San Jose, so we went to Oakland

and some friends of Jack invited us to stay with them. I had grown up with the romantic notion that on a honeymoon you don't stay with people; you stay by yourselves; but anyhow, we stayed with this family, and what do you know? The Globetrotters came to Oakland! So we went to see the Globetrotters play basketball again.

"We've had some delightful honeymoons in later years, but that first one was a riot. I guess we were not unlike millions of other excited young couples who have goofed and bungled their way through a honeymoon. I recall those days and find it difficult to believe that the Jackie Robinson who now sends flowers on every appropriate occasion is the same man who forgot so many things in 1946."

7....The Hospitable South

The American Airlines counter in Los Angeles' Lockheed Terminal was a virtual madhouse the day Jackie and Rachel Robinson began the most important journey of their lives. They were en route to Florida for spring training, which would have a lot to do with the decision on whether or not Robinson was good enough to play baseball with Montreal. As they checked their tickets, Jackie's mother showed up unexpectedly to say good-by to them once more and to promise her son her prayers. Then she handed a shoebox to the young couple.

"What's this?" asked Jack.

"It's a shoebox—and it's full of fried chicken and hard-boiled eggs."

"Aw, Mamma, you shouldn't have brought this. They serve food on the plane."

"I know, but I just thought something might happen and I didn't want you starving to death and getting to that baseball camp too weak to hit the ball."

Remembering the stereotype about Negroes—that they boarded trains and planes to stage picnics—Jackie and Rae were ashamed to board the plane with the shoebox. They could foresee someone pointing to them in derision, or even a newspaper photographer showing up to find them wolfing down fried chicken and boiled eggs in plantation style. But they didn't want to hurt Mrs. Robinson's feelings, so they took the shoebox and got on the plane.

Rachel was uneasy when they left—and she can tell her own story best, for no less important than the incidents are the thoughts and emotions of the young woman making the trip, bound for her first southern exposure, going with her husband to try to help him to fight his way through the most demanding kind of ordeal:

I was worried because I had heard so many stories about the treatment of Negroes in the Deep South that I was bewildered. I knew how quickly Jack's temper could flare up in the face of a racial insult, and I could not be sure but what some incident might occur in which we both would be harmed, or killed, or, at best, we might jeopardize this opportunity to wipe out segregation in baseball.

I soon learned that all the books in the world cannot really make one understand what it means to be a Negro with dignity and self-respect in an area where segregation is entrenched by custom and supported by a maze of laws. I soon came to realize that although there is some prejudice everywhere—and Heaven knows there was no shortage of it in Los Angeles, or in Pasadena, where Jack grew up—there was a world of difference between the communities in which we had lived and those with which we were to become acquainted in the South.

We had reservations to Daytona Beach, with a change of

planes at New Orleans. We reached New Orleans at about
7:00 A.M. and were supposed to leave at 11:00 A.M. When the
eleven o'clock plane came, airline officials told us that we had
been shifted to a twelve o'clock flight. Later they told us that
we would get out on a later plane. We asked if there was
any place where we might rest while awaiting our flight and
found that there was no place for a Negro to rest at the New
Orleans airport. We asked about food and were told that
there was a restaurant where we could purchase sandwiches,
but we would have to bring them out to eat them. Jack
almost exploded at this suggestion. The pride in both of us
had rebelled, so under no circumstances would we accept
food on this basis.

The airline agent suggested that we go to a hotel to relax
until they called us. We went, remembering happily now
that we still had that shoebox full of chicken and boiled
eggs. We ate it with glee. It occurred to us for the first time
that the stereotype about Negro "picnics" on trains probably grew out of just this kind of situation—Negroes pack-
ing a lunch because of knowledge that dining cars and restaurants would refuse them service.

I suppose there must have been a better hotel for Negroes
in New Orleans, but neither Jack nor our driver knew of
it. We entered this place and I was almost nauseated. It
was a dirty, dreadful place, and they had plastic mattress
covers! Lying on the bed was like trying to sleep on newspapers. We gave the airline our telephone number, and
they told us we probably would leave in four hours, but
that if there was any change they would telephone us. They
didn't call, so we checked with them and were told to come
to the airport. When we showed up we were told that
there would be another delay, so we sat for several more
hours. Finally, about 7:00 P.M., we were notified that we
had seats to Daytona Beach.

We were being paged as the plane landed at Pensacola,
Florida, however, and Jackie got off to see why. The
stewardess said to me, "You'd better get off, too." I was

puzzled. I watched closely as she asked another passenger, a Mexican, to get off.

I gathered up my things and went into the airport to find Jack in a heated argument with the manager. "What's the matter?" I said. Jack replied, "We've been taken off the plane. The manager said that they were expecting a storm and had to take three passengers off to load on more fuel."

"Take off passengers to put on fuel?" I said. "Why, I just saw two white passengers get on and take our seats on the plane."

"Well, er, uh, that's another reason. They forgot to leave enough empty seats available in New Orleans for passengers to board at Pensacola."

Jack protested vociferously, but I knew that this would be of little avail in Pensacola. That was one of the big differences, I soon discovered, between injustice in the Deep South and injustice in the North or on the West Coast. In the latter communities a Negro had some recourse, particularly where the law or public opinion was on his side and the side of decency; but here in Florida we realized that the law, public opinion and custom all weighed against us, so there was nothing for us to do but get off the plane. It seemed more than mere coincidence.

We were notified that another plane was coming through the next morning, but that the airline could guarantee us no space on it. Meanwhile Jack was due at spring training the morning after next and under the circumstances—his first visit to spring training, the entire sports world watching him and his conduct—he was anxious to be on time. We asked the airline agent what we should do and he said he would provide a limousine to take us into town and find us a place to stay for the night, and we would have to take a train or bus out in the morning, unless we wanted to gamble on another flight.

The limousine driver was sympathetic, talking at great length about what a shame he thought it was to put us in this position. He said, however, that he hadn't the faintest idea where to take two Negroes to spend the night in Pensacola.

"I'll take you by a white hotel and I can ask some of the colored bellboys if they know where you can spend the night," he said. A bellboy gave him the name and address of a Negro family which would rent us a room. The driver took us to this house, placed our luggage on the porch and drove away. We entered to find that this small frame house was almost overrun with children. The family was using the living room to sleep in, and it was obvious that there was no place for us. But the woman was extremely nice. She said she would make room for us somehow, but we could see there wasn't even room for our luggage.

We learned that a bus would soon leave for Jacksonville, so we decided to take it. When we boarded, only a handful of people were on the bus. They were white, and seated at the front. We were terribly tired and I walked eagerly to the last of the reclining seats near the rear, hoping I could sleep through the greater part of this trip to Jacksonville. Jackie fell asleep before I did. We had traveled only a few miles when, at one of the stops, the driver walked up to me and merely motioned with his hand toward the long seat at the rear. I wondered if it was arrogance or shame that kept him from telling us verbally that the Jim Crow laws of Florida, as he interpreted them, forbade us to sit in the reclining seats that were only one row from the rear of the bus. I woke Jack and we moved to the back seat.

For sixteen hours we bounced and jogged at the rear of this bus, and often I was almost nauseated by the engine fumes that wafted in through the open window. Now I understood why this was the space reserved for Negroes.

At daybreak Negro working men crowded on. The Jim Crow section got so jammed that we took turns standing and sitting, although there were several empty seats in the white section. I looked at my new going-away trousseau suit and the ermine coat that Jack had saved for years to buy me as a wedding gift, and I could see the stains from the overalls worn by men going to work in the fields and the rock quarries. I felt like weeping.

We ate nothing throughout this trip because we refused to ask for food from back doors and windows. I had never been so tired, hungry, miserable and upset in my life as when we finally reached Daytona Beach. And how delighted we were to find Wendell Smith of the *Pittsburgh Courier* and Billy Rowe, a photographer for the same newspaper, there to meet us at the station. I must have sounded almost hysterical as I told them of our ordeal, of what a shock it had been to me to come South for the first time and see these signs that I had heard about but could never really believe.

White people of good will can sympathize, but they can never really understand that hot feeling close to sickness that overwhelms a Negro with self-respect and with a real concern for the institutions of democracy when he or she arrives at a bus station to see signs on separate restrooms saying: FOR COLORED WOMEN and FOR WHITE LADIES; to walk by a water fountain and see a sign saying, FOR WHITES ONLY; to walk the streets and see a sign painted high on a building announcing that WE WASH WHITE FOLKS' CLOTHES ONLY. It was an appalling thing for me, and although Jackie had seen this before, I realized that it affected him deeply too, not just because of his sensitivity to racial insult, but because of what I am sure was a more or less subconscious feeling that in the Deep South, with the deck so completely stacked against the Negro, he would be virtually powerless to protect me from the insults that might come my way.

During that bus ride, when we were alternating between sitting and standing, or first one person would sit forward on the edge of the seat and another would sit far back so as to accommodate more people, I buried my head behind the seat in front of me and wept silently. I didn't want Jack to see me cry, but I was so unhappy; it's just that I had never seen him in that position before, unable to be a man and assert himself, unable to take care of me, having to obey quietly when that driver ordered us to the rear.

The bus station in Jacksonville was a wretched hell hole. As long as I live I think I shall never have a good thought about that place. It was as hot as Hades, and the station was full of flies and jammed with people. We couldn't find a seat inside the Negro section of the station, and we waited there for what seemed an eternity. Except for some apples, we didn't eat from the time we left New Orleans until we got to Daytona Beach.

This experience marked us so that for years we refused to travel on American Airlines. Finally someone wrote American about what had occurred and an executive replied that the incident just couldn't have happened. Actually, we have never forgiven American Airlines completely for that experience, but we do feel that it wasn't the policy of the national management—just the prejudice of some of their personnel along that line.

In Daytona Beach, Smith and Rowe took us to stay with a very interesting Negro couple, Mr. and Mrs. Joe Harris. She was a schoolteacher and he was the leading Negro politician in Daytona Beach, as well as one of the most unusual individuals we ever met. I suppose you would call him a political organizer, because he had cards on every Negro in Daytona Beach and when election time came he would send out a list of recommended candidates. As a result, he said, Negroes had gained the balance of power in Daytona and this was why Negroes had a lot of advantages in Daytona Beach that they did not have in other parts of Florida. For example, we were surprised to see Negro bus drivers.

We didn't stay in Daytona Beach long, for we were late joining the more than two hundred other players in the Brooklyn camp at Sanford. Mr. Rickey had sent word to us by Smith, who was working closely with him, that he wanted Jack in camp immediately. We knew Mr. Rickey wanted no delay in having Jack show what he could do with a baseball bat and glove. Rowe drove us to Sanford, where we were told that during our stay in this town we would be quartered at the home of a Negro doctor named Brock.

Jackie dressed in our room that first day, and I still remember vividly his leaving for that first practice session. I felt so terribly sorry for him. You know how you feel when you send a child out to school for the first time, and when you don't know how he will adjust, or whether the other children will pick on him, or whether he will like the teacher, or just what will happen to him. Well, that's just how I worried about Jack. I wanted to watch the day's proceedings, but I felt that I shouldn't do anything that might embarrass him. I could just hear some antagonistic player shouting, "Hey, Jack, did you bring mama along to be your nursemaid?" or some such remark, and I knew that the less opportunity for an upsetting incident like this, the better Jack's chances would be.

2

Although he said nothing to his wife, Robinson was twice as nervous as she. He felt like that child going to school for the first day.

Robinson, Rowe, Smith and Johnny Wright, a Negro pitcher whom Rickey had also signed to a Montreal contract, were met at the camp by Sukeforth, who gave them a pleasant greeting and took them to the clubhouse, where they got equipment from Babe Hamburger.

Let Jackie tell the rest of the story:

Before going in I glanced at the players out on that field —two hundred men, all of them eager for a place high in the Dodger organization, each of them representing my competition, and a great number of them from the South. They were hitting fungoes, huffing and puffing around the field, with sweat streaming from their faces, throwing balls to each other, keeping up a constant barrage of the chatter

that seems to go with baseball, especially training sessions.
As I made this momentary survey of the situation it seemed
that every one of those men stopped suddenly in his tracks
and that four hundred eyes were trained on Wright and
me.

We walked quickly to the clubhouse, and I don't know
that I ever entered a building more ill at ease. Hamburger
introduced himself.

"Which one of you guys is Robinson?" he asked.

"I am," I said, trying not to betray my nervousness, "and
this is Johnny Wright."

We shook hands as Hamburger said: "Welcome, fellows.
Just want to say that I ain't exactly a part of this great experiment, but I do think I can give you a little advice. Just
go out and do the best you can. Don't get all hot and
bothered. It's what you do on that field that's going to tell
in the long run."

We thanked Babe, although I knew that no amount of
advice could wipe away that fluttery feeling in the pit of my
stomach, could keep us from getting "hot and bothered" in
the race-conscious South.

When we walked onto the field a group of reporters
from northern newspapers began a barrage of questions.

"Jackie, you think you can get along with these white
boys?"

"I've gotten along with white boys at UCLA, at Pasadena, in high school and in the Army. I don't know why
these should be any different."

"What will you do if one of these pitchers throws at your
head?"

"I'll duck like everyone else."

There was a ripple of laughter from the newspapermen.

"Do you think you can win the shortstop job from
Stanley Breard?" Breard, I knew, was the most popular
player on the Montreal team.

"I don't know whether I can win any job or not. I just
mean to do the best I can."

"Do you have hopes of playing with Brooklyn some day?"

"Of course I do, just like all those other players out there."

"That means you're out after Pee Wee Reese's job, since you're a shortstop."

"Now wait a minute—it doesn't mean I'm out after any individual's job. It just means that I'm going to do my darndest to make the team, then I'll play wherever I can best help the team. I'm just like all other players in that respect. Right now, though, I can't worry about Brooklyn. I haven't made the Montreal team yet."

Sukeforth shooed the newspapermen away, telling them that I was late and had a lot of practice to make up. Then he took us to meet Clay Hopper, the Montreal manager. I faced this introduction with a great deal of uneasiness, for I had read that Hopper was a Mississippi plantation owner, and I had heard from several friendly newspapermen that he had something less than the reputation of a great friend of the Negro. I suppose I would have been even more apprehensive had I known of his comment to Mr. Rickey when he first learned I was going to be assigned to the Montreal team.

"Mr. Rickey, please don't do this to me," Hopper had said. "I'm a white man, been living in Mississippi all my life. If you do this to me, you're going to force me to move out of Mississippi."

Whatever Mr. Rickey had told him, however, apparently convinced him that he ought to go through with his job as manager in this situation.

"Clay, this is Robinson and Wright," said Sukeforth.

"Hello, Jackie," Hopper said. I was relieved to see him stick out his hand, for even in those days great numbers of southerners would under no circumstances shake hands with a Negro. After the introduction we made polite conversation about the kind of winter rest we had had and then, in a deep, soft southern drawl, Hopper told us that we were not to do too much that day—just throw the ball around awhile and hit a few. He asked Wright if, in addition to his fast ball and his curve, he knew how to throw a change of-speed pitch. Wright replied that his "change-up" was not very well developed, and Hopper ordered him to work on it because, "You'll never make it in this league without a good change-up."

Sukeforth then introduced me to two players with whom I was to throw. He took Wright over to where the pitchers were throwing. I tried to concentrate on the training exercises, but I was constantly interrupted by photographers —so much so that it was embarrassing. They wanted me to pose leaping to catch a ball, running the bases, sliding, throwing. It bothered me that I remained the center of attention, for I felt that my best chance for success would come if I could get at least some of these people to stop thinking of me as a Negro, to let me fade into the crowd where I then would stand out only because of such fielding and hitting as I might do.

Practice was uneventful for two days. Then, on the second evening, as Rachel, Wright, Rowe, Smith and I sat eating in the Brock home, I sensed a tension and uneasiness, particularly when Smith continued to engage in mysterious telephone calls with Mr. Rickey. I was beginning to resent this newspaperman's meddling and running my business without asking my approval or advice. When Smith left the telephone and said, "Pack your bags. fellow, we're heading back to Daytona Beach," I was ready to blow my top.

"Hurry," he said, "pack your bags. Mr. Rickey has just ordered us back to Daytona. I'll explain later."

Rachel and I had unpacked and settled down for a long stay. Now I threw clothing back into the suitcase in something close to panic. I couldn't believe that Mr. Rickey had given up on me after two days, yet I couldn't help thinking of that phony tryout I'd had with the Red Sox in 1945. I didn't want to believe that a man I had come to respect so much would also use me in a phony tryout, but I could think of no other reason for my being rushed out of Sanford without notice.

Later I was surcharged with mixed emotions—with relief on being told that I was not being dumped by the

Brooklyn organization, yet with acute misery at learning that "race troubles"—no one explained it to us—had caused our expulsion from Sanford. I was disturbed because this was what the people who had worked against desegregation had said all along: "It won't work, for how on earth can you take a Negro player to spring training in the South? There'll be riots and bloodshed if we force a Negro on these white boys." I felt sick inside, for I knew that this was what stood in the way of American progress in race relations, in every aspect of race relations—this timidity on the part of people of supposed good will, this fear that there would be "trouble." It made it easy for the advocates of bigotry and injustice to say, "You can't change this or there'll be trouble," and then to go out and produce the trouble, if necessary, so as to be able to say, "We told you so." I hoped with a passion that Mr. Rickey would have more courage than to be swayed by these difficulties in Sanford, or by indications that there might be trouble ahead. Then I thought back to August, 1945, when Mr. Rickey explained his plan to put me on the Montreal roster. At that time it was I who warned, "There may be trouble ahead—for you, for me, for Negroes and for baseball."

Mr. Rickey rolled that phrase, "trouble ahead," over his lips and said: "Jackie, many years ago the Rio Grande Railroad used to thrill tourists out in Colorado by putting them on a flatcar and hauling them up a canyon. Mrs. Rickey and I took that ride years ago, and the narrow walls so limited our view that all we could see was the sky up at the very end of the canyon. It was a very frightening ride, and I recall that as we neared the top, Mrs. Rickey said to me, 'Branch, there's trouble ahead. Branch, we're going to run right over the top. There's trouble ahead, Branch.'

"Well, Jackie, the engineers had thought it all out. Just before we reached the top, the road veered off and went through a tunnel—so there was no trouble ahead at all. That's the way it is with most trouble ahead in this world, Jackie—if we use the common sense and courage God gave us. But you've got to study the hazards and build wisely."

Remembering this, I felt confident that rumblings of trouble in Florida would not intimidate Mr. Rickey.

The rest of the team soon moved to Daytona and was quartered in a hotel on the ocean. Rae and I went back to the home of the Harrises, and Wright to the home of another Negro family. We disliked this distinction almost as much as we resented being chased out of Sanford, but we knew that there could be no protest. Mr. Rickey had made it clear that, for the success of our venture, we would have to bear indignities and humiliations without complaint. He had said that I would have to be "a man big enough to bear the cross of martyrdom."

It's not easy to be a martyr in this field of race relations. I remember someone saying to me, "Jack, before this is over you're going to conclude that being born black is a curse." I replied that I had never felt that way, that my mother had taught me that God made Negroes black as a challenge and that if we met that challenge it would make better people of us. I hoped that, somehow, I could meet the challenge. There could be no quitting, because so much more than my own sensitivity was at stake. I could tell this just by watching the Negroes at Sanford who came out to watch during those two days of practice. They cheered if I leaned to tie my shoe. Sure, it was embarrassing to me, and it seemed childish on the part of the Negroes, but I understood that my being on that field was a symbol of the Negro's emerging self-respect, of a deep belief that somehow we had begun a magnificent era of Negro progress, a period in which Negroes could walk onto a baseball field, or into another area of life, asking no quarter, no special concessions, and compete creditably with white men.

I went to practice the next day determined to show Manager Hopper that I really could play baseball. I was on the second team. Breard, the fine French Canadian, was first-team shortstop. In trying to impress Hopper, I raced all over the infield trying to make sensational stops, and I pegged the ball to first base as hard as I could, attempting to belie reports that I had a weak arm. Sukie warned me to slow down. "Don't overdo it, or you'll get a sore arm, Jack," he cautioned me.

But I couldn't slow down. Every time I heard somebody mumble, "Beautiful throw," I tried to throw the next one harder. When someone said, "Look at that stop," my rabbit ears picked up the comment and I strained myself to reach even farther to pick the ball out of the dirt.

My first realization of what I had done came when, after a hard peg, a burning sensation throbbed in my right arm. I kept throwing and leaping that day, however, because I didn't want Sukie to know that I was paying so quickly for my failure to heed his advice.

When I got home that night my arm felt as if it was being pulled out of the socket. I couldn't lift it to comb my hair. Rae tried desperately to help by putting on cold compresses, still I tossed and turned all night. Next morning Hopper hit a ball to me, but I couldn't throw it halfway to first. I went to the doctor, who put hot compresses (the nurse and the doctor disagreed) on my arm, but still I couldn't throw. On top of that, I couldn't hit. The harder I tried the more I popped up or pounded the ball into the dirt, where the third baseman or shortstop gobbled it up easily and pegged me out at first. The more I tried the more tense I became. Rae almost became a nervous wreck trying to work the soreness out of my arm. She and I realized later that there is virtually nothing you can do about a sore arm except to let time work it out.

It was even more disturbing to find that Rae and I were not the only ones worried. Mr. Rickey was frantic to have me in the game, showing off my wares.

"Listen," he said, "You've *got* to get in there, sore arm or not. For anybody else it would be all right, but remember that you're here under extraordinary circumstances. You can't afford to miss a single day of practice or some of the other players will start rumors that you're goldbricking that you're dogging off with the pretense that you have *a* sore arm."

He wanted Hopper to try me at second, where the throw to first would be much shorter. I tried that and found to my utter horror that I couldn't even throw from second to first.

Mr. Rickey dropped his head as if in despair. He called me over to the coaching box and told me that he had to keep me in the game even if he had to make a first baseman out of me. So he got me a first baseman's mitt and spent more than an hour showing me how to play the bag, and just what to do under certain conditions. I had no desire whatsoever to play first base, but I had to go along. In practice I felt awkward. I couldn't find the bag with my foot; I goofed easy throws. I was so horrible that one white newspaperman said:

"It's do-gooders like Rickey that hurt the Negro because they try to force inferior Negroes on whites and then everybody loses. Take this guy Robinson. If he was white they'd have booted him out of this camp long ago."

Branch Rickey was acutely aware of such mumblings, by newspapermen and by Montreal players, so he deserted the Dodger camp to keep a close eye on Robinson and his progress. He notified Rachel that it would be all right for her to attend practice sessions, hoping that her presence might inspire Robinson. During practice Rickey would post himself along the first base line and shout to Jackie in a hoarse whisper: "Be daring! Be daring!" or "Run it, run it out with all you've got!" He would sit there with an old battered hat slouched on one side of his head and a stubby cigar between his fingers, demanding that Robinson take more chances, that he loosen up and give his natural athletic ability a chance to take over! "Take a bigger lead—take a bigger lead!" "Get off that base!" "Worry that pitcher!" "Make him think you're going to steal second!"

Prior to the first game between the Dodgers and Royals there were rumors that Robinson and Wright would not be allowed to perform. However, Rickey had secured promises from Mayor William Perry and other city officials that as far as the Dodgers' training activities went there would be no racial difficulty whatsoever.

Not knowing this, Jackie stepped onto the field at Daytona Beach expecting boos and catcalls. Instead he was greeted with loud cheers, not just from the Negroes jammed into the Jim Crow section of the park but from the white section. He felt good, and thanked heaven that his arm seemed to be all right. So did Rickey, who sat watching the game with Clay Hopper. When a batter smashed a hot grounder between Robinson and the shortstop (Robinson was playing second now), and it appeared certain to be a hit into center field, the Negro dashed with catlike agility onto the grass behind second base, scooped the ball up with his gloved hand and flipped it backhandedly to Breard, forcing the runner coming down from first.

Wham! Rickey slapped Hopper on the shoulder and commented: "Look at that! That's an aptitude play!"

Days later, in an intrasquad game, a batter slammed the ball between first and second for what looked like a sure runscoring hit. Robinson dashed toward the right field line in that clumsy-appearing gait, but he grabbed the ball deftly and, still off balance, pegged it to first to nab the runner by half a step.

Wham! Rickey slapped Hopper on the back. "Clay, no other human being could have made that play!"

Still later, Jackie made a belly-slide stop of a sizzling grounder, and snapped the ball to second to force the runner going down and start a crucial double play.

Wham! Hopper cringed under this back slap. "Clay, there's coordination, agility. You're seeing the aptitude play, the best play in baseball. That is a superhuman play!" Rickey looked with enthusiasm at Hopper, who was in a tremor, as if about to break emotionally. Then Hopper asked the question that Rickey and Robinson were to remember so vividly.

"Mr. Rickey," he said, "do you really think a nigger's a human being?"

Branch Rickey bristled momentarily. Then, as he tells it, "I saw that this Mississippi-born man was sincere, that he meant what he said with tears, that this regarding the Negro as being subhuman was part of his heritage, that here was a man who had practically nursed racial prejudice from his mother's breast, so I decided to ignore the comment."

Despite these fielding gems, Robinson was unhappy because he was not hitting. It was almost unbelievable that a man could go to the plate so often, or try so hard, and not be able to hit just one safe ball.

What made it even worse was that there was almost nothing he could do in this Florida town to get his mind off his baseball troubles. There was a Negro movie to which he and Rachel went so often that they began to think it was affecting their eyes. Then they made a few friends at Bethune-Cookman College, founded and headed by the late and beloved Negro educator, Mary McLeod Bethune, and they were asked to private homes occasionally for dinner. But Jackie had no opportunity to talk baseball with the white players, to hear them laugh and kid each other out of slumps. His only consolation was that he could commiserate with Wright, who, it now was becoming obvious, was even less enchanted with life as a guinea pig.

A few days later Robinson got his first hit of the spring. Rae was so delighted that she left the park early and went to the agricultural school at Bethune-Cookman to pick some vegetables for a celebration dinner. When she told faculty members that Jackie had just gotten his first hit, they insisted on giving her a couple of chickens. That night Rachel asked Mrs. Harris if she might just this once have the privilege of cooking (the Robinsons heretofore had eaten in a greasy little restaurant). She cooked the chickens and the vegetables and invited Smith, Rowe and one other Negro newspaperman in for the celebration dinner.

Following days showed, however, that Robinson still was not hitting at an International League pace. Hopper told Rickey that the only honest thing to do was take Robinson out of the line-up, race relations project or not. If this had happened, it would have been the end of the world for Robinson. Whether a tip as to Hopper's attitude shook him out of his slump, Jackie does not recall, but something shook him up. Sports writer Bill Roeder has told a fascinating story about how Robinson came into his own—a story that almost certainly is apocryphal (and a thousand such stories were told about Jackie) since Robinson has no recollection of it. According to Roeder, a couple of southerners supposedly conspired to stir up in Jackie the competitive fire that sent him winging toward a magnificent debut. As the story goes, a few days before the Royals were to break camp and head north for the opening game of the season, they played an exhibition game with the Indianapolis Indians. Pitching for the Indians was Paul Derringer—a southerner, an old friend of Hopper, and a big star for the Cincinnati Reds before coming down from the majors. Before the game, Hopper and Derringer were discussing Robinson's tenseness, and Hopper's fear that the Negro just didn't have the guts to play topnotch baseball.

Derringer grinned a sly grin and drawled to Hopper: "Tell you what I'm gonna do, Clay. I'm gonna knock your colored boy down a couple of times and see how much guts he's got."

The first time Robinson came to bat, the story goes, Derringer winged a fast ball at his ear. Robinson sprawled back with his feet flying in the air and sat down hard on the seat of his pants. He stared angrily at Derringer from this prone position for a few moments, then got up and dusted off the rear of his trousers. He picked up a handful of dirt and let it ooze through his fingers as he gazed at the pitcher, then stepped back into the batter's box, the bat cocked high behind his right ear. Derringer fired a curve that broke over the inside corner. Robinson lashed out angrily and socked it into left field for a single.

Two innings later the Negro strode back to the plate, noting the mischievous grin on Derringer's face. This time the huge right-hander really winged one. Robinson hit the dirt just in time, as that fast ball whizzed by his head and pounded into the catcher's glove with a loud plop. Robinson mumbled a few words under his breath, remembering Rickey's admonition to keep his mouth shut even when thrown at. He got up and stepped back into the batter's box. When Derringer came over the plate with a low fast one, Robinson socked it deep into left center field for a triple.

After the game Derringer said to Hopper with a grin, "Tell you what, Clay. Your colored boy is going to do all right."

Any hope that these hits would mark the end of Jackie's troubles was woefully short-lived, for a few days later the Royals traveled to Jacksonville to meet the Jersey City Giants in an exhibition game. They found a huge crowd milling around a padlocked baseball park. Dodger representatives were notified that the game had been called off. Jacksonville's Bureau of Recreation had declared that the Royals could not play in a Jacksonville park because Negroes were not allowed to compete against white athletes in that city. (A scheduled game at De Land, Florida, was canceled when city officials said the stadium lights were out of order. It was to have been a day game.)

At Sanford, where the Royals were scheduled to play Indianapolis, it had been rumored that Negroes would be forbidden to play, but Rickey insisted that Robinson and Wright go along with the team. Throughout infield and batting practice no one made any objections. Hopper figured that the rumors were false, so he started Robinson at second base. As the visiting team, the Royals were up first. Robinson batted second in the line-up and his first time up he singled to center. With Sukeforth encouraging him from the sidelines, Robinson danced off first, pestering the pitcher, then dashed down the diamond, stealing second. The next hitter, Tom Tatum, slapped a single to left center. As Robinson sped into third he saw Hopper wave him on home. Wheeling around the bag at full speed he roared toward the Royals' first tally, but he could tell by the way the crowd jumped to its feet that it would be a close play. Robinson breathed deeply and left his feet for a flying slide, reaching the plate just before the throw. Loud cheers went up in the stands, and a nice warm feeling surged through him.

When he returned to the dugout, the applause still tingling in his ears, Robinson noticed Manager Hopper moving toward him. "At last, I've got a word of praise coming," he thought.

Instead, Hopper said, "I'm sorry, Jackie, but I'm gonna have to take you outa the game."

"Outa the game?"

"Yep, a member of the local constabulary says you and Wright can't stay."

"What have we done wrong?"

"Nothing that he could tell me. It's just—well, you know. The man says whites and colored can't play together here."

Robinson and Wright strode to the shower to a mixed chorus of boos and cheers.

3

April 14 meant a private emancipation proclamation, for when the Royals packed their bags, the Jackie Robinsons could say good-by to Florida and the Deep South. They were headed for Jersey City and the opening day of the 1946 baseball season, and Robinson remembers it well:

There was a lot of fanfare at Roosevelt Stadium. Mayor Frank Hague was there, with a lot of school children he had "liberated" by declaring a holiday. I remember the parades, the brass band's playing "The Star-Spangled Banner" and the marvelous beauty of this "day of destiny" for me. Nothing else mattered now—not even the people who, I now knew, had ordered me out of Sanford, not even the insults and humiliations, the days and nights of strain. None of this would show up in the records of the years to come—only the hits, runs and errors of this day. As they played "The Star-Spangled Banner" and Old Glory rolled slowly toward that azure blue sky, I stood on the base line with a lump in my throat and my heart beating rapidly, my stomach feeling as if it were full of feverish fireflies with claws on their feet. I was remembering what Mr. Rickey had said to me in spring training: "Jackie, we scouted you for a long time. So I know what you can do, and I want you to do it. I want you to run those bases like lightning. I want you to worry the daylights out of those pitchers. Don't be afraid to take a chance, to try to steal that extra base. Sure, sometimes you'll get caught but just remember this: I prefer the daring player to one who is afraid to take a chance. Just remember the best base runners get caught, even Ty Cobb. Just go out there and run like the devil."

Yes, I thought, how I'll run like the devil—if I can ever get on base!

Hopper called us into a semicircle for a pep talk: "O.K., boys, let's get off to a flying start. The game you lose the first day of the season hurts just as much as the game you lose during the pennant stretch drive. So let's go out there and pile up such a big lead that no team will be able to catch us. I'm going to start off today with this line-up. Breard leading off at shortstop, Robinson batting second at second base . . ." I was thrilled to hear my name. Apparently Manager Hopper and Mr. Rickey still believed in me, although I had not beaten the hide off the ball during the spring training session. Now I knew that this was more than just a phony attempt to appease Negroes and those elements of the press which had demanded that baseball really become the American pastime. I was within reach of what I am sure is the dream of every boy who ever strode to the sand lot with a glove: the major leagues.

The umpire shouted, "Play ball!" and the Jersey City team dashed onto the field to a deafening roar by fans who packed every seat in this stadium. This was the golden period for baseball, when magnates couldn't find enough seats for the fans who wanted to come.

Breard stepped to the plate and I crouched on one knee in the batters' circle, awaiting my turn. I watched the pitcher closely, as Mr. Rickey had told me to do, so as to be able to get the jump on him when I decided to steal—if I got on. Breard slapped a grounder to shortstop and was thrown out. As I strode to the plate there was an ear-splitting roar. I felt weak in the knees. My palms felt too moist to grip the bat. I was afraid to look toward the stands for fear I would see only Negroes applauding—that the white fans would be siting stony-faced, or yelling epithets.

The pitcher threw five times, I think, before I got the

rubber out of my knees. Luckily the count was three balls and two strikes. When he threw again I swung with all my might and dribbled an easy grounder to the shortstop, who threw me out by at least four steps. Another loud roar came from the stands, and this time I could see that the great portion of the cheers were from Negro fans—apparently Negroes who had never before given two hoots about a baseball game, but who had come out in order to say that they were present on the historic day when the racial barriers were broken in organized baseball. Thus they hardly knew the difference between a safe hit and an easy ground-out to the shortstop.

I went back to the bench, unhappy, of course, that I had not gotten on base, yet a little relieved to get the ice broken, to be able to run down that base line in front of all those people and have nothing awful happen. After the third out of the inning, I trotted out to my position, thinking about the importance of this day, about the fact that watching this minor league game were more sports writers than would be watching any opening-day major league game—sports writers present because they knew that unfolding here on this diamond was a story much bigger than baseball, a story as far-reaching in essence as the very idea of democracy and the equality of men. Some of them were there, I knew, with a social conscience that went no deeper than the hope that something fantastic, perhaps even a riot, would occur, and that they would have "good copy" for the morning editions. Others were there because they felt that this scene represented the success of a newspaper crusade in which they had played a part. I prayed that before the day was over I might do something to justify the applause of those fans and the support given me by those sports writers who believed that baseball belonged to all the American people. While I stood daydreaming, thinking of what was happening to me and the nation that day, I heard the slap of the bat against the ball and "awakened" just in time to see the ball screeching along the grass between the first baseman and me. I dashed toward the ball as quickly as my reflexes would permit, but could do no better than wave. Duke Bouknight had just drilled a single into right field. I wondered how long I had daydreamed, whether I could have gotten that ball had I been more alert. I quickly rationalized that it was too well hit and too perfectly placed for me to get it.

We held Jersey City scoreless in the second inning. In our half of the third I found myself in the first clutch situation of my baseball career. There were two men on base as a result of a walk and a single and I knew what the people in the stands were wondering: "Can he hit when there are ducks on the pond?" "Can he deliver when the opposing pitcher is bearing down?"

I stepped to the plate determined to move those men. Word was already around that I was a good bunter, and Manager Hopper decided to try to outguess pitcher Warren Sandell. He figured that the Giants would be looking for me to sacrifice the two runners to second and third. Hopper guessed right, because Sandell's first pitch was a fast one, letter-high down the middle. I swung with all my might and knew when the bat met the ball that I really had connected. As I dashed toward first, the roar of the crowd told me that this one was going all the way. It sailed more than 340 feet over the left-field fence. I had hit my first homer and driven in my first three runs in organized baseball. I was so excited, so exhilarated, as I circled those bases that it seemed all the oxygen had left my brain and for a moment those stands were just a blur in front of me. As I crossed home plate two teammates were waiting to shake hands.

"Atta boy, Jackie. Atta boy," said one. "That's the old ball game right there."

I got a warm reception from the Royals as I returned to the bench. I peeked into the stands for a look at Rae, who was beaming broadly. I felt even better.

I sat beside Marvin Rackley, a speedy young outfielder from South Carolina. He slapped me on the shoulder and said, "That's the way to hit 'em, Jackie." A third baseman,

These family photographs show the Robinsons soon after they moved to California. In the group photograph: Mack, Jackie, Edgar, Mrs. Robinson, Willa Mae, and Frank. At the right: Jackie.

Robinson's military career during the Second World War was just as stormy as his baseball career; it included a court-martial that grew out of Robinson's refusal to accept segregation in an Army-camp bus. Robinson, Number 14 in this photograph, is shown in Officers Candidate School at Fort Riley, Kansas. He and other Negroes got into OCS only after Joe Louis appealed to the War Department in Washington to remove the ban on officer candidates.

Barney Stein

The Deep South bleachers in the background were empty when this photograph was taken, but the whole world was watching Jackie and pitcher John Wright, left, in their first days of spring training with the Montreal Royals.

Jackie Robinson and Rachel Isum were married February 10, 1946, shortly after Jackie signed with the Montreal team.

above right: All the worries about "social equality" and the predictions that Jackie's teammates would refuse to associate with him off the diamond were quickly destroyed by members of the Montreal squad, who urged Robinson to join in card games, as above, and in similar activities.

right: During Robinson's rookie year with the Dodgers he was subjected to severe "jockeying" from players around the League, but no other team gave him as much abuse as the Philadelphia Phillies and their manager, Ben Chapman. After the baseball commissioner ordered the abuse toned down, Branch Rickey asked Robinson to pose shaking hands with Chapman "for the good of baseball." Chapman refused, and would only pose holding a bat. Robinson says that he had to swallow more pride to agree to this photograph than in any other instance he can remember.

Barney Stein

In the early days of Robinson's ordeal, one man who stuck by him and helped him weather the storm was Clyde Sukeforth, the Dodger coach. His scouting was largely responsible for the fact that Rickey selected Robinson as the first Negro to play in modern organized baseball.

"Run! Be daring! You've got to show them what you can do!" Branch
Rickey, left, told Jackie Robinson.

International News Photos

"Ty Cobb in Technicolor," was the label pinned on Robinson by the late Bill "Bojangles" Robinson. Baseball experts agree that no player since Cobb has run the bases with the same daring and skill.

right: Branch Rickey had forewarned Jackie that balls thrown at his head would be part of what he would have to withstand in order to destroy Jim Crow in the national pastime. During his early days in baseball the Negro star was hit more often by pitched balls than any other batter in the League.

Jackie, Rachel, and Jackie. Jr., in front of their apartment in Brooklyn.

above left: One of Jackie's constant problems was keeping his weight down. Branch Rickey is shown here patting Robinson's stomach with approval after Jackie reported for spring training in 1949 at his best playing weight.

left: Robinson and Charlie Dressen, one-time Dodger manager, quickly formed a mutual admiration society. Jackie rates Dressen as the best of the men who managed him, and Dressen once said, "Give me five players like Robinson and a pitcher and I'll beat any nine-man team in baseball."

JACKIE ROBINSON   FAYE EMERSON

Robinson was what newspapermen called "good copy" because he almost always gave straightforward answers to their questions. Appearing
on the "Youth Wants to Know" program in 1952, he gave his usual direct
answer—"Yes"—when he was asked whether or not he thought the New
York Yankees were discriminating against Negroes. The next thing he
knew he was in the middle of a press hurricane. Faye Emerson, right, was
moderator of the television show.

above left: This is the infield that sent the Dodgers winging into a period
of perennial contention for the pennant—a period that matched very
closely Robinson's tenure in the majors. Left to right are Spider Jorgensen,
Pee Wee Reese, Eddie Stanky and Jackie. Robinson says that the gentle-
manly qualities of the "Kentucky Colonel," Reese, and Eddie Stanky's
courage and team loyalty were major factors in helping him to make good.

left: "I hated nothing the way I hated to lose, and this picture indicates
that my teammates didn't like defeat either," says Robinson, shown here
with Wayne Belardi, left, and Carl Furillo, with pitcher Chris Van Cuyk
and first baseman Gil Hodges in the background. The Dodgers had just
lost a heartbreaker to Philadelphia's 1950 whiz kids.

Photo by Look Magazine

On December 8, 1956, when Robinson received the 41st Spingarn medal from the National Association for the Advancement of Colored People, he called it justification for his policy of speaking out whenever and wherever he saw racial injustice. Ed Sullivan, noted columnist and televison star, is shown draping the medal about Robinson's neck as Dr. Allan Knight Chalmers, NAACP treasurer, left, and Roy Wilkins, NAACP executive secretary, look on.

above left: The crucial struggle of Negroes today, as Jackie Robinson sees it, is that of trying to secure adequate housing in decent neighborhoods of their choice. Finally the Robinsons were able to purchase this house in Stamford, Connecticut.

left: After retirement from baseball, Robinson became vice-president of Chock Full O' Nuts. He is shown here with William Black, president of Chock Full O' Nuts, after Robinson was named personnel director of the New York restaurant chain.

Jackie and Rachel Robinson

Johnny (Spider) Jorgensen, said: "Nice going, Jackie." I felt great, and I couldn't help but wonder whether these players were complimenting me out of baseball instinct or reflex, or whether they were consciously saying these things to make me feel a part of the team. Whatever the reason, I knew that it would make Mr. Rickey feel good to see that even Montreal players from the Deep South didn't object to a Negro hitting a three-run homer for their team.

When I came up in the fifth inning I decided to cross up the Jersey City team. Instead of trying to slam the ball over the fence, I dropped a bunt down the third base line that caught the third baseman flatfooted. By the time he reached the slowly dribbling ball I had crossed first base. I remembered Mr. Rickey's advice to run those bases like crazy, so as the pitcher took his stretch I dashed daringly off first, then plunged back on my belly as the catcher faked a throw to first. When the pitcher began his stretch for the second pitch I dashed off recklessly again, but I kept going this time and stole second easily.

I dashed off second now, still trying to worry Larry Higgins, the New Jersey pitcher. He broke off an inside curve which Tom Tatum slapped hard on the ground to the third baseman. A standard rule in baseball is that a man on second does not try to advance when the ball is hit to third base or shortstop. I acted as if I were going back to second, but when third baseman Norm Jaeger threw to first I dashed toward third. The first baseman fired right back to Jaeger, but I slid into third, beating the throw by an eyelash. I had now stolen one base officially, and had "taken" third, although it never would appear in the record as a stolen base. I figured now was the time to be daring. I would try to steal home!

Phil Otis came in to pitch for Jersey City. After his warm-up throws, I began to dance down the base line. He looked toward home plate, then threw hard to third, but I slid back in safely. I danced down the line and he threw to third again, but I slid back safely. I knew now that Otis was worried. He watched me closely and then fired to the plate as

I ran halfway down the base line, dashing back to third before the catcher could throw me out. On the next pitch I again dashed down the base line. Otis was so frustrated that he stopped his delivery toward home plate—a balk. The umpire waved me on to the plate and a score.

Now the crowd went wild. Not just the Negroes, but thousands of whites, including many Jersey City fans, screamed, laughed and stamped their feet, and I knew that this was no tribute to a Negro; this was people proving Mr. Rickey right: they liked daring baseball.

The applause loosened me. I felt that somebody had underestimated the decency of the American people, else baseball would not have been a Jim Crow institution for all these years.

When Robinson's first day in organized baseball was over he had four safe hits in five trips to the plate, one of them a home run; he had stolen second twice; he had scored four runs, two of which were awarded by the umpire when the pitcher balked after becoming unnerved by Robinson's dashes down the third baseline. Montreal had won its opening game, 14 to 1.

At 6:05 P.M., a smiling Jackie Robinson walked out of the Royals' dressing room to find Rae with her face aglow. Tears glistened in her eyes as she kissed him. Sports writers clustered around to ask an amazing assortment of questions about how it felt to be a Negro in a white man's world.

Afterwards, Joe Bostic summed up the day by writing in the New York *Amsterdam News:* "The most significant sports story of the century was written into the record books today as baseball took up the cudgel for democracy and an unassuming but superlative Negro boy ascended the heights of excellence to prove the rightness of the experiment. And prove it in the only correct crucible for such an experiment—the crucible of white-hot competition."

4

The first three games against Jersey City gladdened the heart of Jackie Robinson and all who prayed that his debut in organized baseball would be a success. More than 66,000 fans attended those games, and many of them stormed the field afterwards, grabbing at Jackie's cap, jerking at his glove, eager just to shout a greeting, to be able to say that they were there when baseball history was made.

Still, there were those who said that three games in Jersey City proved nothing—that Robinson still had to go to Baltimore, to come up against teams with many southerners on their rosters under circumstances not nearly as favorable as Jersey City's carnival-like opening-day atmosphere. One of those who wished Robinson and integrated baseball well, but who held deep and honest fears that the worst was yet to come, was Frank Shaughnessy, president of the International League.

Shaughnessy had telephoned Rickey before the opening game in Jersey City to ask, "Branch, if I could convince you that Robinson's playing with Montreal in Baltimore would produce rioting and bloodshed and wreck organized baseball in that city, would you let him play there?"

Rickey thought for a while and replied, "If you could convince me of that, Frank, of course I would not."

"Then for God's sake, Branch, don't let that colored boy go to Baltimore. There's a lot of trouble brewing down there."

Rickey had scoffed at Shaughnessy's talk of trouble but promised to discuss the matter in Jersey City on opening day. Shaughnessy had brought to Jersey City a batch of newspaper clippings, some of which played up the comments of rabid racists. Rickey looked the clippings over and said: "Frank, if Robinson is good enough to help this Montreal team he's going to Baltimore. As far as I'm concerned, these clippings are just another indication of supposedly sensible people crying, 'Trouble ahead, trouble ahead!' when the only thing that really endangers them is their own fear."

"Look, Branch," said Shaughnessy, "this is no time for philosophical mouthings and silly platitudes. The people are up in arms in Baltimore. This could wreck not only baseball in Baltimore but the whole International League."

"I'm sorry, Frank, but I just don't foresee all the trouble you do. Anyhow, the time has come for us to give democracy a chance. We solve nothing by backing away—in fact we'll encourage every agitator in Maryland if we show fear."

Baltimore provided the first really bitter experience the Robinsons faced after the beginning of the official season. First there was no place they could stay except with a private family. The night of the first game in Baltimore, Rae sat near the Dodger dugout. When the Montreal team took the field, a man sitting directly behind her shouted, "Here comes that nigger son of a bitch. Let's give it to him now!"

Rae cringed. In Florida people had called Robinson insulting names behind their hands, but in Baltimore they were openly shouting them. The man behind her and a companion of his continued to shout loudest of all, perhaps for her benefit. Rae was determined not to look around at them, nor to leave, because she didn't want them to think they had driven her away. She wondered if Jackie heard—if it would affect his playing.

Periodically these agonizing thoughts were broken by the scream of other epithets in which the racists were making derogatory remarks about Jackie's mother, his family, his color, his odor, and anything else they could think of.

What was worse, only about 3,000 fans were attending, and in view of the publicized threats that Baltimoreans would boycott the Orioles if they played against a Negro, the Baltimore management almost surely would say that Jackie had cost both teams money.

Jackie was so busy watching Baltimore hits and base runners go by that he had little time to worry about the attendance. And what hurt him far more than the insults was the fact that he got just one hit in three times at bat—and the Orioles breezed to a 12-to-7 victory over his team.

The boycott fear was short-lived. The next day, for an afternoon doubleheader, 25,396 fans (about 10,000 of them Negroes) jammed into the stadium to see Jackie get just one hit in seven tries as the Royals and Orioles won a game each.

Referring to the crowd, Lloyd McGowan of the *Montreal Star* wrote that "Jackie Robinson is paying his keep anyway . . . He is playing adequately, but no more, they say."

Rickey was quite satisfied, however, for there was no rioting, no bloodshed, because, as usual, the bigots had a bark much worse than their bite. Even though Baltimore was— and is—a Jim Crow city, unable to make the kind of progress that Washington, a much more southern city, was making, the bigots did not have the tacit approval of city authorities or police officials, and it is usually only when hoodlums are given the go-ahead sign by the power structure of a community that they resort to violence. In addition, there were many Negroes out to see Robinson play in Baltimore, and most rabble-rousers prefer violence only when the victim is outnumbered.

After the Baltimore series, which seemed, compared with the dire predictions, uneventful, Jackie and Rae joined the team for the journey north to Montreal, convinced that the worst was over; if Baltimore could take it, surely the other cities could.

In Canada the Robinsons' first problem was finding an apartment, an ordeal for any young family in that time of acute housing shortage, but a particularly severe one for a Negro couple. For about a month the Robinsons lived in a tourist home, because the first apartments available in Montreal were allocated to families with children. Rae was pregnant, but their child would not be born for several months. It was cold as the dickens in that tourist home, for the calendar said it was spring, no matter what the weather. Finally Montreal team officials notified the Robinsons that an apartment was being advertised in the newspaper and urged them to apply. Rae and Jackie read the ad together and figured the location of the apartment to be quite a distance from the ball park and in a neighborhood where few if any Negroes lived. And everybody would speak French!

The language problem did not worry them nearly as much, however, as the conditioning they had received in the States. In an American city, only the most courageous or foolhardy Negro would answer a housing ad without some advance information that the property might be available to colored people. So the Robinsons went to check on this apartment with many misgivings. Rae was sure that as soon as the landlord saw her he would declare, as in a typical United States city, that the apartment had already been rented, or say frankly that the apartment was not available to Negroes.

When Rachel rapped on the door a woman answered with a pleasant smile and asked her in for a cup of tea. The apartment was lovely, clean and sunny, and Rae's heart pounded nervously as she speculated as to whether they would get it. As they discussed the price the woman told her that she would leave all her linens, pots and pans, dishes, all her housekeeping utensils, and that she was happy to rent to them.

Rae was delighted. As she discussed their good fortune with Jackie, she said: "How can a few miles, a mere border, make that much difference in people?"

The apartment actually was half a duplex, built like the row houses of Baltimore and Philadelphia. When several French-speaking women called on her in a body, Rae knew even though she could not understand what they said, that they came in friendship. She scanned their friendly faces thinking how easily, at another time or place, this might have been a delegation of protesters to lecture about property values or intermarriage and urge them to leave the neighborhood. An English-speaking member of the group explained that they had seen that Rae was pregnant and had come to offer any help they could give. Also, since food rationing still existed, they had come to offer her ration coupons for anything she needed and couldn't get with her own ration books.

The Robinsons were objects of curiosity—not hostility, but an intense curiosity on the part of people who had had no association with Negroes. When Jackie left for the baseball park, often someone in the adjoining house would say. "Here he comes!" and then the signal would go down the block as people banged on the wall, alerting the occupants of the next-door row house. As Jackie strolled down the street, heads would pop out of windows and doors in almost perfect cadence as the people stared at him, the black ballplayer who was the celebrity of their neighborhood.

Youngsters on the street were a source of great amusement for Jackie and Rae as they tried to explain to each other what these people of color were. Some called them Dutchmen, others called them Chinese, some called them Africans, and others simply did not know what to think. Very often the cry would go down the block as Rachel left the apartment to do a bit of shopping, "Here comes the black lady!" A parent would correct the child and say, "No, the brown lady."

Some youngsters in the block would always meet her at the store and carry back her heavy packages. Rae kept a bowl of fruit on the kitchen table by the screen door. The young-sters would poke their noses against the door waiting for her to invite them in for a piece of fruit. It did not take them long to learn to ask in English for the fruit they liked best.

Rae and Jackie soon fell in love with Montreal, a city that was warm and friendly, that had made delightful for them what might have been a nightmare.

Yet a baseball team plays only half its games at home. The rest of the time Jackie was traveling to Baltimore, Syracuse, Newark, Jersey City, Toronto, Buffalo and Rochester.

Although Baltimore produced the most vicious crowd re-action, far-north Syracuse, ironically, was where Robinson was abused most because of his race. Players on the Syracuse bench hurled all sorts of racial epithets at him. Once, as he leaned in the batter's circle awaiting his turn at bat, a Syra-cuse player pushed a black cat out of the dugout and shouted, as the cat skittered across the field, causing the umpire to call time: "Hey, Jackie, there's your cousin clowning on the field! Get him off so we can get on with the ball game."

Although the abuse took its toll, Robinson proved that he was a competitor in the greatest sense of the word. When Syracuse hauled out the black cat, for example, Robinson gritted his teeth and slashed a double down the left-field line. When the next player singled to center he dashed home, shouting toward the Syracuse dugout, "I reckon my cousin's pretty happy now, huh?"

Robinson provided dash, fire, for a Montreal team that was already great by the highest minor league standards, and Montreal became a Mecca toward which sports writers beat a path of pilgrimage, eager to say then and certainly in the future that they had played at least a small role in baseball's big experiment.

Jim Coleman of Toronto's *Globe and Mail* went down for a look at this new "attraction" and wrote: "With all due respect to the boys in the back room, [I just saw a baseball player] who is too good for the International League. He is a black man. His name is Jackie Robinson . . . when he first appeared rival players and southern scribes predicted that he wouldn't last through one complete trip around the League. Well, he has fooled them, and it looks as if his next step is into a big league uniform."

Coleman went on to relate that watching Robinson with him was a former New York Yankee named Herb Crompton, who had watched Robinson dip to his right to scoop up a ball seemingly destined for center field as a base hit, wheel gracefully and throw out the runner. "A great ballplayer," Crompton said to Coleman. "Yes, indeed, a truly great ballplayer. Too bad he's black."

Robinson read that comment and wondered how many times under how many different circumstances that last sentence had been uttered. How did they put it? "That Pullman porter—a smart fellow; college degree with honors. Too bad he's black."

Yet Robinson knew that the American racial tragedy was not only that white people saw a black skin as a calamity, but that some Negroes echoed them with the despairing wail, "Too bad I'm black." He hoped that somehow he could render this dirge meaningless, could let the nation and fifteen million Negroes see that barriers that men refuse to cower before cease to be barriers.

Some sports writers might still believe that because Jackie Robinson was black and baseball had been what it had been, Montreal would be the end of the line. Yet there were writers already putting the pressure on, as Rickey had hoped they would, saying that Jackie had to get his chance in the majors. A sports columnist for the *Newark Evening Telegram* wrote that Ted Williams, Bob Feller, Dixie Walker and Hal Newhouser might be named players of the year, but "the greatest performance being put on anywhere in sport . . . is being supplied by . . . Jackie Robinson of Montreal who is playing great baseball under pressures that would have crushed a less courageous man."

And there were baseball people saying what Branch Rickey hoped they would be saying. For example, Bruno Betzel, manager of the Jersey City team, told J. G. Taylor Spink, editor of the *Sporting News*, that Robinson was the best bunter in baseball, "even better than Ty Cobb was." Betzel, a southerner, said to Spink: "I would like to have nine Jackie Robinsons playing on my team. If I had only one . . . I would room with him myself and put him to bed nights to make sure nothing happened to him."

By the end of July the Royals led the league by a dozen games. In less than a month they would clinch the pennant and a place in the playoffs to determine which International League team would meet the playoff winner of the American Association for the title of "Little World Champions." When the Royals clinched the pennant, Robinson was batting .360; he was the best-fielding second baseman in the league; he was number two in the league in stolen bases, second only to his fleet-footed teammate, Marvin Rackley.

Only Rae knew that Jackie was weary, bedraggled, worn out physically and mentally. For weeks he had carried himself only on his tremendous competitive spirit. He was having trouble sleeping; he was nauseated; on many days he was unable to eat. The Negro's future in baseball rested with Robinson alone now, for the Negro pitcher had been dropped early in the season.

"Jack, I think you've got a nervous condition," said Rae.

"Aw, honey, I'm all right. My nerves are fine."

"Jack, I never saw a healthier specimen than you. This nausea, this loss of appetite, has to be a nervous condition. Why don't you take a few days' rest?"

"Aw, I'm all right, Rae; I'll be fine in a couple of days."

Finally both she and Manager Hopper insisted that he see a doctor. The physician said sharply, "You're on the verge of a nervous breakdown." He ordered at least ten days' rest, and that Robinson do nothing but relax and play golf, indulge in the activities he enjoyed—and under no circumstances was he to attend baseball games or even read the sports pages.

Rae was delighted at the thought of having Jack home for ten days. There was a large park near their apartment and she talked gaily of how they would have a picnic in the park every day and then they would go to the driving range where Jack could hit some golf balls.

But the next morning when Rae got out the picnic basket and began to prepare sandwiches, Jack mumbled quietly, "Rae, let's not go on a picnic today." She acceded to his wishes, assuming at first that he preferred just to sit at home and chat with her. A few minutes later, however, she noticed that his head was buried in the newspaper. Later the radio was on and Jack was hanging close to the play-by-play broadcast of the Royals' game.

"Please, Jack, why don't you take the doctor's advice? I know baseball's your bread and butter. I know it's in your blood now. But you can't wreck your health."

"I'll be all right. I'm worried about the team."

"My goodness, Jack, the pennant's clinched, there's nothing to lose. Why worry about the team?"

"You don't understand," he said. "I'm leading the league in batting. The way things stand I'm subject to win the batting crown. I'm afraid if I stay out for ten days the players will start whispering that I'm trying to protect my batting average by staying out of ball games. I don't want that kind of talk going around."

"O.K., I suppose you understand those things better than I do, better even than the doctor does. Do what you think you must," said Rae with a gesture of hopelessness.

The next day Robinson was back at the ball park, telling Hopper that he just couldn't stay away for ten days. Hopper argued that he shouldn't feel obligated to play, and shouldn't worry about what some players might think, but he insisted that he wanted to play.

"You see, Skipper, as soon as that doctor told me that I wasn't dying of anything horrible like cancer, that it was just my nerves, I was all right. I wasn't nervous any more. So I'm ready to go now, if you want me."

Hopper assured Robinson that he did want him, and Jackie rejoined his team.

Robinson finished the season as the top batter in the league, as the best-fielding second baseman, in a tie for the most runs scored, and second in stolen bases. Beyond this, though, there were other measurements of his success. One was that in Baltimore, where he had been the target of such bitter abuse early in the season, the fans and players now accepted him as a player to be respected and admired. Seldom had he felt so good inside as on that late-season night when he stole home in a close game and the Baltimore fans gave him a thunderous standing ovation. He was doubly convinced that Branch Rickey was a very smart man, that he knew what he was talking about when he said that, in time, courage and dignity, coupled with some stellar baseball playing, would win over even the most prejudiced fans.

The season over, newspapers were filled with speculation that Robinson would be called up to help the Dodgers in their desperate struggle with the St. Louis Cardinals for the National League pennant. Rickey put a quick stop to that. He announced that Robinson belonged to Montreal, and that Montreal fans had every right to expect Robinson to remain with the team in an effort to help them with the playoffs and the Little World Series.

Rickey later remarked that in addition to these charitable feelings toward Montreal, he felt that to bring Robinson up late in the year would conflict greatly with his plans to bring him into the majors under conditions where he was more likely to have the support of the Brooklyn players.

And that was how, in just twenty-seven years, a Negro lad had risen from the hopelessness of Georgia plantation life, the grinding poverty of youth, to the role of stardom in the Little World Series. With the thrill of that Little World Series triumph over Louisville still throbbing in his chest, the acclaim of that wonderful Montreal crowd still tingling in his ears, Jackie Robinson could look back over his life and conclude that it was a long road from stealing grapes and running from cops in Pasadena to stealing bases and running from a lovely, lovable mob in Montreal. Yes, he had come a long way. But Jackie knew that, thanks to men of courage like Branch Rickey, so had men of integrity like Clay Hopper. Which meant that his country had come a long way in the twenty-seven years of Jackie's life. Robinson was proud, but more than anything, he was grateful.

8....The Wall Comes Tumblin' Down

Soon Jackie's memories of a triumphant first season gave way to worry about the future. Funny, he thought, how much more important the future becomes when you have a child. In November Rae had given birth to a son, Jackie, Jr. They laughed often about how she "barely got home for the delivery," for she traveled with Jack until she was eight months pregnant, knowing that he wanted her with him. Now Jack would scold himself occasionally for having been so engrossed in his baseball pioneering that, until after the baby was born, he had no idea that Rae had frequently been ill, but managed to hide it from him so as not to add to his burdens.

Throughout the winter of 1946-47, which they spent in Los Angeles with Rae's mother, one question about the future overshadowed everything else before them: Would Jackie be promoted to the Dodgers in the spring? The young couple discussed this question repeatedly, reaching the same conclusion every time: that Branch Rickey was a man of integrity, a man who refused to use the platitudes, clichés and alibis used by so many leaders of industry as a reason why a Negro "can't" be given this job or that one.

Rickey had already indicated to them that he had confidence in Jackie and his ability to play the kind of baseball and be the kind of man, on and off the field, necessary for the success of this experiment. No one had done more to convince Rickey of Robinson's ability to do the job than Clay Hopper. After the 1946 season, when Rickey met Hopper in St. Louis, he felt he had waited long enough for some voluntary comment on whether Robinson ought to be brought up. Finally he decided to draw Hopper out by expressing vague doubts about whether the Negro was of big league caliber.

The Mississippian looked at Rickey for a while, then blurted: "Mr. Rickey, I want to tell you something. If you give that fellow Robinson a try, he'll make it with Brooklyn. You don't have to worry about him. But if you don't care to give him a try at Brooklyn, I'd be tickled to death to have him back at Montreal."

"Wait a minute, Clay," said Rickey. "A year ago you were begging me not to crucify you by putting a Negro baseball player on your squad . . ."

"I know, I know," Hopper interrupted. "But I'm here to tell you today that you don't have to worry about that fellow Robinson. He's a great ballplayer and what's more he's a real gentleman."

Rickey smiled broadly. Hopper was living proof of what he had said from the start: *Prejudice runs away from truth. Prejudice is a coward in the face of fact. Proximity is the solution to this race problem if only we can get enough of it.*

Rickey had told the Robinsons of Hopper's recommendation, and this seemed to them ample evidence of what Rickey had in mind. But could he buck successfully what they knew would be strong opposition by the owners to a Negro entering the majors? Few people outside the circle of major league owners knew that, after Jackie's year at Montreal, at an owners' meeting in Cleveland, a report was presented which said that admission of Negroes to organized baseball would wreck the investments of the clubs. Fifteen owners had voted to approve the report. Rickey, who declined to vote, left that meeting burning inside.

Now Rickey was maintaining strict silence about his intentions as far as Robinson was concerned, even though he was constantly pestered by newspapermen who wondered why he was taking so long to go through a five-minute bookkeeping routine of transferring a contract from the Royals to the Dodgers. In January, 1947, Associated Press polled sports editors across the country and a whopping majority said that the number one question of the year was whether Robinson would become the first Negro player to make the grade in big league baseball.

Frank Shaughnessy, who had warned Rickey that there would be riots and bloodshed if Robinson played in Baltimore, asked Rickey about his intentions. Rickey was noncommittal.

"Well, Branch, I just want to let you know that I'm man enough to admit I was wrong last year and to say that I'd be more than delighted if you decided to give Robinson another year in Triple-A baseball," Shaughnessy said.

Rickey noticed the sly grin on Shaughnessy's face and replied, "Yeah, I'll bet you *would,* considering the fact that with Robinson for a drawing card the Royals played before a record attendance of more than 800,000 at home and on the road last year."

Late in January, Robinson was ordered to report to the Royals for spring training. This raised new doubts in the Robinson household, yet Rae and Jackie could detect many signs that Rickey was paving the way into the majors. He had announced that the Dodgers and the Royals would train in Havana, Cuba, an obvious effort to prevent Robinson's having to face the insults and abuse he had received in Florida the year before. Someone told Jackie that arrangements had also been made

for the Dodgers to play exhibition games against South American teams with Negroes on their rosters, and he figured that
this was Rickey's way of getting the Dodgers accustomed to
playing with Negroes. Both Jackie and Rae had seen that one
of the things Rickey was most concerned about was the reaction
of the Dodger players, for Rickey felt that a bitter reaction,
which might become highly publicized, would be greatly
detrimental to the cause of integration.

However, Rickey knew that there was another threat to the
successful movement of Negroes into big league baseball, and
that threat was the Negro fan. Rickey discussed this problem
with Dr. Dan Dodson, a sociologist at New York University
who had been extremely helpful to him in bringing Robinson
into the International League. They agreed that there were
many understandable reasons why some Negroes might abuse
the situation. "What on earth would be more reasonable
than for a people supposedly free for ninety years, but with no
recognition, to see one of their own men stand up boldly
among whites and be proud? Lord Almighty, it's the most
natural thing in the world," said Rickey. Yet he knew that Negroes would have to resist the temptation.

Rickey talked to Mordecai Johnson, president of Howard
University; to Wendell Smith and Mrs. Jesse L. Vann of the
Pittsburgh Courier; to Judge Myles Paige; to Herbert Miller,
executive secretary of the Carleton branch of the YMCA in
New York City, and they all agreed that they should do something as quietly as possible to try to make the Negro fans
aware of the terrible responsibility faced, not just by Jackie
Robinson, but by every Negro who went to the ball park to
cheer him.

Miller told Rickey that it would probably be helpful to meet
privately with prominent Negro citizens to explain what they
could do to help promote the successful integration of Negroes in baseball. So on the evening of February 5, 1947,
about thirty prominent Brooklyn Negroes assembled for a
meeting with Rickey, who had brought along his assistant,
Arthur Mann, Dodson, and his good friend and adviser Judge
Edward Lazansky.

Several of the guests viewed the dinner as a festive occasion; they expected to be told that Robinson would be a Dodger in 1947. Rickey did not say what they had hoped to hear. After dinner he arose to a great ovation and began to speak haltingly—something rare for Rickey—as if he did not know how to say what he needed to say without offending those present. Finally he discarded any pretense of giving a prepared speech and said that he wanted to talk to the Negroes man-to-man, as friends with whom he could speak frankly about some very distressing problems.

"I think all of us here tonight have courage enough to face the facts of life, to discuss things that may sting our pride—if they are things that must be discussed. You see, I have a ballplayer named Jackie Robinson with the Montreal team of the Brooklyn organization. He may play another year with Montreal or he may be asked to join the Brooklyn Dodgers. I can't tell you tonight which will happen. But I do know this: if he is brought up to the Dodgers, one big risk to his success is that the Negro people themselves will ruin it."

The Negro leaders sat in anxious, wide-eyed silence.

"I know that I am saying it as cruelly as it can be said," Rickey continued, "but I must make you appreciate the weight of responsibility that rests upon the shoulders of leading Negro citizens of this community. I don't need to tell people like you how racial progress is made, for every gain that you have made in this country was won by sacrifice, sorrow, and sometimes bloodshed. This step we would like to take in organized baseball is certain to benefit greatly every Negro in this nation, and this step is being made for you by a single individual, by a young man who has already had to undergo racial barbs and humiliations that are sickening to any human being with a heart; by one young man whose wounds you cannot see or share.

"So I'm here tonight to beg you to do what you can to see that no Negro adds to the burdens of Jackie Robinson. We don't want Negroes to form gala welcoming committees, to form parades to the ball park every night. We don't want Negroes to strut, to wear badges, to hail Jackie Robinson's movement into the major leagues as a victory by Negroes over white people. We don't want any premature 'Jackie Robinson Days' or 'Jackie Robinson Nights,' because you must remember that white ballplayers are human beings too. That old green-eyed monster, jealousy, also moves among them, and it is only natural that they will resent the heaping of praise and awards upon a Negro who has not been in the major leagues long enough to prove himself. We cannot have Negroes in the stands drunk, gambling, fighting, being arrested. We don't want Jackie Robinson wined and dined until he is fat and futile. We don't want what can be another great milestone in the progress of American race relations turned into a national comedy and an ultimate tragedy."

The round man with the wrinkled face and the bushy eyebrows was interrupted by thunderous applause. A Negro stood to tell him that he need have no worry about his audience being sensitive about the things he had said, because Negroes were discussing these things constantly; because Negroes had always been acutely aware of the damage one ignoramus could do to the cause of the whole race.

There followed a long discussion about the ways in which these Negro leaders could help the Brooklyn organization. A committee was formed to spearhead a campaign throughout Brooklyn and Harlem with the slogan, "Don't spoil Jackie's chances," and the Negro press began an editorial campaign urging Negroes to "take this tremendous victory in stride."

2

It was reasonable, perhaps, to hope that Negroes could take Robinson's entry into major league baseball with a measure of sanity, but who really could expect them to "take it in stride" when no one else in the nation could? The whole sports world was excited, and even Robinson was no picture of calmness the morning he was to depart for spring training in Havana. He wished Rae were going with him, but the cost and the presence of Jackie, Jr., made this out of the question. He admitted to her that he was as uneasy as he had ever been in his life, that his year at Montreal had not conditioned him to the point where he could look forward to going to camp with anything but nervousness and uncertainty.

"I'm just as nervous as you are—probably more so," said Rae, "but so much is at stake, and you're so deeply involved now that you couldn't back out if you wanted to."

"Well, I'm not nervous enough to try to back out."

"Before you leave would you make me one promise?" asked Rae.

"What?"

"Promise that throughout spring training you'll be just plain Jackie Robinson."

"Of course. Who else would I be?"

"Jack, you know what I mean. I want you to be the thoughtful, calm and considerate person that I know at home."

"You want me to be nice, sweet, docile—and play in the Three-I league this summer," Jack teased.

"Please, Jack. You know I want you to play baseball as hard as you know how, but I want you also to remember that every eye in America will be on you. I want you to remember that many sports writers will be looking for incidents, will be out to prove that, in effect, integration won't work in baseball."

Jackie understood, for nobody knew better than he that despite his behavior at Montreal in 1946, a lot of people still considered him a source of trouble for baseball. It was human nature for ballplayers to sound off, to cry "murder" in the heat of battle, and in that respect, Robinson was more "human" than most, but he was going to Havana with Branch Rickey's warning still echoing inside him: "We can't fight through this . . . We've got no army . . . We can win only if you can convince the world you're a great ballplayer . . ." For Rae, for Rickey, for the millions of Americans who hoped so desperately that he would make good, Robinson would try in Havana to be a baseball player and nothing else.

At the airport he kissed Rae good-by and insisted that she and Jackie, Jr., not wait until the plane took off. Rae agreed and went home. Robinson entered the airport just in time to hear an announcement that his flight had been canceled. It was like an eleventh-hour reprieve, he thought, as he grabbed a taxi and returned home.

Rae looked up in disbelief as Jack walked back into the house, and asked, "What on earth are you doing here?"

"The planes aren't flying," he said, "so I won't have to leave you till tomorrow."

"Well, that doesn't make me happy—I hate to see you get another start like this. You were late last year and you ought to be there on time this spring. You know how important first impressions can be."

"What do you mean, 'first impressions'? It isn't as if I'm meeting Clay Hopper for the first time in my life, you know. He'll give me a couple of days' grace."

"Jack, you know that although you're reporting to Montreal it's little more than a sham. In effect, you're reporting to the Brooklyn Dodgers, because you know and I know that you're going to be a Dodger in April. And I should think you'd want to make every effort not to do anything that will handicap Mr. Rickey."

Robinson knew that Rachel was right. He looked at their son, just three months old, and he could picture him as a lad in his teens, playing baseball on some sand lot, being ridden by the players on the opposing team with this taunt: "Hey, Jackie, what makes you think you can play baseball any more than your pappy? He had a chance to be a big major-leaguer but he flopped. Isn't that right, Jackie?"

That night Robinson could barely sleep for fear his plane would be delayed another day. It was not, and Jackie got to Havana on time, only to find that the season was starting off wrong as far as he was concerned. The Royals had signed three other Negro players, Don Newcombe, a huge fast-balling pitcher; Roy Campanella, touted as one of the best catchers in the business; and Roy Partlow, another pitcher. Although Montreal was quartered at the Havana Military Academy and the Brooklyn team at the plush Nacional Hotel, the Negro players were housed separately at a hotel some fifteen miles from the Royals' practice field.

Robinson was indignant. "I thought we left Florida to

train in Cuba so we could get away from Jim Crow," he said to a member of the Dodgers' staff. "So what the devil is this business of segregating us Negro players in a colored nation, Cuba?"

The staff member explained that segregation had not been demanded by the Cuban government or by hotel authorities, but that Mr. Rickey figured too much was at stake to risk any incidents and that he was being extra cautious by quartering the Negroes separately.

"He realizes that you stayed with the Montreal team last year and are on good terms with the players, but there are quite a few new fellows on the Montreal squad, some of whom may be quite prejudiced. Mr. Rickey figures that rather than run the risk of some half-baked rookie starting a squabble he'd just separate the team this way for a while."

"Well, I don't like segregation, but I'll go along with Mr. Rickey's judgment. He's been right so far."

Rickey's hope was that Robinson would play such standout baseball in spring training that even Dodger players reluctant to associate with a Negro on anything close to a position of equality would put their mercenary interests first and say that they wanted him on the Brooklyn team because he might be the difference between a second- or third-place finish and winning the pennant.

Rickey had studied the Brooklyn club carefully, noting that the most difficult way to move Robinson onto the team would be to have him compete for a spot at either second base, which he played at Montreal, but where Eddie Stanky, the aggressive holler guy, was holding forth for Brooklyn, or at shortstop, which was being held down by Pee Wee Reese, one of the best ones in the business. Rickey knew that more than pure baseball ability was involved, that even to succeed in dislodging two such established and popular stars would be a mistake. Already talk was circulating that one reason Negroes ought to be kept out of baseball was that they would end up with most of the jobs. One newspaperman had tried to arouse such fears in Reese by pointing out that Robinson was a shortstop. Another player had said, "These Negroes have a natural rhythm, and they can run faster than white guys. First thing you know they'll run us out of the game."

Rickey telephoned Mel Jones, then general manager of the Royals, and ordered that during spring training Robinson be placed at first base. Dodger manager Leo Durocher was convinced that none of his candidates for first base would play baseball up to big league caliber and he had told Rickey that the Dodgers couldn't possibly win the pennant without a better first baseman. He offered to help, in any way Rickey suggested, to smooth the way for Jackie to join the Bums.

When Jones handed Robinson a first baseman's mitt, the puzzled Negro said, "What's this?"

"You're to get all the practice you can with this, and Manager Hopper will be explaining to you later that you're to play first base this spring."

Robinson let Jones know that he was plenty irked with the shift. Just when he hoped to play well enough in spring training to justify a promotion to Brooklyn, he was being shifted from a position he knew, and where he felt confident, to one he didn't know. Except for that brief period when he had a sore arm during his first spring training with the Royals, Robinson had never played first base. When he got Rickey's explanation, however, he promised that he would do his best. But Robinson never felt that his best was good enough at first. For one thing, he had a sore back and a toe that was giving him trouble, and first base required a lot of bending and running back and forth. He was having a devil of a time physically. Besides this, he was never sure whether he was playing the runner properly. As a result of all this he spent most of his time on the field hoping the ball wouldn't be hit to first base, whereas at second he had always hoped that the ball would be hit to him. He also sensed that Manager Hopper and some other members of the Royals squad were a little irked. They obviously felt that Rickey was disrupting their team in the interest of a sociological experiment. Hopper wanted to play at first base the man who would eventually be playing first base for the Royals, but Rickey's desires prevailed.

What everyone interested in Robinson was waiting for was

the games to be played between the Dodgers and Royals in Panama. This was where Rickey hoped Robinson would shine so brightly that Dodger players would demand that he play first base for them. Rickey called Robinson aside and explained to him: "Jackie, you can forget about what you did at Montreal last year. That's ancient history, for as far as these men are concerned, your minor league record doesn't mean a thing. You'll have to make the grade on that field against major league pitching, so I want you to be a whirling demon against the Dodgers. I want you to concentrate, to hit that ball, to get on base by any means. I want you to run wild, to steal the pants off them, to be the most conspicuous player on the field—but conspicuous only because of the kind of baseball you're playing. Not only will you impress the Dodger players, but the stories that the newspapermen send back to the Brooklyn and New York newspapers will help create demands on the part of the fans that you be brought up to the majors."

"I'll do my best," said Robinson.

Not many hours later, however, Branch Rickey received a jolt that cast a cloud of doubt on the question of whether Robinson would even show his wares against the Dodgers. Rickey learned that someone on the Dodger squad was trying to get other Dodgers to sign a petition saying they would not play on the same baseball team with Robinson. Kirby Higbe, a South Carolinian, had drunk a few bottles of Panama beer and discovered that his conscience was bothering him. The Brooklyn organization had plucked him out of oblivion when virtually everyone else in baseball had given up on him, and Higbe had fought his way back to stardom.

"Old Hig just can't do it; Old Hig just can't be a part of it," he said to Harold Parrott, the Dodgers' traveling secretary, and he went on to explain what was happening.

Rickey set out to squelch the uprising. "I have always believed," he said later, "that a little show of force at the right time is necessary when there's a deliberate violation of law. I knew that a reasonable show of force would be the best control of this thing. I believe that when a man is involved in an overt act of violence or a destruction of someone's rights, then that is no time to conduct an experiment in education or persuasion."

Rickey knew that while we may not change men's morals or wipe away their prejudices by fiat, when the penalty is costly enough most men prefer not to exercise their prejudices. He found that the players involved were Hugh Casey, a Georgian and a mighty valuable relief pitcher; Bobby Bragan, who had a southern background and was a third-string catcher but a ballplayer Rickey respected because of his guts and the fire he instilled in the squad; Cookie Lavagetto, who was mixed up in this for reasons Rickey couldn't understand; and Dixie Walker, an Alabaman who was a ringleader of the rebellion. But Walker was temporarily away from the squad in the States, and to Rickey's amazement, the substitute leader was Carl Furillo, a good outfielder but a man Rickey believed could be easily swayed. Rickey was pleased that Pee Wee Reese was neutral and that Gil Hodges had refused to have anything to do with the petition. Rickey called in each one of those involved and read the riot act. Bragan opposed Rickey openly in an angry scene that left Rickey nervous, yet determined not to wreak revenge on Bragan because he considered him an intelligent man who could be changed by proximity to Robinson and other Negroes. Bragan had at least promised Rickey that while he would not welcome a Negro with open arms, he would not put any more stumbling blocks in his way.

Rickey says he did not even bother to talk to Furillo, because "I regarded him as a man in whom talk could arouse no moral dilemma because he had no basic moral concept of his own. I would almost wager that today Furillo will argue as rabidly in Robinson's behalf as he was arguing against Robinson in those days."

The protest was silenced, and the Dodgers succeeded in keeping it out of the papers. Robinson, although unnerved by the furor, managed to play magnificent ball during seven games between the Royals and the Dodgers. He batted .625 and stole seven bases, a fantastic performance not only superior to that of any of his Montreal teammates, but far above anything displayed by any of the Dodgers.

Rickey was unhappy that there was no demand from the Dodgers that Robinson be brought up, but he had his plans well laid. The Dodgers and Royals were supposed to play two exhibition games in Ebbets Field on April 9 and 10. Rickey's plan was to have Durocher meet the press on the ninth and state, more or less offhandedly, that all Brooklyn needed to win the pennant was a good first baseman, that Robinson was the best thing in sight, and that he was "going to put pressure on Mr. Rickey to get Robinson." Durocher never got to discuss Robinson with the press. On April 9, Commissioner Chandler shocked the sports world by announcing a one-year suspension of Durocher for "conduct detrimental to baseball."

Rickey was stunned, but he knew it was time to make his move anyway. The next day, in the sixth inning of the game between the Royals and the Dodgers (just as Jackie had bunted into a double play), one of Rickey's aides walked through the press box handing releases to the newspapermen. The notice said: "Brooklyn announces the purchase of the contract of Jack Roosevelt Robinson from Montreal. He will report immediately. Signed, Branch Rickey."

Newspapermen leaped frantically, completely forgetting the exhibition game, and raced to relay to the sports world the big announcement of the year.

9....Hits, Hates, and Hallelujahs

When the excitement, the flurry of telegrams and telephone calls from well-wishers, had subsided, Jackie thought about the months ahead, about what 1947 would mean to him and the future of the Negro in baseball. He was confident that he would make good. In fact, he thought, playing in the majors would have to be a lark compared with his year at Montreal. Sure, Mr. Rickey had warned him to be prepared for all sorts of provocations, but it was difficult for Jack to take at face value Rickey's assertion that all his glowing tributes from Montreal, the base hits, the base running he had done there, would go for nought when he found himself among a bunch of calloused old-timers who doubted his ability to hit a major league curve, to stay in the batter's box against a major leaguer's brush-off pitch, to keep his balance when crafty old veterans tossed in their slow "junk"—veterans who would hold these doubts until Robinson had proved himself in major league competition.

Early on the morning of April 15, 1947, Robinson left the Hotel McAlpin, in Manhattan, for Ebbets Field.

"You coming to the game today, Rae?" he asked.

"I wouldn't miss it for the world!" It was a cold, almost wintry day—but not too cold for little Jackie, she hoped, because she had no one to leave him with, and she had already decided to bundle him up and attend the game.

"Just in case you have trouble picking me out, I'll be wearing Number 42," said Jack.

Rae chuckled and kissed him. "I'll have another way of picking you out—that pigeon-toed walk."

For Robinson this opening game was not the spectacular success that the one with Montreal had been. Crafty old Johnny Sain, pitcher for the Boston Braves, practically stood him on his ear. After grounding out to the third baseman, flying out to left field, and bouncing sharply into a double play, Robinson laid down a bunt trying to advance a runner to second. Earl Torgeson, the Braves' infielder, made a hurried throw in an effort to get Robinson, but hit him on the shoulderblade and the ball caromed into right field, allowing Jackie and the other runner to advance to second and third, from where Pete Reiser doubled them home to win the game 5 to 3.

What most sports writers were more interested in than Robinson's hits and runs that day, however, was whether his Brooklyn teammates were accepting him. Writers peered into that dugout and saw many different reactions, ranging from "natural acceptance" to "coolness." Arthur Daley of the *New York Times* reported: "The muscular Negro minds his own business and shrewdly makes no effort to push himself. He speaks quietly and intelligently when spoken to and already has made a strong impression . . . A veteran Dodger said of him, 'Having Jackie on the team is a little strange, just like anything else that's new. We just don't know how to act with him. But he'll be accepted in time. You can be sure of that. Other sports have had Negroes. Why not baseball? I'm for him. If he can win games, that's the only test I ask.' "

For several days, however, Robinson went through one of those unexplainable and agonizing slumps that afflict base-ball players, and many people began to doubt that he could win ball games. In the first five Dodger contests, Robinson went to the plate twenty times without a safe blow. Burt Shotton, the quiet, homespun, grandfatherly baseball veteran who had answered Rickey's S.O.S. to manage the Dodgers after Durocher was suspended, knew that he was under pressure to pull Robinson out of the line-up and give his post to either Ed Stevens or Howard Schultz, who had split first-base chores in 1946. But Shotton, whom Robinson liked and respected, and Sukeforth, who next to Rickey and Rachel had done most to steer Robinson over the rough spots, kept encouraging him, expressing their confidence in his ability to help the team.

Robinson knew, though, what some members of the squad were whispering: "It's just like Bob Feller said. This guy's good field, no hit." Another player remarked, "I don't even know that he's good field. Did you see that game the other day where Hal Gregg almost blew his top and would have if Pee Wee Reese hadn't pulled him out of the hole Robinson put him in?" He was referring to a game in which Gregg was trying to hold a one-run lead in the ninth inning. With two men out, he had given the opposition only one hit. The third batter of the inning hit an easy ground ball and Robinson muffed it. Gregg stared sullenly at Jackie for what seemed like fifteen minutes to Robinson although it was only a few seconds. Many Dodgers knew that if that man advanced to score, Gregg's wrath would be vented on Robinson, and many people would consider it racial rather than a manifesta-tion of any pitcher's disgust at losing a shutout because of an error. Fortunately, Reese went deep into the hole to back-hand a grounder, peg out the next batter and preserve Gregg's shutout.

It was in those tough days, Robinson remembers, that "the little brat," second baseman Eddie Stanky, rose above his background and put loyalty to baseball and the team first.

Stanky shared with Robinson his great knowledge of baseball, continually shouting little tips about how to play this runner or that one. Even though Robinson was in a slump, Stanky made him feel that he was a part of the team. Eventually this made the difference and Robinson went on a tremendous hitting spree, but there were some rough moments before this happy day.

In April, with the season barely under way, the Philadelphia Phillies invaded Ebbets Field for a three-game series. When Robinson started to the plate in the first inning he heard shouts from the Phillies' dugout: "Hey, nigger, why don't you go back to the cotton field where you belong?" "Hey, snowflake, which one of those white boys' wives are you dating tonight?"

Robinson stood at the plate fuming, almost forgetting Rickey's advice that he must turn the other cheek. As the language became more foul, he looked around to see that leading the barrage was Ben Chapman, the Alabama-born manager of the Phillies.

Robinson was so tense, so filled with rage, that he was an easy out. But he made no complaint. Some of the epithets hurled by the Phillies reached the ears of newspapermen, however, and they watched eagerly to see whether this would be the incident to cause organized baseball's first blow-up. Dan Parker of the *New York Daily Mirror* was one of the first newspapermen to report on the race baiting by the Phillies. He wrote: "Ben Chapman, who during his career with the Yankees was frequently involved in unpleasant incidents with fans who charged him with shouting anti-Semitic remarks at them from the ball field, seems to be up to his old trick of stirring up racial trouble. During the recent series between the Phils and Dodgers, Chapman and three of his players poured a stream of abuse at Jackie Robinson. Jackie, with admirable restraint, ignored the guttersnipe language coming from the Phils' dugout, thus stamping himself as the only gentleman among those involved in the incident."

After two days of this abuse, with Chapman and his "bench jockeys" now shouting at the other Dodgers ("Hey, you carpetbaggers, how's your little reconstruction period getting along?"), Stanky figured he'd had enough. He shouted: "Listen, you yellow-bellied cowards, why don't you yell at somebody who can answer back?"

Robinson listened with a lump in his throat, feeling that here was a man of intrinsic decency. He would remember and appreciate Stanky as long as he lived. It was funny, and good, he thought, that with the passage of time, your appreciation of a little act like that grows bigger and bigger, while your anger, your hatred of foul acts like Chapman's, grows smaller and smaller. Jackie remembered better than any of the humiliating experiences in Florida in 1946 the happiness given him by one little white boy. In those first days in the South, he remembered, he was reaching out for even the tiniest straw of hope. During an exhibition game against Jersey City, Robinson was on second, after stealing, when a pitch got past the catcher. As Jackie rounded third, Hopper waved him home. The catcher made a perfect throw and Robinson was out at the plate. As he walked toward the dugout some white fans booed him and a few hurled insults. A white kid of nine or ten was hanging over the roof of the Royals' dugout. Above the chorus of boos Robinson could hear him shouting, "Atta boy, Jackie, nice try! Atta boy, Jackie!" Robinson paused to look into the face of this young fellow, who smiled and waved his hand. Robinson winked at him and gave him a broad grin. He knew that never in his life would he forget the face of this boy who was honest at heart, not yet filled with the poison of prejudice, who shouted a word of encouragement above the cries of the mob. That little boy had shamed a crowd as Stanky had shamed the Phillies—so much so that some apologized to Jackie.

Robinson came to understand, also, that the press could be a potent ally, for sports columnists all over the nation ridiculed Chapman. The press furor became so great that Chapman agreed to meet with Negro newspapermen to explain his actions. Nathan Alexander, road secretary and public relations man for the Phillies, announced to the general press:

"Chapman met the Negro writers, and after admitting that

the name-calling incidents had taken place, asked: 'You fellows want Robinson to become a real big leaguer, I suppose. Well, so do we, and we're treating him just the same way as we do any other player on a rival club. When we're playing exhibitions with the Yanks, DiMaggio is always "The Wop"; and when we meet the Cards, Whitey Kurowski is "The Polack." The Phils ball club rides the devil out of every team it meets. That's our style of baseball. We hand it out and we expect to take it too. If you want us to lay off Jackie and treat him like a guy who can't take his medicine the way the rest of us have to in this slam-bang game of baseball, then we'll do it—but that isn't the way a big leaguer is made. And remember, all that stuff is forgotten the minute the ball game is over.' "

Many people, including a great number of editorial writers, were not willing to swallow this explanation. Neither was Commissioner Chandler, who warned the Phillies' management that there could be no more of the venomous insults.

Rickey watched all this with sardonic amusement, for almost no one else knew that the Philadelphia president, Bob Carpenter, had telephoned him earlier to say that the Phillies would refuse to take the field if Robinson played with the Dodgers. "Fine," he had said to Carpenter, "then we'll win all three games by default. That's fine with us." So Rickey knew that Chapman's "explanation" was pure malarky, that the insults hurled at Robinson did not represent an effort to help the Negro, but deep prejudices on the part of Chapman and other members of the Philadelphia organization. Rickey was delighted, however, for he felt that this incident did more to consolidate Robinson's position as a member of the Dodgers than any lecture he might have given the players, or anything else anyone might have contrived. Even today, Rickey can lecture for an hour about how Chapman, a prejudiced man from Alabama, unwittingly helped to consolidate the position of the Negro in organized baseball.

"Chapman did more than anybody to make Dixie Walker, Eddie Stanky and other Dodgers speak up in Robinson's behalf," he says. "When he poured out that string of unconscionable abuse he solidified and unified thirty men, not one of whom was willing to sit by and see someone kick around a man who had his hands tied behind his back. Chapman created in Robinson's behalf a thing called sympathy, the most unifying word in the world. That word has a Greek origin; it means to suffer. Thus, to say I sympathize with you is meaningful only because it means 'I suffer with you.' That is what Chapman did. He caused men like Stanky to suffer with Robinson and he made this Negro a real member of the Dodgers."

Watching these results with pleasure in 1947, Rickey was willing to be generous. He told Jackie that it would be good for baseball if he would help take Chapman and the Phillies off the spot. Chandler and Rickey both asked Robinson to pose shaking hands with Chapman in order that photographers might present to the nation a picture of restored harmony in baseball. Chapman, a racist to the bitter end, indicated that rather than shake hands with a Negro he preferred to pose holding a bat with him.

Robinson recalls: "I can think of no occasion where I had more difficulty in swallowing my pride and doing what seemed best for baseball and the cause of the Negro in baseball than in agreeing to pose for that photograph with a man for whom I had only the very lowest regard. But I did it, although deep in my heart I could not forgive Chapman and the Phillies for what they had tried to do."

According to Pee Wee Reese, a few years later Jackie got a chance to say what he'd wanted to say that day in 1947. It was at an exhibition game in Tampa, Florida, where one of the men who had heaped racial insults upon Jackie was now a baseball coach. He was standing on the base lines while Robinson and Reese snapped the ball back and forth to each other. Reese threw a hard one that hit Robinson's glove with a loud plop.

"Yow!" said Robinson.

The former Philadelphia "jockey" said in a mock-feminine voice: "Be careful out there, Pee Wee. Don't throw so hard or you'll hurt Mr. Robinson's hand."

According to Reese, "Robinson strolled over to this coach

and pushed his chin up into his face and barked: 'Listen, you yellow son of a bitch. I haven't forgotten those days in 1947 when you called me some unprintable, filthy names, and I couldn't talk back. Well, I can talk back now, and I just want to tell you that if you say one more word to me or about me I'll kick the hell out of you.'

"I tell you the truth," said Pee Wee. "For some strange reason I felt good right down to my toenails to see that, years later, this guy finally got what was coming to him. When Robinson challenged him he shriveled up like a snail and we never heard another peep out of him."

Chapman and the Phillies were only the beginning of Robinson's ordeal of 1947. Every day's mail brought a number of crank letters, many involving threats to kidnap Jackie, Jr., to assault Mrs. Robinson, to kill Robinson.

The press learned of these letters on May 9, after Rickey turned several of them over to the police, who concluded that they came from crackpots. There was another development of far greater implications on May 9, however. Stanley Woodward of the *New York Herald Tribune* wrote a story that hit baseball like a bomb. He announced that the St. Louis Cardinals had planned a protest strike against Robinson's presence in the Brooklyn line-up when the Dodgers visited St. Louis on May 6 for the first game of the season between the two clubs. In addition, Woodward said, some Cardinals had been trying to instigate a league-wide strike against the "invasion" of baseball by Negroes. Woodward reported that Ford Frick, president of the National League, had gotten wind of the protest movement and squelched it with a stern announcement that players participating in it would be indefinitely suspended from baseball.

Woodward reported that Frick sent this message to the Cardinal players: "If you do this you will be suspended from the league. You will find that the friends you think you have in the press box will not support you, that you will be outcasts. I do not care if half the league strikes. Those who do it will encounter quick retribution. They will be suspended, and I don't care if it wrecks the National League for five years. This is the United States of America, and one citizen has as much right to play as another.

"The National League will go down the line with Robinson whatever the consequence. You will find if you go through with your intention that you have been guilty of complete madness."

Frick later confirmed Woodward's report that Cardinal owner Sam Breadon had told him of a movement among the Cardinals to stage the protest. Frick said that Breadon was the one who relayed his message to the players that they would be dealt with severely if they went ahead with their plans. Breadon, however, more or less denied the Woodward story.

Woodward followed up with this assertion: "The blast of publicity which followed the revelations that the St. Louis Cardinals were promoting a players' strike against the presence of Jackie Robinson . . . probably will serve to quash further strolls down Tobacco Road. In other words, it can now be honestly doubted that the boys from the Hookworm Belt will have the nerve to foist their quaint sectional folklore on the rest of the country . . ."

Many baseball writers believe that singlehandedly Woodward saved baseball from an incident which might have become one of the most infamous in the history of the sport. Some newspapermen said that by writing about Robinson's problems, and racism generally, Woodward was doing what the nation's daily press should have been doing for years.

There were influential writers, however, who had not given up their belief that bringing a Negro into organized baseball would be detrimental to baseball and the Negro. The *Sporting News*, for example, hauled out its 1942 editorial to restate its opposition to integration in baseball: "The *Sporting News* carried an editorial on August 6, 1942, which expressed the opinion that the use of mixed teams in baseball would benefit neither the Negro nor white professional games, because of the possibility of unpleasant incidents.

"This view, five years later, takes on new interest in the light of the stir caused by the recent stories . . . about an abortive strike by some of the Cardinals over playing against Jackie Robinson . . . as well as criticism directed against manager Ben Chapman of the Phillies for regarding Robinson as just another player, subject to the jockeying that any performer might receive . . .

"The *Sporting News* has not changed its views as expressed in 1942, but feels that with the majors having taken the step of introducing a colored player into their ranks, the situation calls for tolerance and fair play on the part of players and fans."

2

The public read the *Sporting News* and the sports pages of the daily press, and sympathized with a young man who they saw was under tremendous pressure—but the public could not know the full story, could not know all the mental and emotional dimensions of the pressure. How could fans sense the strain of a young ballplayer, circling the bases after Dixie Walker has hit a home run behind him, wondering whether to follow custom and stop at home plate to shake Walker's hand, or to congratulate him in the relative privacy of the dugout so as not to embarrass him by putting him in the position of having to shake hands with a Negro before thirty thousand people? How many could appreciate the daily toll of the requirement that Robinson be meek (children and Negro rookies should be seen and not heard!)? And there was a special kind of control involved in pretending to read a book on the train so as to have an excuse for staying out of the players' poker games, which Jackie and Rickey recognized as possible sources of the trouble they wanted to avoid at almost any cost.

As the weeks passed, however, Robinson found it virtually impossible to keep rejecting invitations, and he began to play poker occasionally. On one road trip, Hugh Casey, a great relief pitcher and a southerner, had a few too many drinks under his belt and apparently couldn't see his poker hands well enough to play them properly. He was losing money on every deal. Finally he said to Robinson, who had now agreed to join his teammates at cards:

"Jackie, man, am I in lousy luck today! Got to change my luck, Jackie. Tell you what I used to do down in Georgia when my poker luck got bad. I'd just get up and go out and I'd rub me the teat of the biggest, blackest nigger woman I could find." He reached over and rubbed Jackie's head.

Robinson felt his muscles tense. For a few seconds his eyes did not focus properly as rage welled up in him. Then he looked at this Georgian leaning back in his seat, then at his teammates who sat in silent disbelief, yet with an obvious fear on their faces that this was the beginning of the racial conflict people said had to occur, the trouble that was supposed to be inevitable when a Negro traveled, ate, slept and played cards with white men.

Robinson concluded that, although it might not seem possible, his teammates were more embarrassed, more pained, than he. He shook his head gently and said, "Deal, man, deal." The game went on.

Perhaps Mr. Rickey was right, Robinson thought later; perhaps it is a measure of higher courage to be able to turn the other cheek, to swallow a remark like Casey's without protest. He just hoped that the other players understood; he couldn't bear to think that they might consider him a coward.

No matter what, he would go on heeding Mr. Rickey's advice to let his bat and his glove speak for him. Still, these days brought dozens of occasions when Jackie had to fight the urge to belt someone, to vent his wrath against an opponent, to sound off at an umpire, to let off steam because baseball players need to let off steam. He came close to getting into a brawl in Chicago early in the season. He had heard rumors that some of the Chicago Cubs, too, had expressed their dislike of playing baseball with a Negro, and had hinted that they might try to do something about it. Yet apparently they got the same word that the St. Louis Cardinals got, so the players who had boasted in spring training that they would never play against Robinson had dropped the subject.

The jockeying was lively during the first games against the Cubs, although not at the scurvy level reached by the Phillies. In the last game of a hard-fought series, Robinson was on first when the batter following him hit a ground ball to second base. Len Merullo, Cub shortstop, took the throw to force Robinson at second, but as he drew back to throw to first to complete the double play, Robinson slid into him in a typical baseball block, sending Merullo flying through the air and breaking up the double play. As Robinson got up and dusted himself off, Merullo shouted angrily. Holding on to Rickey's advice once more, Robinson trotted silently toward the Brooklyn dugout to a chorus of boos and shouts from the Cubs.

In the ninth inning Robinson got his second hit of the game. He danced off first trying to worry the Cubs' pitcher, Bill Lee. When Lee finally threw to the plate, Robinson dashed to second, stealing successfully. Lee then made several attempts to catch Robinson off second base. When Robinson took a long lead, Merullo dashed in behind him and Lee whirled quickly and fired the ball. Robinson had to slide back in on his hands and stomach, moving in safely under Merullo. Some sports writers wrote that as the two players were untangling they could see Merullo kick Robinson and then the Negro raise his right arm as if to punch Merullo. Robinson apparently changed his mind just in time to avoid what could have been an unhappy fracas.

Because the little incidents of conflict and tension on the ball field were played up in the press, most fans were aware of this aspect of Jackie's ordeal during his first year in the major leagues. Yet very few knew that his private life was far from that of a national celebrity, or even a typical major league ballplayer.

Rickey had signed Robinson to a first-year contract at Brooklyn, paying him $5,000 per year. This would not have been so bad had Robinson been permitted to accept even a small portion of the many thousands of dollars worth of commercial endorsements that he was requested to make that year. Rickey felt, however, that Robinson's name on billboards and in radio and TV commercials shortly after his entry into baseball would not only cheapen him in the eyes of the public, but would enable those who opposed the Negro's entry into baseball to complain that Robinson was less interested in playing the game than in exploiting it commercially.

Roscoe McGowen wrote in *Sports Magazine:* "The Rickey policy, incidentally, of attempting to keep Robinson out of the limelight has cost the player a great deal of money. Until almost midseason Jackie had been denied the privilege of endorsing any product—a common and remunerative practice among prominent ballplayers and other athletes—nor was he allowed to appear on radio programs or for any sort of article appearing under his name . . .

"Jackie Robinson is paying quite a price for the privilege of playing baseball in the major leagues, but he thinks it well worth the price."

Even McGowen did not know, perhaps, that at the beginning of that season the Robinsons and their young son were living in one room at the McAlpin Hotel. They could not afford a baby sitter, so they were not able to go out together at all. They could not afford to have meals sent to their room, so Rachel baby-sat while Robinson hurried to a cafeteria behind the hotel. Then he baby-sat while she went to eat.

This is how Rachel remembers that period:

It was an utter nightmare living in that one hotel room with a baby who was suffering from a terrible cold caught when I took him to the ball park to see that opening-day game. To add to our troubles, Jackie, Jr., suffered from diarrhea for a month because of the change of water from California.

We had lived with my mother during the winter because we were not yet able to establish a home on the East Coast. In fact, we had been so uncertain of Jackie's future status with the Brooklyn organization that we probably wouldn't have done so if we had been able to afford it. In any event, moving from Montreal to California and then back to Brooklyn had also been a drain on our meager financial resources.

As if all this were not enough, we were plagued almost every hour by newspapermen rapping on our door. It would have been comical if it hadn't been such a burden on us to go through this constantly recurring ritual of pushing utensils under the bed and rushing to close the bathroom door so newspapermen would not see the diapers hanging over the shower rod. Then as quickly as we'd get the utensils out from under the bed and resume making formula, or as soon as I was busily engaged in washing more diapers in the bathtub, another newspaperman would arrive.

After a few weeks of this we became determined to get more suitable accommodations. Thus we were delighted when we were offered an opportunity to share an apartment in Brooklyn.

It turned out that not only was the place less than desirable, but that rather than sharing an apartment, all we got was a bedroom, a corner of a hall in which the baby was to sleep, and the use of the kitchen. We had virtually no access to the living room, because the woman with whom we shared the apartment seemed to entertain friends constantly, day and night. It was there that I really learned the distress of young mothers who must struggle with getting a baby carriage up and down stairs; trying to keep cool in a Brooklyn tenement; heating water in all the available pots and pans on the stove in the evening because the water is shut off in the building after 4:00 P.M.

Jackie and I took bus rides or we pushed the baby carriage up and down the street late at night for recreation, because we had no car, no baby-sitter, and virtually no friends.

Mr. Rickey had cautioned us not to accept the many invitations we received that first year and to concentrate on our job. He felt that for us to get snowed under with social obligations would adversely affect Jack's playing, so we more or less stayed to ourselves.

3

Many observers maintained that in 1947 Jackie Robinson was the loneliest man in baseball. Said McGowen: "If you were Jackie Robinson, you probably would feel a twinge of loneliness once in a while. On train trips you might play a game of hearts now and then with three other ballplayers who look upon you as just a nice kid. But mostly you'd sit and stare out the window.

"Occasionally you might eat at the same hotel dining room table with another Brooklyn player, but mostly you'd eat by yourself.

"The games of hearts, and the infrequent meals with a teammate, along with a conversation in the clubhouse, would make up most of your social contact with the other Dodgers.

"You would be among them, rather than of them."

Yet Robinson felt that he was far from the loneliest man in baseball. Not nearly so lonely, so anguished, as Hugh Casey, who was drinking himself to death. Casey, the "mixed-up" Georgian, had made that racially insulting remark during a losing streak in a poker game, but days later he wanted to rush onto the field and fight Enos Slaughter of the Cardinals after Slaughter had spiked Robinson. Seeing such evidence of worse kinds of loneliness than his, Robinson could not feel sorry for himself, no matter how many people speculated about his isolation as a black man in a white man's world. Even in that drab apartment, even in his worst moments on the field, he knew that he was a happy man. There was a further reason to be happy, too: the Cleveland Indians had signed Larry Doby as the first Negro player in the history of the American League, and the St. Louis Browns had taken on two Negroes, Willard Brown and Henry Thompson.

"We're winning the battle, Rae. The walls will crumble fast now. The day may not be too far off when I can be just a player, and play the way I think baseball ought to be played."

"I hope so," Rae replied. "I live for the day when you

won't be 'Jackie Robinson, first Negro player in organized ball' any longer. But I'm afraid that day may be farther away than either of us imagines."

At the end of the season, nothing gave Jackie and Rachel more satisfaction than the feeling that he had carried his share of the load as a baseball player. They knew the strange psychology that made whites seeking to prove their liberalism often say of some Negro in a key job: "Everybody knows that for a Negro to get that job he has to be twice as good as a white man," then say of a Negro in *their* firm who has won a coveted position: "Someone was being particularly nice to him because he was a Negro."

The record was such that no one could justifiably say that about Robinson, for his heavy hitting on a western road trip in September had helped assure the pennant for the Dodgers. When the team returned to New York, it was Jackie who was besieged by the wildly cheering throng of Brooklyn fans. He went into a phone booth to call Rae and couldn't get out until he was rescued by policemen.

Robinson had played in more games (150) than any other Dodger; had scored 125 runs, 27 more than Eddie Stanky, the Dodger nearest him; had hit safely 174 times, 14 times more than Dixie Walker, who was Flatbush's hitting hero until Robinson came on the scene; had batted a creditable .297, had hit 12 home runs to tie Pee Wee Reese for the team lead; had led the team in stolen bases. It was no great surprise to the baseball world that the *Sporting News,* which had expressed such grave doubts about the wisdom of admitting Negroes into organized baseball, selected Robinson as the National League Rookie of the Year.

Explained the *Sporting News:* "In selecting the outstanding rookie of 1947, the *Sporting News* sifted and weighed only stark baseball values.

"That Jackie Roosevelt Robinson might have had more obstacles than his first-year competitors, and that he perhaps had a harder fight to gain even major league recognition, was no concern of this publication. The sociological experiment that Robinson represented, the trail-blazing that he did, the barriers he broke down, did not enter into the decision. He was rated and examined solely as a freshman player in the big leagues—on the basis of his hitting, his running, his defensive play, his team value.

"Dixie Walker summed it up in a few words the other day when he said: 'No other ballplayer on this club, with the possible exception of Bruce Edwards, has done more to put the Dodgers up in the race than Robinson has. He is everything Branch Rickey said he was when he came up from Montreal.'"

Near the season's end even Rickey agreed that it was proper for fans to hold a "Jackie Robinson Day" at Ebbets Field. Before a game between the Dodgers and their much-hated rivals, the Giants, thousands of fans paid tribute to the Negro lad who had made good. There to honor him alongside home plate were Ralph Branca of New York, Joe Hatten of Iowa, Clint Hartung of Texas, Dixie Walker of Alabama.

Rachel sat in a box, an orchid pinned to her lapel, tears gleaming in her eyes, as she watched the procession. Some might care who won the game that night, but for her it was an anticlimax. Democracy, decency, sanity—these had won a lopsided victory in the big game, the one that really counted.

4

Who could have written a more story-book finish to the first Negro's first year in modern organized baseball than the one in which Jackie Robinson and Brooklyn's zany Dodgers hurled themselves against the awesome New York Yankees in the World Series? It was Hollywoodish enough that Brooklyn should be there, considering how long Flatbush fans had had to cloak their disappointment in the cry, "Wait till next year." That this Negro lad whom the sports world had been watching so intently should help make "next year" 1947 was almost too good to be true.

With the whole world watching and listening in, Jackie Robinson gave a series performance of which Rickey, the nation's Negroes, and he himself could be proud. Almost every Negro who had ever heard of baseball followed that series, knowing almost instinctively that because Robinson was still thought of as a Negro first and a ballplayer second, his triumph would be the Negro's triumph, his failure that of black men everywhere.

In the opening inning of the first game, 73,365 fans screamed wildly as Jackie drew a base on balls from pitcher Frank Shea. When he stole second there was bedlam in Yankee Stadium and joy in the hearts of millions around the world. Then, when Pete Reiser bounced to short, Robinson violated a cardinal baseball rule by moving toward third. He was trapped—but the crowd got a display of his uncanny ability to run the bases as he dashed back and forth to give Reiser time to reach second, from where he later scored the game's first run.

In the third inning, Robinson worked Shea for another walk and then so upset the fine Yankee pitcher that the latter balked, sending Robinson to second. But he was left on base, as several other Dodgers were that September day, and the Yankees won, 5 to 3.

The following day the Yanks whipped the Bums 10 to 3, and as the scene shifted to Ebbets Field, few people figured the Dodgers could make a serious contest of the series. Then Brooklyn smashed out six runs in the second inning of the third game, in which Jackie singled twice, scored once, sacrificed once and completed two double plays, and the Dodgers won, 9 to 7.

Then came a fantastic fourth game in which Cookie Lavagetto smashed a double off the wall in the ninth to break up Floyd Bevens' no-hitter and give the Dodgers a 2 to 1 triumph. The sports world now knew that this Dodger team had guts and determination, no small amount of it supplied by Robinson, who promptly singled in a Brooklyn tally in the fifth game. But this was not enough against the magnificent Shea, who won 2 to 1.

Despite little Al Gionfriddo's magnificent catch of a smash by Joe DiMaggio to save the sixth game for Brooklyn, in the end the Dodgers could not cope with Joltin' Joe and the great relief hurler, Joe Page, and the Yankees won the seventh game and the world championship.

Jackie was disappointed—but he emerged from this most exciting of all World Series as the most talked about and written about Negro in the world, something no one knew better than the postmen who lugged the thousands of invitations to Jackie to speak here, to give exhibitions there, to sing, dance or do just about anything imaginable—just as long as he showed up. Two Chicagoans, Mr. and Mrs. David Wallerstein, had become the Robinsons' close friends. Wallerstein, a theater executive, arranged for Jackie to appear onstage at a Chicago theater, an arrangement that Jackie accepted happily since it permitted him to earn some much-needed money. Jackie continued on celebrity circuit all winter, with the result that, as Rickey had feared two years earlier, his admirers had fed him until he was fat and futile.

Time to go south for spring training in 1948 arrived almost before Robinson realized what was happening to him; it caught him twenty-five pounds over playing weight. This is how Jackie remembers the next few months:

I was almost afraid to face Leo Durocher, who was back as manager, when I got to the Dominican Republic, where we were training to avoid racial incidents in the United States. Just as I feared, Durocher took one look at me and noted sarcastically that I had been eating as if it were going out of style. Newspapermen quickly filed stories that were beefed up far more than I was, telling the baseball world how angry Durocher was at me.

I could understand how Durocher felt. Here he was, back after a year's banishment from baseball with his future hanging in the balance, and I show up too fat to run bases or play the game up to my normal ability. I felt sick with sorrow, for Durocher had gone to bat for me in 1947, trying to make it easy for Mr. Rickey to promote me to the majors. He must have felt that I was an ingrate to have stayed in condition for Shotton and then show up so fat for him.

Whatever Leo thought, I had no intention of making him look bad or of giving anything but my best for him. I had simply forgotten that nothing withers faster than laurels that have been rested upon—and had spent a winter exploiting the past season's laurels without giving proper concern for the future.

Durocher hauled me out under that blazing West Indies sun and engaged me in a little tossing game called high and low. He would throw high to my left, then low to my right, and as I bent and groaned the perspiration poured off. Then he would station me between first and second and hit ground balls to my left, then to my right. My tongue was almost dragging the ground, but Durocher kept me running while he yelled at the top of his voice, "Move, Robinson, move. There's more lard where you got that, so leave some in Santo Domingo."

It was no fun being chewed out in front of rookies, reporters and anyone else who happened along, and some newsmen wrote that "bad blood" was developing between Leo and myself. This wasn't true, because I knew that Durocher was right and that I had been foolish. I respected him as a manager, because he hated to lose more than anything, and in that respect we were cut from the same cloth. So I swallowed Leo's sarcasm and sweated off fifteen pounds, but at the time we broke camp and headed home I was hauling around ten pounds that I just couldn't shake.

Then I was stunned to read that Mr. Rickey had put me on the waivers list of players for sale at the bargain price of $10,000, but I soon learned that he hadn't the remotest notion of selling me. Perhaps he wanted to see what other teams were now willing to take a Negro—or he could have wanted to tell me in a dramatic way that he was disappointed in my physical condition. He didn't need to tell me that if I had reported to camp so overweight in either 1946 or 1947 I never would have made it to the majors.

One thing that convinced me that Mr. Rickey wasn't eager to trade me was that he had booked several exhibition games in the Southwest and even the Deep South—in cities where interracial games had never been played. It required no great measure of vanity for me to sense that fans in these cities wanted to see what was still a freakish situation of Jackie Robinson playing ball with white men. In two games at Fort Worth we drew 23,070 fans, the Sunday crowd of 15,507 being the largest ever to witness an exhibition game there. Half the 11,370 fans who turned out in Dallas were Negroes. I was proud that a sport like baseball could induce people to cast off age-old prejudices.

My weight problem obviously affected my playing early in 1948, and to add to the difficulty, the whole team was playing poorly. Durocher fumed, as he was known to do when things weren't going his way. At the end of May we were lounging in the cellar, and I could not help but feel that I was largely to blame. By the time I started to hit, the team was stunned with the announcement that Shotton was returning to manage the Dodgers and that Leo Durocher was taking over the Giants. Leo's shift to our hated rivals set the stage for a feud between him and me that became one of the worst in baseball history. We goaded each other to the point of coming to blows, and newsmen wrote a thousand fantastic stories of the origin and extent of our little spats. Actually, there was nothing involved other than the natural crabbiness of two guys who weren't winning and had to let off steam somewhere.

The feud was intensified, of course, by the fact that by the time Shotton took over I was down to normal weight and playing the kind of baseball that I had played in 1947. If Leo ever thought that I was giving my all for Shotton and goofing off for him, this coincidence was enough to convince him.

My return to form wasn't enough to pull the Dodgers out of the doldrums, however, and we finished a disappointing third. I had led the team in batting with a .296 average, doubles with 38, triples with 8, runs scored with 108, total bases with 260, runs-batted-in with 85 and hits with 170, but deep in my heart I was miserable, because I knew

that I should have done better—much better. I made myself a solemn vow to redeem myself and the Dodgers in
1949.

Branch Rickey also wanted to assure that there would be
no more mediocre years for Robinson. Feeling that the Negro's position in baseball was secure (at least five had now
played in the majors, and a dozen or more were in organized
ball), Rickey felt that he could take off the mental and emotional strait-jacket in which he had bound Robinson and
let him be the daring, competitive athlete Rickey knew him
to be.

"All along I had known that the point would come when
my almost-filial relationship with Jackie would break with ill
feeling if I did not issue an emancipation proclamation for
him," Rickey recalls.

"I could see that for two years the tensions had built up,
that this young man had come through with courage beyond
what I ever could have asked. Yet I knew that burning inside him was the same pride and determination that burned
inside those Negro slaves a century earlier and had made them
rise up to shout, 'The nigger ain't no slave no more, he's
free.' I knew also that whereas the wisest policy for Robinson
overall for those first two years was to turn the other cheek,
not to fight back, there were many in baseball and out of it
who, because they did not accept Papini's philosophy, would
not understand Robinson's employing it. They could be
made to respect only the fierce competition, the fighting
back, the things that are the signs of courage to men who
know courage only in its physical sense. So I told Robinson
that he was on his own.

"Then I sat back happily, knowing that, with the restraints
removed, Robinson was going to show the National League
a thing or two."

In 1949, the emancipated Robinson became the sensation
of the league. He was awesome at bat, slick in the field and a
plain terror on the bases. At the midseason break, he led the

league in batting, stolen bases, runs-batted-in and number of hits. He was second in runs scored and third in both doubles and triples. Fans across the nation gave him 1,891,212 votes —tops for the National League—in naming him to the All-Star team. Robinson had scored another first for the Negro.

10.... A Patriot's Purgatory

Robinson was exultant over his baseball triumphs, thrilled by the torrent of votes proclaiming him the National League's best second baseman, but to his surprise, that summer of 1949, the All-Star game did not turn out to be the biggest event of his year. Unaware of how much more was still being asked of him than what went into the box scores, he was jolted by a telegram from Representative John S. Wood, a Georgia Democrat and chairman of the House Un-American Activities Committee. Wood was asking, as the congressman explained to newsmen on July 8, that Robinson testify before his committee and "give the lie to statements by Paul Robeson that American Negroes would not fight in case of a war against Russia."

Jackie was college-trained and he made at least a minimum

effort to keep well informed, but this telegram stunned him into a realization that the nation had much more on its mind that summer than bunts and batting averages. People were worried about Communist expansion abroad and possible Communist subversion at home; and suddenly he was thrust into the center of these fears. He was being asked to denounce publicly a Negro who had once held almost exclusively the limelight in which he now basked, a man he had admired greatly in childhood. Jackie read that when Robeson heard the committee's plans he had commented with a chuckle that it would "do better to summon any of the millions of Negroes who are suffering from unemployment, privation and oppression, rather than some who, like Robinson, have no complaints." He was faced with perhaps the deepest soul-searching of his life:

I knew that many Negroes welcomed Robeson's remarks, not because of disloyalty, or of any tender feelings toward the Soviet Union, but because they feared that white America would never grant the Negro a position of equality simply out of a sense of justice and decency. These Negroes believed that the only way to get Americans to do right was to frighten them, to hold a big stick over their heads. The Soviet Union appeared to be that big stick.

Yet as I turned these things over in my mind, I could not convince myself that the average American white man was so devoid of a sense of justice that he would do right only out of fear. In fact, I feared that the threat implied in Robeson's remark might warp whatever sense of justice American white men possessed.

I could not help but sense the irony of the fact that I, a Negro once court-martialed for opposing Army Jim Crow, should now be asked to pledge the Negro's loyalty to the Army, to the nation's military ventures. Yet life is full of ironies.

Against the facts, Robeson's Paris remarks seemed silly to me. Even in those days of legalized peonage, when my mother was battling for a minimum standard of decency on that plantation in Georgia, Negroes had stormed the hills of San Juan with Teddy Roosevelt, for whom I was named; in the First World War, Negroes had gone to the Marne, to Château-Thierry, and to Belleau Wood, where they had proudly borne the burden of second-class citizens playing second-class soldiers, even as they pledged allegiance to the same noble causes other Americans professed in fighting this war. And in the Second World War, even in the face of insults, attacks on soldiers in their homeland, and work-horse duties in the farthest corners of the globe, the Negro had fought some, though not always with his heart in it; had sung some, even if the song was the "Bug-out Boogie," dedicated to Negroes who ran cowardly because someone had convinced them that Negroes were supposed to be cowards; still the Negro was there, as an American.

But what about Robeson? With what was I to take issue specifically? Had Robeson betrayed me? The *Negro?* The *nation?* The *cause of freedom?* How much justification was there in the things that Robeson had said in Paris and elsewhere?

Rae and I remembered how, as children, we had thrilled to Robeson's success, had hummed the tunes made famous by his booming bass-baritone voice. Now a white man from Georgia was asking *me*, a "refugee" from Georgia, to denounce Robeson, who spoke from a well of bitterness that few white people ever would understand. Thus white Americans would not understand my dilemma, or that of any Negro faced with the task of passing judgment on Robeson. What Negro, by 1949, had not heard Robeson tick off the background to his bitterness? "Man, in Princeton, New Jersey, where I grew up, they used to push Negroes off the sidewalk. It was like darkest Alabama!" We had heard Robeson recall the episodes that he could not or would not forget: the resentment of having to sit out a football game against a southern college which refused to play against a Negro; the jolt of leaving college and law school a Phi Beta Kappa and a football hero only to find that when he went to white law firms looking for work he was "just another Negro"; the anger of being invited to sing in city after city where his sponsors did not have the courage to make it possible for him and other Negroes to stay at the local hotel without eating their meals in their rooms or riding the freight elevator.

I was an impoverished lad not yet in my teens, filching grapes and plums in Pasadena and running from ever-suspicious policemen, when Robeson delivered his first really bitter blast at Jim Crow in the United States and announced that he would make England his home. It was three years later, in 1934, that he visited Russia for the first time and came back to declare boldly that he "walked the earth for the first time with complete dignity." And it was three years later still, after taking his son, Paul, Jr., to Russia for study, that Robeson announced: "When we returned to Moscow we were quite surprised to find him a different kind of child. He was no longer shy or sensitive or moody, always unconsciously defending himself against the possibility of being rebuffed. Instead, he was one of the children, and he thoroughly enjoyed this great experience."

It was a sordid, seemingly unending story in which the life of every Negro is a tear-tinged little chapter, and I knew that even Negroes who considered Robeson politically naïve and tactless would sympathize with him.

Yet there was the question of responsibility—not "patriotism," but responsibility—to the bigger issue of personal freedom, to the future of humanity involved in an ideological struggle that would be the world's most consuming issue for years. How best could a Negro right the glaring wrongs of his native land? Certainly to give the impression that no Negro would go to war against Russia, that all Negroes were waiting eagerly to betray the United States, was not only a lie, but a gambit designed to push millions of frustrated white Americans into replacing error with terror. Even more tragic, to imply that a bright future for the Negro was possible only through violent revolution most surely would convince millions of whites that the only way to retain the noble part of America's past would be through blind reaction. And how tragic this would be, not just for Negroes, but for all Americans, and all those who had begun to look to America for wise leadership.

Yes, I thought, it was this same anti-change, anti-Communist hysteria during the 1920's that ran my family out of Georgia. I could sense that in 1949 the nation was already on the way to a series of witch hunts, inquisitions, character assassinations and ideological lynchings that would make the rabble-rousing of the 1920's look like a Sunday school discussion. I was certain that Representative Wood, the Georgian, was not so interested in establishing the patriotism of American Negroes as in furthering the notion that anyone speaking out violently against racial discrimination and segregation was a tool of world communism. I couldn't escape the feeling that if I helped him smear Robeson I would have helped him smear all Negroes who protest boldly.

During the next few days, as Rae and I searched our hearts and minds, letters, telegrams and telephone calls of advice poured in. There was a well-organized volley of correspondence from those pushing the Communist cause, warning that I would be "a traitor to the Negro" if I became a "tool of the witch hunters." What added to our mental strain was the messages from people we respected, some urging me to testify, others insisting that I tell the Un-American Activities Committee to "go to hell, where it most likely was conceived." Negroes warned that I should beware of letting myself be used in "that old white man's plot to divide and conquer" the colored peoples of the world.

No one had to tell me that I did not know all I needed to know about political alignments in the United States, or about our country's position in the cold war, or the overall state of race relations, to say what I really wanted to say about communism. I had not yet had enough experience handling delicate problems of Negro progress to articulate for the nation the Negro's aspirations, especially when they had to be outlined against a background of political fear.

Yet I knew that Mr. Rickey wanted me to go to Washington. He figured that an appearance before that committee, in which I would speak boldly but wisely, would be the final stroke necessary to establish forever the Negro's place in baseball—and possibly in America.

I asked the help of Lester Granger, executive director of the National Urban League and a man with many years' experience in helping to solve ticklish social problems, including the ending of segregation in our military forces. With Rickey, Granger and Rae, I explored idea after idea, went into details of what seemingly was the most insignificant phraseology, and finally arrived at a speech that I felt I could give in Washington with pride and a clear conscience, without any feeling that I had sold out either those anguished Negroes still groping for even the smallest place in the sun, or those Americans who looked with great horror upon a congressional committee that they viewed as a threat to the liberties enshrined in the life of this nation for many decades. I shall be forever grateful to Lester Granger for his contribution to that speech. I needed his help because even though I had and still have the greatest respect for Mr. Rickey, I felt that no white man could sense fully the agony that I was going through, or understand the little nuances of what I knew I had to say frankly, yet so carefully. Mr. Rickey felt this deeply himself.

Even after Granger helped prepare the speech, my agony continued. A week before I was to go before the committee, someone handed me a copy of the *Nation* in which there appeared the following editorial:

"On the day that Jackie ('The Clutch') Robinson contributed his sixth home run of the year to a Dodger victory in Pittsburgh, Dr. Ralph J. Bunche called on the President in Washington and was asked by him to become an Assistant Secretary of State. Thanks a lot, said Dr. Bunche, but no thanks . . . Dr. Bunche, for all the immunity he has won by virtue of internationally recognized ability and stature, has had enough of the Jim Crow life he and his family must lead every day in our fair capital . . . On the day that Jackie Robinson hit his seventh home run of the season to break up a thirteen-inning thriller against the Giants in New York, a 'pretty troublesome sort of Nigra' named Caleb Hill, Jr., was taken by two unmasked men from the second-floor room 'that passes for a jail' in the home of the sheriff of Irwinton, Georgia, and escorted to a nearby creek. There he was beaten and shot to death, thus becoming the first lynch victim of 1949 . . . Most of the 53,053 white and colored people who saw Robby ruin the Giants on the day of the lynching are surely numbered among the millions of Americans who are bitterly ashamed this week of Georgia justice, Washington *mores*, and the rule of white supremacy, and who will not rest until it has been wiped out in every field, as it has, to all intents and purposes, in that of entertainment."

The implication was clear: many people would say that in going to Washington to disown the remarks of Robeson, I was "selling out" Negroes like Caleb Hill, Jr., and the millions of others who, in Washington, D.C., and places farther south, had not been so fortunate as to receive the breaks that had come my way. Rae and I felt deep in our hearts that under no circumstances could any amount of money or success wipe away our feeling of kinship for the Caleb Hills, or ease our hatred of enforced racial separation to the extent that I should become even the faintest ally of the segregationists. Yet it did not seem right to me that even in bitterness over the murder of a helpless Negro anyone should become so filled with despair as to say that fifteen million Negroes had given up on America.

2

On July 18 Jackie Robinson went before the House Un-American Activities Committee after much the same kind of careful preparation that preceded his entry into organized baseball. But in this testimony, as in his baseball debut, the crucial moment would be Robinson's alone. As he sat before the committee and began to read his statement, newsreel cameras picked up a pretty face behind him—his wife Rachel mouthing every word as Robinson spoke it, fearful that he might skip just one.

But Robinson missed nothing that day as he said to the Congressmen: ". . . I don't pretend to be any expert on communism or any other kind of political 'ism' . . .

"But you can put me down as an expert on being a colored American, with thirty years of experience at it. And just like any other colored person with sense enough to look around him and understand what he sees, I know that life in these United States can be mighty tough for people who are a little different from the majority—in their skin color or the way they worship their God, or the way they spell their names. I'm not fooled because I've had a chance open to very few Negro Americans. It's true that I've been the laboratory specimen in a great change in organized baseball. I'm proud that I've made good on my assignment to the point where other colored players will find it easier to enter the game and go to the top. But I'm very well aware that even this limited job isn't finished yet. There are only three major league clubs with only seven colored players signed up, out of close to four hundred major league players on sixteen clubs.

"But a start has been made, and progress goes on . . .

"We're going to make progress in other American fields besides baseball if we can get rid of some of the misunderstanding and confusion that the public still suffers from. I know I have a great desire and I think that I have some responsibility for helping to clear up that confusion. As I see it there has been a terrific lot of misunderstanding on this subject of communism among Negroes in this country, and it's bound to hurt my people's cause unless it's cleared up.

"The white public should start toward real understanding by appreciating that every single Negro who is worth his salt is going to resent any kind of slurs and discrimination because of his race, and he's going to use every bit of intelligence he has to stop it. This has got absolutely nothing to do with what Communists may or may not be trying to do. And white people must realize that the more a Negro hates communism because it opposes democracy, the more he is going to hate any other influence that kills off democracy in this country— and that goes for racial discrimination in the Army, and segregation on trains and buses, and job discrimination because of religious beliefs or color or place of birth.

"And one other thing the American public ought to understand, if we are to make progress in this matter. The fact that it is a Communist who denounces injustice in the courts, police brutality and lynching when it happens doesn't change the truth of his charges. Just because Communists kick up a big fuss over racial discrimination when it suits their purposes, a lot of people try to pretend that the whole issue is a creation of Communist imagination. But they are not fooling anyone, with this kind of pretense, and talk about 'Communists stirring up Negroes to protest,' only makes present misunderstanding worse than ever. Negroes were stirred up long before there was a Communist Party, and they'll stay stirred up long after the Party has disappeared—unless Jim Crow has disappeared by then as well.

"I've been asked to express my views on Paul Robeson's statement in Paris to the effect that American Negroes would refuse to fight in any war against Russia because we love Russia so much. I haven't any comment to make, except that the statement, if Mr. Robeson actually made it, sounds very silly to me. But he has a right to his personal views, and if he wants to sound silly when he expresses them in public, that's his business and not mine. He's still a famous ex-athlete and a great singer and actor.

"I understand that there are some few Negroes who are members of the Communist Party, and in event of war with Russia they'd probably act just as any other Communists would. So would members of other minority and majority groups. There are some colored pacifists, and they'd act just like pacifists of any color. And most Negroes—and Italians and Irish and Jews and Swedes and Slavs and other Americans—would act just as all these groups did in the last war. They'd do their best to help their country stay out of war; if unsuccessful, they'd do their best to help their country win the war—against Russia or any other enemy that threatened us.

"This isn't said as any defense of the Negro's loyalty, because any loyalty that needs defense can't amount to much in the long run. And no one has ever questioned my race's loyalty except a few people who don't amount to very much.

"What I'm trying to get across is that the American public is off on the wrong foot when it begins to think of radicalism in terms of any special minority group. It is thinking of this sort that gets people scared because one Negro, speaking to a Communist group in Paris, threatens an organized boycott by fifteen million members of his race. I can't speak for any fifteen million people any more than any other one person can, but I know that I've got too much invested for my wife and child and myself in the future of this country, and I and other Americans of many races and faiths have too much invested in our country's welfare, for any of us to throw it away because of a siren song sung in bass. I am a religious man. Therefore I cherish America where I am free to worship as I please, a privilege which some countries do not give. And I suspect that nine hundred and ninety-nine out of almost any thousand colored Americans you meet will tell you the same thing. But that doesn't mean that we're going to stop fighting race discrimination in this country [before] we've got it licked. It means that we're going to fight it all the harder because our stake in the future is so big. We can win our fight without the Communists and we don't want their help."

3

Robinson's testimony was the tremendous success that Rickey predicted it would be. Newspaper headlines screamed, "JACKIE HITS ROBESON'S RED PITCH"; "JACKIE HITS A DOUBLE—

AGAINST COMMUNISTS AND JIM CROW"; "JACKIE ROBINSON, AMERICAN"; "JACKIE ROBINSON HITS ANOTHER HOME RUN."

Said the *St. Louis Post-Dispatch:* "Jackie Robinson's statement . . . was distinguished by its good sense and moderation. As we have said before, it is a pity that Negroes have felt called on to repudiate Paul Robeson's statement that they wouldn't fight for their country against Communist Russia; the fact that Robeson was talking through his hat should have been taken for granted. But as long as they are called upon to say the obvious, Robinson has said it about as well as it could be said.

"One thing the Brooklyn Dodgers' second baseman said could serve as a counsel of wisdom to the white majority as well as the minority consisting of his own race. He said Negroes don't want the Communists' help and can win their fight without them. In these days when dollars and hopes are being spent lavishly to keep despair from pushing whole nations into nationalist Russian Communism, it's up to every American to see to it that when Jackie Robinson says Negroes can win their rights without Communist help he is absolutely correct."

As the editorial writers pondered and pontificated, Jackie Robinson was back at Ebbets Field, walking through an applauding crowd (from which came cries like "You gonna be a politician now, Jackie?" or "You gonna lead the league this year, Jack?")—back to the business of baseball.

After scoring what the editorial writers called an afternoon victory over Robeson, he put on a spectacular show to help Brooklyn score an evening victory over the Chicago Cubs.

With 25,595 fans in the stands, Brooklyn's Joe Hatten was locked in a tense pitching duel with Bob Rush, the Cubs' top pitcher. With the Dodgers holding a precarious 1-0 lead in the sixth inning, Robinson drew a base on balls. He danced off first, taking dangerous leads, and dashed to second when he got the jump on the frustrated pitcher. Mickey Owen, the Chicago catcher, hurled the ball to second in a desperate effort to get the flying Negro, but the throw was wild. Robinson had slid, but was on his feet in a split second as he noticed the ball skittering into center field. By the time the fielder had retrieved the ball, Robinson was on third.

Now, with the daring that made him the most exciting player in baseball, Robinson danced off third, acting as if he intended to steal home. Rush and the Cubs almost certainly would figure that nobody would try to steal home with only one man out, for a ground ball or a fly to the outfield would score him easily. But Rush went into a long windup and again Robinson dashed down the base line—only this time he didn't stop. The amazed Rush fired the ball toward the plate like a bullet—but over the head of the catcher. Robinson had scored a badly needed insurance run—and he had scored it on a play that didn't make sense as far as the "book of percentages" is concerned; but this was the kind of unorthodox leadership with which Robinson had so often pushed this Brooklyn team to the heights. In the eighth inning Robinson was on base again, dashing up and down the base line so menacingly that relief pitcher Bob Muncrief committed what Larry Goetz called a balk, only to be overruled by umpire Beans Reardon, who ruled that the batter, Carl Furillo, had stepped out of the batter's box. Robinson scored anyhow when Gene Hermanski tripled. When it was over, Brooklyn had won 3-0 to take a two-and-a-half-game lead over the St. Louis Cardinals.

The game over, sports writer Milton Gross observed that the only person to "stop" Robinson that day was the umpire who overruled the balk. "Maybe an umpire's decision is the only way to stop Robinson," wrote Gross. "Singers, pitchers and Congressmen can't."

4

Jackie Robinson remembers 1949 as one of the great years of his life. His turn-the-other-cheek restraints lifted, he batted .342 and stole 37 bases to lead the league in both departments. Besides being named to the All-Star team, he was selected by the Baseball Writers Association as the league's most valuable player for his key role in leading the Dodgers to another pennant.

From the moment we left spring training camp, I knew that 1949 was my year. Just the way obstacles were cleared and things fell into proper place, even in the Deep South, made me know that things were going my way.

For example, we were all filled with anxiety as we approached Atlanta, where Mr. Rickey had scheduled exhibition games against the Atlanta Crackers on April 8, 9 and 10. Dr. Samuel Green, grand dragon of the Ku Klux Klan, had threatened to block Campanella and me from playing on grounds that it was illegal for interracial teams to perform in Georgia.

The Atlanta owner, Earl Mann, was courageous enough to ignore the Klan, and Atlanta papers gave Green a going over, still the Klansman predicted riots and bloodshed.

I'll never forget the tension at the press conference called by Mr. Rickey before our first game in Atlanta.

"Mr. Rickey, do you think Jackie Robinson will be assaulted if he plays here?" asked John Drebinger of the *New York Times.*

"Yes, I think he will be . . ." Mr. Rickey began, and newsmen dashed madly for the door.

"Hold it, hold it," cried Mr. Rickey. "I think Robinson will be assaulted by autograph seekers, and their weapons will be fountain pens."

He was right. They held up the bus twenty minutes after the first game while I signed autographs.

We played before record-smashing crowds totaling 49,-299 in those three games in Atlanta, and there were no incidents. Almost 14,000 Negro fans overflowed a special section and stood ten-deep around the outfield for the Sunday game. I told a friend that the Klan could start anything it chose that day and I wouldn't worry; I'd run straight into that throng of Negroes in center field and see what Klansman was brave enough to come and get me.

We played in Greenville, South Carolina; Beaumont, Texas; Macon, Georgia, and several other southern cities that spring. I left the South believing that substantial racial progress had been made since my first year in Florida. I was proud to have had even a small part in producing that change.

Jackie Robinson was no longer the "freak" of baseball after 1949. Men of all manner of racial views agreed that he was a great baseball player, that as he went so went the Dodgers. He batted .328 in 1950 and .338 in 1951 when he set a fielding record for second basemen with a percentage of .992. He set a record of 133 double plays in 1950, then broke it in 1951 with 137.

More important than his hitting and fielding, however, was the fight Jackie put into the Dodgers—the fact that he was the one his teammates expected to keep the opposition from getting out of line.

Probably one of the best "bean-ballers" to pitch against the Dodgers during Robinson's years on the team was Sal Maglie, then of the New York Giants. Maglie's success derived largely from his uncanny ability to keep opposing batters off balance by throwing them an assortment of "junk," or "cute" pitches, and whiz in, just at the right moment, a fast ball that would shave the batter's chin so closely that Maglie became known as "The Barber."

Although the Giants were not always Brooklyn's number one rival for the pennant, they were the team that seemed to work hardest to hurt the Dodgers, to beat them in the crucial game with the hope of giving the pennant to the Braves, the Phillies, or whoever was hottest in pursuit of the Dodgers.

One of Robinson's biggest rhubarbs came about because, in a crucial game, Maglie was unusually bold in throwing at the heads of Dodger players.

Reese said to Robinson: "Jack, we've got to do something about that guy throwing at us. If we don't somebody's going to get hurt, or at least we're going to lose this game. When you come up this inning, drop one down the first base line and dump him on his butt."

Without giving any thought whatsoever to what it would mean to him individually, to whether or not it would involve him in a press furor, Robinson nodded to Pee Wee that he would. If it was good for the team, Robinson figured, it was good for him, because he had come to win. As Robinson waited in the batters' circle, however, the Dodger batboy knelt beside him.

"Don't you drop that bunt and run into Maglie, Jackie," he said. "You're always the one that gets the team out of trouble and yourself into it by taking on a pitcher who's throwing at the batters. Let some of the other guys do it."

Robinson thought about these remarks. He *was* usually the guy to take on the opposing pitcher. "I've been in enough rhubarbs lately," he said to himself, "so I'll let someone else do it." As he walked to the batter's box, however, he heard a teammate shout, "Don't forget, old boy, we're counting on you to give him the works."

"They're counting on me," Jackie said to himself. "I think I'll lay it down."

He dumped a bunt down the first base line, hoping that Maglie would come over to field it. The bunt was perfect, but Maglie refused to come to first to cover, so the hard-charging Robinson barreled head-down into the base only to send the Giants' second baseman, Davey Williams, sprawling on his back.

When the players got up, Robinson was disappointed to see that it was Williams, not Maglie, whom he had sent sprawling. Some of the Giant players shouted, "You're asking for it, Robinson, and we're going to give it to you."

In the next inning Alvin Dark, the Giants' shortstop, slapped a line drive deep to the outfield. As the fielder retrieved the ball, Robinson, who was playing third, saw Dark rounding second, trying to stretch the blow to a triple. As the infielder took the relay and fired the ball toward third, Dark was steaming in like a freight train. The ball hit the dirt and bounced once to third—a perfect throw—just as Dark left his feet, sliding into third. Robinson took the throw and stationed himself as if to take the full impact of Dark's lunge. But after Dark had completely committed himself, Robinson stepped back quickly and jammed the baseball against Dark's nose, only to have it bounce out of his hand, leaving the runner safe. Later, as the Dodger players rushed off the field to their dugout, some slapped Robinson on the back, shouting, "That's the way to play it, boy, that's the way to play it if they want to be nasty about it."

Maglie didn't throw at any more Dodgers that day, and the dressing room of the victorious Dodgers was bedlam as player after player pummeled Robinson and laughed loudly that "you sure put the fear of God in that Maglie.'

"The only thing I hate about the deal is that I had to get involved with a nice guy like Al Dark," said Robinson. "I really didn't mean to tag him in the nose."

A little later Joe Reichler of A.P. came by to act as peacemaker between Robinson and Dark, a Louisianan who had a high regard for the Negro star.

"Dark wants you to know that he had no malicious intentions when he stormed into third," Reichler said. "But he was surprised and hurt that you would bowl into Davey Williams, a kid who already had a sore back and couldn't defend himself."

"Joe, you tell Alvin that I don't want to carry on any feud or squabble with him, and I don't blame him for taking up for Davey Williams. That's what good baseball players are supposed to do. When I dropped that bunt I had no intention whatsoever of knocking down anybody but Maglie. I was charging to first with my head down and didn't even know it was Williams I'd bowled into until he was sprawling on the ground."

It was this daring, competitive spirit, this willingness to do whatever was good for the team, that made Jackie Robinson an invaluable man to the Dodgers.

In 1949, sports writer Tom Meany said: "Who would you pick as the most dangerous player in baseball today? Stan (The Man) Musial? Ted Williams? Let's not kid ourselves, fellows, the most dangerous player in baseball today is . . . Jackie Robinson. Before anybody blows a gasket, Robby isn't a hitter with the authority of Musial or Williams, or maybe

several others, but Jackie can beat you more ways than any
other player in baseball today. He can beat you with his
power (.353 and seven home runs) or with his great speed.
And there isn't a better second baseman in the National
League . . .

"Robinson is closer to Cobb in his baseball technique than
any of the modern players. There have been base runners since
Ty and before Jackie who upset pitchers, but nobody since
Cobb, except Robinson, who upset entire ball clubs . . ."

Robinson seemed at his greatest in the clutch. As a result,
he not only gave a lift to the Brooklyn team, but often took
the heart out of the opposition. Si Burick, sports editor of the
Cleveland News, went to Cincinnati in 1950 to watch the
Dodgers meet the Redlegs in a very important double-header.
In the seventh inning of the opening game the Dodgers were
struggling to hold a 4-3 lead. With a runner on second, first
base open and one man out, the Dodgers had Duke Snider,
the powerful left-handed swinger, coming to the plate. A
home run by Snider would break the game open. Cincinnati
manager Luke Sewell knew that baseball percentages indicated that he should walk Snider intentionally in view of the
fact that on the mound for Cincinnati was Ewell Blackwell, a
right-hander. This was particularly so since following Snider
was Robinson, a right-handed hitter who had stated publicly
that he always had difficulty hitting Blackwell. Sewell put
Snider on first, leaving Blackwell to pitch to Robinson.

"What I have to say now is not a second-guess," Burick
wrote. "Snider might have hit a home run, had he been
pitched to. Robinson might have followed with another home
run. But Robinson is a man who has spent his life facing personal challenges—and beating them down.

"Blackwell pitched a ball, then he threw one down Jackie's
alley—and there was never any doubt about the destination
of that delivery once Robinson's club met the horsehide.
Over the center-field fence, of course, for a home run. And
then there was dancing in the aisles.

"What else could Sewell have expected when he chose to
walk a left-hander for a right-hander who happened to be his

league's top hitter with a batting average in the .400 vicinity? What else could Luke expect in challenging a man who thrives on challenges?

"HE BROKE THE REDS' SPIRIT. That's how Jackie broke the first game wide open and, in a sense, the second, too. The Reds had little stomach, or heart, for competition the rest of the way, to say nothing of the rest of the day. They played with a 'what's-the-use' attitude thereafter."

What made that home run more spectacular than Burick or the spectators realized was that Robinson clubbed it under pressures that would have been unbearable to many men. Upon arrival in Cincinnati he learned that someone had sent to the Cincinnati Police Department, to a Cincinnati newspaper and to the Brooklyn baseball club a letter signed "The Three Travelers," announcing that if Robinson played at Crosley Field that day he would be shot by a high-powered rifle from a nearby building.

FBI agents questioned Robinson upon his arrival in Cincinnati, but Jackie knew of no one in or near Cincinnati who had any reason to be gunning for him—except, of course, people who disliked him because he was a Negro. Jackie explained that there had been other letters of that nature, all of which he had thrown into the waste basket because efforts to check them out always wound up at vacant lots, or something of the sort. However, the FBI checked thoroughly in this case because there were buildings overlooking Crosley Field from which a gunman could easily operate.

Members of the Dodger club heard about the letter and began to kid about it, partly as a means of relieving the tension on Jackie.

Gene Hermanski bellowed out in the clubhouse before the game, "I've got it, gang, I've got a way we can protect Robinson from those gunmen. We'll all wear Number 42 today."

The Dodgers roared with laughter.

"A heck of a lot of good that'll do," shouted Robinson. "Now if you'd brought along a little soot to paint your faces black and had practiced walking pigeon-toed you could use Number 42 and be some help."

The Dodgers roared with laughter again.

When Robinson smashed that game-clinching homer right in the direction of a building from which the gunmen could easily have shot, he rounded third base happily, soaking up the cheers from the fans who had come from Louisville, Nashville and towns far and wide to cheer him and the Dodgers. As he touched home plate and stuck out his mitt to shake hands with outfielder Cal Abrams, the latter laughingly reminded him: "My God, Jack, let's get into that dugout quick. If they're ever going to shoot at us, now is the time."

In the clubhouse between games, the Dodgers had another session of banter and laughter about how to keep Robinson from getting shot, but at the end of the day, most of them had forgotten the threatening letter.

The team had a few hours to kill before moving to the next city, and most of the Dodgers checked out of their rooms and went to a movie, as they often did. Robinson usually joined them, but this time he decided to read in his room. At about 8:30 P.M. he was engrossed in his book when he heard a key rattling in his door. He was about to call, "It's not locked," when the door swung open and three men stepped in carrying small black bags. The first thing that came to Robinson's mind was "The Three Travelers." He gasped a couple of times until he saw the bellboy standing behind the three men.

"Awfully sorry," said the bellboy, "but we thought you had checked out, Mr. Robinson."

The three men did happen to be travelers—salesmen, in fact—but their only interest in "assaulting" Jackie Robinson was to jerk out their fountain pens and vow that their children would never forgive them if they let go this chance to get his autograph.

5

Jackie's greatest day in baseball was the last day of the 1951 season, when he showed, beyond any doubt, that he was often the difference between victory and defeat for Brooklyn. Early in the year the Dodgers appeared to be running away with the pennant, piling up a 13½-game lead over the New York Giants. Then the Dodgers went into a tailspin. The Giants were coming on strong, like a miracle team, whittling down the Dodgers' lead until the last days of the season, when the two teams were running neck and neck. The Dodgers went to Philadelphia with their confidence shattered, fighting for the team's life, struggling to preserve a pennant that every man long ago had figured was in the bag. On Saturday night, the day before the season ended, the Phillies threw their ace, Robin Roberts, at the Dodgers. Brooklyn countered with Newcombe, a man later to be derided and laughed into virtual impotence by sports writers declaring that he never won the "big ones." Big Don won a big one that night, for he beat Roberts and the Phillies, 5 to 0.

The next day was made for drama, with the Brooklyns battling the Phillies and the Giants playing Boston. In the early innings of that game against the Phillies, Robinson was just another baseball player. The Dodgers fell behind 6-1 and seemed destined for defeat. Then, in the top of the fifth, with the Dodgers trailing 6-2, Robinson came to bat with a Dodger on base. He lashed a triple to deep center field, scoring that runner and later scoring himself as the Dodgers put together three runs to make the score 6-5.

But the Phillies bounced back in the bottom of the fifth and scored two runs to take an 8-5 lead. As the inning ended, the Dodgers looked at the scoreboard disconsolately to see that the Giants had beaten the Braves. They knew that if they failed to beat Philadelphia they would have lost the pennant; there would be no tomorrow. In the eighth inning the Dodgers stormed back and scored three runs to tie the game. Now it was Saturday night all over again, with Roberts and Newcombe coming in as reliefers to continue their grueling battle of the night before. These two magnificent right-handers mowed down batters until the bottom of the twelfth inning. Then Newcombe seemed to tire. With two out, the Phillies loaded the bases. Eddie Waitkus strode to the plate. Big Newk reared back and fogged in his fast one. Waitkus swung and caught the ball squarely, whacking a clothesliner that seemed ticketed for center field. If it got there, the game, the season and the Dodgers' dreams were ended. But Robinson, in magnificent desperation, moved speedily to his right, then flung himself into a full-length dive and got his glove on that ball. As he fell to earth his right elbow crashed into his stomach, knocking him all but unconscious. By instinct, however, he held on to that ball long enough for the put-out.

Reese ran to his teammate and started rubbing him. Trainer Doc Wendler and Manager Charlie Dressen rushed to the field, worked on Robinson and finally got him back to the dugout.

The Dodgers failed to score in the thirteenth inning. As they started to the field again, Robinson lay slumped in the dugout, the energy and eagerness drained out of him. Pain marked his face and he seemed utterly weary as Wendler waved a piece of cotton soaked in ammonia under his nose.

Reese paused at the top of the dugout steps as he looked around and saw that Robinson had made no effort to get back to second base. "Let's go, Jackie; we need you now, boy; we're playing for all the marbles now, and we've never needed you more. Push him up here, Doc. He'll be all right as soon as he gets on the field."

"I'm not sure I can help the team," said Jackie.

"If you can't I don't know who can," said Reese.

Robinson wobbled up the steps and moved waveringly toward second base. The Phillies were retired in the bottom of the thirteenth. Then, in the top of the fourteenth, Roberts retired the first two Dodgers easily and it looked as though the game would go on interminably.

As Robinson knelt in the batters' circle, he looked at that scoreboard: Giants 3, Braves 2. The Dodgers with a 13½-game lead, he thought, and then the big change. The Giants kept winning, winning, winning. Brooklyn kept losing, losing, losing. Then neck-and-neck with two days of the season left. Tied, with one game to go. And now, on the last day of the season, Brooklyn involved in a desperate struggle to hold on for a playoff. Two out, nobody on base, and Robin Roberts out there pitching, pitching as brilliantly as he had ever done. Robinson tired, sick to his stomach.

Robinson dusted resin on his bat handle and stepped to the plate as he eyed Roberts cautiously. When the great Philadelphia pitcher broke a curve over the inside corner, getting a little too much of the plate, Robinson swung with every ounce of energy in his body, his mind on just one thing: those seats beyond the left-field fence. When the bat met the ball he knew that he had done it. He ran recklessly toward first, peeking at that little white spheroid that zoomed rocketlike out toward left field. As he neared first, the Dodger coach jumped up gleefully, and Robinson knew that it had reached the seats. Brooklyn held the Phillies in the last of the fourteenth. Now they would go into a crucial playoff with the Giants.

Sid Freidlander of the *New York Post* would look back on this game many years later as Jackie Robinson's finest hour and conclude that "Jackie Robinson must be rated as one of the greatest clutch players of all time."

Nobody agreed more than Dressen, with whom Robinson had formed a sort of mutual admiration society. Both were tremendous competitors who preferred winning to all else. Robinson admired Dressen's savvy and credited the manager with teaching him many of the little tricks of base running and fielding that made him a star. Dressen praised Robinson for the indomitable spirit that was displayed in Philadelphia and elsewhere.

"Give me five players like Robinson and a pitcher," Dressen told a sports writer, "and I'll beat any nine-man team in baseball."

11....The Colonel from "Old Kaintuck"

In 1949, 1950 and 1951, when Robinson was at his peak and his every hour was filled with the world's acclaim, he was quick to say, with no pretense of modesty, that he had not gotten that far alone. There were Branch Rickey, Clay Hopper, Rae, Lester Granger and a host of other people who had boosted him over barrier after barrier, given him courage when his troubles seemed all-consuming. There was one man who, unlike all these, had no personal interest of any sort in seeing that Robinson made good, but who, nevertheless, had been a prime figure in Jackie's development. That man was Pee Wee Reese, the Dodger shortstop.

Robinson had held up under the mental strain of 1947 and played baseball of major league caliber largely because of Reese, the "Kentucky colonel" whose decency and courage in seemingly insignificant situations had buoyed him up and kept him believing that America is populated mainly by decent people who justify the Negro's continued optimism. Not that Reese was a crusader, a lecturer about the heritage of freedom or the rights of a minority, or the necessity for baseball to operate on a democratic basis; actually, when Robinson joined the Dodgers in 1947, Reese was a puckish-faced young man of twenty-seven who looked as if he had just been munching on a green persimmon, and as if he were much too young to be playing baseball in the majors. Yet it was Reese more than anyone who led Robinson to believe that a courageous man is the noblest work of God—not a man of physical courage, for some of the most daring physical feats in history have been the work of fools, but a man of moral courage. Robinson soon saw that courage was what Pee Wee had, although the two had played together for years, had become one of the greatest keystone combinations in the history of baseball, before Robinson realized fully how much courage it had required for Reese to treat him as just another ballplayer and to insist in his own way that others do the same.

Actually, Reese was thrust under moral and social pressure from the day Robinson signed a Montreal contract, for that day a newspaperman located Reese to get his views on the signing of a Negro. Reese was thoughtful for a while, then he asked the newspaperman whimsically: "What position did you say this guy played?"

"Shortstop."

"Well, that's the old Reese luck for you. There're nine positions and this guy has to play shortstop."

Pee Wee watched the writer's face, noting that he seemed to take this remark as denoting fear by Reese that Robinson might get his job. "However," added Reese, "there may be room enough in baseball for both of us."

Later some of Pee Wee's Louisville friends expressed disgust that he should be so calm about the prospect of playing alongside a Negro, or even competing against a Negro for a job. As his friends harassed him on the subject, Reese says he thought: "What will my Louisville friends say about me playing with a colored guy? Probably won't like it, but I say to hell with anyone who doesn't like it. I don't even know this fellow Robinson; haven't met him; but I do know that he deserves a chance, same as anybody else."

So by the time the proposed Dodger rebellion in Panama came to his attention, Reese had made up his mind that he would have no part of any anti-Negro demonstration. One ex-Dodger reports that an anti-Negro player barked, "What the hell's the matter with you, Reese? Don't tell me we've got a nigger-lover up from Kentucky?"

"Listen," said Reese in a voice that seemed unbelievably stern for a man with such a young and pleasant face, "you've got your views and I've got mine. I haven't thrown any insulting remarks at you because of what you believe and I don't expect you to throw any at me. If you want to know where I stand I can put it to you quite simply. I've thought about this thing a great deal and I ended up putting myself in Robinson's place. I said to myself, suppose Negroes were in the majority in this country and for years baseball had been closed to white players, and somebody gave me a chance to be the first white player on a Negro team. Well, I'd be awfully damned scared and lonesome and I sure would appreciate the guy who didn't go out of his way to give me a kick in the teeth. So when I put myself in Robinson's place I made up my mind I wasn't going to be the one out to give him any kicks in the teeth."

It was this kind of courage, along with the work of Eddie Stanky, that thwarted that Dodger rebellion.

Reese was thoughtful because to him there was a principle involved. It was more than just doing something for the team, or currying favor with Branch Rickey. He did things because he felt they were the things a gentleman ought to do. He said to one newspaperman: "I don't know how to explain my feelings toward Robinson. It's nothing for which I think *I* deserve any great credit. It just happens that there are some southerners on this team who were born into the most violent kind of racial prejudice. They've had this thing crammed down their craws for all these years. I understand that for them it may be impossible for anyone to say overnight, 'Well, here he is, boys, and this is the way it's going to be.'

"But all my life, even though I had members of my family who held a low regard for Negroes, I never had any deep prejudices against Negroes. Some boys in my group would throw stones at Negroes or shout insulting remarks as they passed by the park in which we played in Louisville, but something made it impossible for me to participate in the stone-throwing or epithet hurling."

Reese was perceptive, he had concern for the rights and feelings of others. Because of these qualities, he made it possible for Robinson to step out of the role of baseball's two-headed monster—Brooklyn's one-man circus—and really become a member of the Dodger squad. Reese was one of the first to insist that Jackie join him in a card game. Robinson noticed that in baseball, as in life generally, the courage of one man can be a powerful force upon individuals who have consciences but not much backbone. Thus, after Reese asked Robinson to join him at cards, the latter quickly became a poker companion of other players like Preacher Roe, Billy Cox and Billy Loes.

Thus, three months after Rickey squelched the rebellion in Panama, Robinson was accepted as a valuable member of the Dodger organization. The fans and sports writers began to see this in many ways. One of the best indications—and Reese was the main figure here, too—occurred in Danville, Illinois, in late June, 1947, when the Dodgers stopped to play a night exhibition game. The Dodgers arrived just before noon, which left them the afternoon free. After a luncheon in their honor at a country club, most of the players decided to get in a round of golf. Robinson found that he and Wendell Smith, the Negro sports writer, were left to play together. A crowd followed the Negro twosome, not only because Robinson was the biggest news in baseball but because many spectators had heard that he was also a first-rate golfer. After about four holes, Robinson and Smith caught a foursome composed of Dodger pitcher Rex Barney, Harold Parrott, the Dodgers' secretary, Roscoe McGowen of the *New York Times*, and

Reese. Reese saw the Negroes waiting for them to hit their shots and move out of range. He waved to them to hit up. As Robinson and Smith came toward the foursome, Reese shouted, "Why don't you two join us? We can make this a six-some. That's against the rules, I know, but there aren't many people playing out here today and there's practically no one behind for us to hold up."

Robinson and Smith accepted the invitation happily because, although they enjoyed playing together, each was aware that many viewers would notice the two Negroes playing alone and conclude, as some writers had declared, that Jackie Robinson was "the loneliest player in baseball."

The writers who peddled that line talked quite a bit about Robinson's needing a Negro or two with whom to associate, about Negroes naturally preferring to be with each other under social circumstances, or conditions of great intimacy. Pee Wee Reese was showing gradually and naturally that people simply prefer to be together when they have a common interest.

The incident Robinson remembers best as illustrating Reese's innate decency occurred in Boston, however, shortly after Jackie was shifted to second base. The Boston bench jockeys decided that rather than give Robinson the works, they would goad Reese—and possibly knock off two horses with one bit of jockeying.

"Hey, Pee Wee, you and your pal going to dinner together tonight?" someone would shout as the Dodgers took infield practice.

"Hey out there, Kentucky boy. When yo' grandpappy finds out how you up heah socializing and fraternizing with cullud folks he's gonna cut you off from yo' mint juleps," another player bellowed.

For a while Reese ignored the calls, spitting in the pocket of his glove and pounding it with his fist while staring straight ahead. As the calls got louder, however, he strode over to Robinson and put his arm around his shoulder. They talked for a minute in buddy-buddy fashion—oddly enough, neither Robinson nor Reese remembers a single word they said—and the Braves' players fell silent. Reese had said, simply but with force: Robinson and I are teammates, and we came here to play baseball. We came to beat the living daylights out of Boston. If the Braves want to spend their time throwing silly barbs while we play baseball, that's all right with us. That ended the race heckling.

Reese soon got close enough to Jackie to discover that he was not "unsociable," or the "lone wolf" that many sports writers described, but was merely being extra cautious and considerate of the racial views and backgrounds of some of his teammates.

"You see, Pee Wee, I sympathize with some of these players," Robinson once said. "This experience isn't new to me because I've played baseball, football, basketball and track with white boys practically all my life. But there are some white fellows on the squad who practically never said 'how do you do' to any Negro other than some yard boy or servant. So you see, while many people may think that this is an ordeal for me, it may be a greater ordeal for some of the white guys."

"That's a mighty thoughtful attitude for you to take," said Pee Wee. "I've never told you before, but I've had my own troubles. Jack, you don't know how I hate to go to Cincinnati. My mother and relatives and some of my friends always come up from Louisville to see the team play, and so help me God the subject always gets around to the fact that I'm a little southern boy playing shortstop next to a Negro second baseman and possibly in danger of being contaminated. Jack, I get so goddamned mad I just about explode. I can't understand how any relative of mine could be so—"

"Don't be too hard on them," Robinson interrupted. "We mustn't forget that you had some educational opportunities that they haven't had, and I'm not referring to schooling. You were in the Navy; you traveled a lot; now you've played baseball with a Negro. So you've had a chance to see first-hand that not every Negro's like the street-corner clowns on which a lot of these people want to base their picture of the entire Negro race."

"Yeah, Jackie, I always end up giving my relatives the benefit of the doubt, because I do understand the way these views —fears, really—have been drilled into some of them. So I say to them, 'If you people would ever go to the trouble of meeting Robinson, you'd probably come to the conclusion that you were pretty damn proud to have your little Kentucky boy playing shortstop alongside him."

Reese never gave up until he convinced his mother and some of his other relatives that they ought to meet Robinson. His relatives were soon won over completely—so much so that Reese's meetings with them were no longer filled with emotional talk about whether Pee Wee would want his daughter to marry a Negro, but with conversations about how silly people can act and talk when they just don't know.

Yet Reese had a lot of friends in Louisville who never got to meet Robinson or any other Negro with an education, with convictions, with the ability to articulate his own aspirations or those of his race. So in the minds of these friends of Reese, Robinson remained a symbol of a strange race of burly, smelly, obnoxious creatures who lived only for Saturday night when they might get a fish sandwich, a bottle of moonshine whiskey and a chance to use their switchblades. Reese and his wife were continually badgered and pestered by people caught up in this myth, even when attending some of the most sedate social parties in their home town.

Discussing these things with Robinson helped to tie the bond of friendship between the two, and this made them a better second-base combination. Not that a shortstop and a second baseman have to be buddies to do their job well, for Joe Tinker and Johnny Evers, the Chicago keystone combination that made "Tinker to Evers to Chance" a baseball byword, went for years without speaking to each other, on or off the field; but the friendly relations between Reese and Robinson added pleasure to the practice sessions in which one would study the other's movements, each gauging the other man's speed in reaching second base from a given position, each figuring to the finest detail just where each man should receive a toss so as to pivot most quickly in order to complete a double play. The two worked out their own special signals for the double steal, which made them twin terrors to opposing pitchers when both got on base, or for the hit-and-run play, at which both were extremely adept. Soon they became such friends that they were able to kid each other about their respective contributions to the Brooklyn team.

Once they went to a recording studio together to make an album of records for children. Robinson, who was in a dreadful batting slump at the moment, said to Reese, "Brother, have I got nerve, posing to the kids as a baseball player when I can't hit the ball out of the infield."

Reese smiled and replied, "You're right, and you'd better get going, because if you don't hit when I'm on base I don't score runs. And if I don't score runs, how'm I going to beat you out of the scoring championship this year?"

There were several occasions when, but for this natural, easygoing relationship, the Dodgers might have been split by trumped-up racial jealousies. In 1951, for example, not only was Robinson playing exciting baseball, but Roy Campanella had joined the Dodgers, quickly to become recognized as one of the best catchers in the game, and big Don Newcombe was having a magnificent season as a pitcher. Someone was barraging the white players of the Brooklyn team with letters pointing out that Negro players were getting all the headlines and that if the white players weren't careful they'd be "run and written out of baseball."

Reese told Robinson about these letters in Cincinnati while the team was on the bus from the hotel to the ball park. This led to an open discussion in which the team talked out the situation. Reese said without fanfare: "I think everybody here knows that some crackpot has been writing anonymous letters to all the white players trying to stir up racial animosity. I don't think anybody on this squad is so insecure that he feels Negroes are going to take over baseball, and I don't believe anybody here is so jealous that he resents the publicity being given the Negro players on this squad. You know what the record shows; you know what Robinson, Newcombe and Campanella are to this team. I think the sports writers are basically fair and every man is going to get what he deserves. But one thing we must be sure of: that we don't let some outsider—possibly some guy working for our opposition—sow dissension with any stupid kind of propaganda like this."

There was general approval of what Reese had said, and Gil Hodges, an extremely quiet man, spoke up: "I'm glad you brought this into the open, Pee Wee, because I knew that there'd been some mumbling about these letters. They seemed awfully silly to me; now maybe we can just laugh them off and forget it." That is what the Dodgers did.

2

There is no greater sign that race has ceased to be a barrier between men than when they are able to talk freely about matters of race. Robinson and Reese reached this happy stage in 1949. In spring training that year, the Dodgers were playing an exhibition game in Beaumont, Texas, where an unusually large crowd of Negro fans came to see the Negro stars. When Campanella poked two tremendous drives to left field during batting practice the Negroes practically went wild. There was shouting and jumping and stamping and yelling and whooping and hollering and a general atmosphere that seemed to say: Are you looking, white folks, at the way that boy hits that ball? He's colored, you know!

Jackie and Pee Wee were standing side by side on the infield and Pee Wee could sense that Jackie was wishing the Negro fans would show a little more restraint, would not make him so conscious of being a Negro.

"Pee Wee," Jackie said, "watch me when I get up there to hit. I'll try to sock a long one to left to see what the Negro fans do. Then I'm going to swing like hell and miss one on purpose to see what kind of reaction I can get from the white crowd. I think you'll get a pretty good indication of how racial jealousy and frictions are developed."

Jackie slapped the first pitch against the left-field fence, and the Negro stands shook with cheers. On the next pitch Robinson swung so hard his cap spun off but the ball went kerplop into the back of the batting cage. Many white fans laughed, sounded catcalls and booed; the Negro fans sat in silence. Robinson winked at Reese.

After Jackie left the batting cage he and Reese talked at length, in seriousness and laughter, about the suspicion, the almost subconscious contest of racial prides, the fears that grew out of the fact that in that grandstand two races were kept so completely apart that they had no chance to know each other. Robinson admitted that it embarrassed him to have Negroes cheer his every move, but he tried to explain that in a way the Negroes were compensating for and protesting against the stigma of having to sit in those Jim Crow bleachers. They were saying in effect: Look at Jackie and Campy; they don't have to play second fiddle to any white ballplayer. They're proving that Negroes are men. So why do you white folks keep pretending we're inferior by forcing us to sit in these bleachers?"

Because of conversations like this, Reese had begun to appreciate Robinson as something more than an athlete, had begun to admire him not only because he had the courage to take the abuse and tension that Reese felt he would not have been able to take, but because Robinson stood for something —and that made him not only Pee Wee's kind of ballplayer, but Pee Wee's kind of man.

Once, during night practice in Macon, Ga., no one but Reese seemed to be aware that Robinson was bothered by some of the threats to his family, and particularly by a recent threat that if Robinson took the field in Macon he would be shot.

Jackie was aware, though, that Reese was practically shadowing him. He looked at the Dodger captain as if to say: What the hell's going on here? Why don't you get off my back? Reese said with a smile, "Why don't you get away from *me*, Robinson? I don't want to be shot." Robinson laughed, realizing that Reese was saying to him and to the letter-writing crank: You don't scare me with your threats to shoot out on this field, so I know you don't scare Robinson.

There were several attempts to drive a wedge between Reese and Robinson, some by sports writers who may have acted solely out of insensitivity and a callous disregard for the feelings and reputations of others rather than from malicious intent to harm the Brooklyn team. One wrote that while all the Dodgers respected Robinson's ability, the vast majority, including Reese, never stopped thinking of him as a Negro. The implication was that the Kentuckian was doing only what he felt he had to do, and that personally even he had not truly accepted Robinson. Another writer speculated that if Reese became Dodger manager, Robinson would have to be traded or else there would be constant friction growing out of Robinson's feeling of baseball superiority to the Little Colonel.

When Milton Gross of the *New York Post* reached Robinson by telephone in Jacksonville, Florida, and told him of this story, Robinson was "an angry and anguished man who felt that an injustice was being done not only to him, but to his teammate who had been his benefactor in his most difficult days."

"I want the people in Brooklyn to know that I'm hoping it will be Pee Wee," said Robinson. "I would work harder for Pee Wee than anybody I can think of because I would want him to be a success. Ever since I joined the club Pee Wee has been as close to me as anybody possibly could be," Jackie continued. "I don't feel superior to anybody, so how could anybody claim that I feel superior to Reese? Pee Wee's got to know that he doesn't have a better friend than Jackie Robinson."

Reese understood, for nobody knew better than Reese how writers liked to put words into Jackie's mouth, or to twist and distort even his most innocent remarks into a sensational story.

Robinson recalls that Reese was not the only teammate who made his baseball days pleasant to remember:

I'll never forget Carl Erskine and how he came to symbolize, at least for me, what a Christian is supposed to be. If Rae or just a Negro friend of mine was around, Carl was never too busy to stop to chat. In difficult times, he seemed by instinct to know the right thing to say. There was no condescension, no conscious effort to be nice, about him. I got the feeling that because of his religious principles and upbringing, race truly meant nothing to Carl.

Then there was Billy Loes, a pitcher who had as much "stuff" on the ball as any, but who never quite found that drive, that motivation, that produces greatness. I played cards with Billy a lot, and I often thought how, unwittingly I am sure, Billy was proof that the common interest of two men can be so unifying a force that talk about race and social equality seems silly.

As I look back and recall the days when the tensions were finally waning, I cannot minimize the contributions of Campanella, Newcombe and my former roommate, Jim Gilliam. I was happy to have them join the team and even happier to see them achieve stardom. As the number of Negroes on our team and in baseball increased, I knew that the day had come—thanks to guys like Reese, Erskine, Loes, Hodges and others—when Negro players would rise or fall on merit. Much sooner than either Mr. Rickey or I ever would have dreamed during that unforgettable first meeting in 1945, we were fast approaching the day when all that would count was what was in the box scores.

12....After Faint Praise, Damnation

Pee Wee Reese saw early a side of Jackie Robinson that sports writers and the public did not see until 1949, when Branch Rickey told Jackie that he was on his own. Reese saw the fighting, uncompromising, win-at-any-cost attitude that made Jackie a superior athlete; he saw also that these attributes sprang from a deep and smoldering personal rage against social injustice. Reese understood, then, as few sports writers ever would, that in "liberating" the fighting ballplayer Rickey had also liberated the social crusader.

Rickey took this step with trepidation, knowing that a Jackie Robinson free to say what he pleased to whom he pleased was certain to be a joy to newspapermen looking for "hot news," especially since Robinson was not only the most newsworthy player in baseball, but one of the most articulate.

Rickey was aware that many influential writers and other powerful forces were not resigned to Negroes' presence in baseball in 1949; they simply hadn't found any basis except race on which to attack Robinson and the other Negroes, and the mood of the country was not such that they could afford a purely racial assault. A "liberated" Robinson would surely give them some reasons. Yet Robinson was eager to cast off his shackles, and Rickey set him free, opening up a chain of events that was to create a new public image of Jackie Robinson, "social firebrand," "hothead," and "troublemaker."

Shortly after spring training began in 1949, Jackie remarked casually to a newspaperman, "They'd better be rough on me this year, because I'm going to be rough on them." He went on to explain that he had reported to camp in good physical condition, and he intended to make good Rickey's prediction that this would be the year Robinson would run the opposition dizzy. "I'm going to steal 'em blind," he laughed.

Newspapermen did not even consider the remarks worth an item in their columns until a few days later, on March 10, when Robinson almost had a fist fight with a Dodger rookie pitcher, Chris Van Cuyk. The trouble began when Van Cuyk and another rookie, Gale Wade, began to "ride" Robinson during an intrasquad game between teams led by Reese and Bruce Edwards. When Robinson booted a ground ball, Van Cuyk and Wade shouted rapid-fire taunts and barbs at him.

"You'll be a twenty-year man in Class D!" Robinson shouted back at Van Cuyk.

"Why don't you be quiet, you bush-leaguer!" Wade yelled back.

When Robinson next came to bat he slapped a single off Van Cuyk. Then he danced off first, up and down the base line, unnerving the young pitcher. The next time Robinson came to bat, Van Cuyk whizzed a fast ball past his head. Robinson hit the dirt. He stepped back into the batter's box and Van Cuyk whizzed another fast ball close to his chin. This led to a bitter toe-to-toe quarrel with Robinson threatening (according to reporters) to punch the six-foot-five, two hundred-pound rookie if he ever threw at him again. A coach prevented any fisticuffs and later Robinson and Van Cuyk shook hands and agreed to forget the incident. Van Cuyk admitted that he had thrown the first ball at Robinson deliberately "because he tried to embarrass me, to make me look silly when he was on the bases," but said the second ball had slipped out of his hand.

Robinson and Van Cuyk learned, however, that while they were willing to forget, the newspapermen were not. Two days later Bill Roeder of the old *New York World-Telegram* wrote: "The temper display pitting Jackie Robinson against a . . . farmhand pitcher means little to the Dodgers as far as intracamp harmony is concerned, because the participants are willing to forget, but it should serve as another hint that this is no longer the meek, inoffensive, uncomplaining Robinson who first appeared in the big league. The present Jackie is in no way a Milquetoast.

"In the future those who step on him, or on his feelings, are likely to hear about it just as young Chris Van Cuyk did yesterday. What began as a barbering session, a once-over-lightly from one bench to another, grew into a genuinely nasty name-calling, bean-balling spat brought on because Robinson decided he was being ridden too hard."

Robinson was irked that his "sensitivity" was blamed for the dispute, but he was enraged to pick up a wire-service story linking with the Van Cuyk incident his comment that "They'd better be rough on me because I'm going to be rough on them," making it appear that his comment that he was going to play hard baseball actually meant that he was going to be involved in fisticuffs and brawls throughout the season. Thus he was not surprised when, in Miami a few days later, Commissioner Chandler confronted him with a clipping of the wire-service story and warned him not to become aggressive. "I just want to warn you, Jackie," he said, "that if anybody starts getting rough in baseball I'm going to get rough on all of them.

"Your conduct during your brief career in baseball has been exemplary. Don't ruin everything by some foolish action now. I don't want to give you the worst of it, but neither do I intend to give you the best of it. I think you would be smarter to continue acting in the same manner you did during your first year in baseball.

"Just remember that such remarks could easily result in a riot."

Many writers agreed with Chandler, feeling that a quiet, docile Robinson fit the pattern they preferred, but one columnist, Bill Mardo, was incensed. He wrote: "Chandler's tête-à-tête with Robinson was in the same vein of absurdities that have become typical of the ex-Senator. Except in this case it was strongly tinted with the patronizing habits common to the Bourbon. Robinson must not be 'aggressive' is another way of saying a little freedom is okay for Negroes so long as they stay in their place. You're in the majors, Robinson, but don't try and do everything a white major leaguer does . . .

"By asking Robinson to behave as he did in 1947, Chandler is asking everyone to keep the clocks timed to that point in baseball history when Robinson was being presented very much as a ticklish 'experiment.' "

In the years ahead, Jackie Robinson was to learn with anguish that not many sports commentators thought as clearly or spoke as fairly as Bill Mardo, for few would concede that Robinson ought to be able to play with the same finesse and also the same fallibility as other players. He learned with even greater anguish that the criticisms expressed by certain newspapermen began to have their effect on the fans, so it became a common occurrence for Rachel to sit watching a game and hear a fan shout, "Hey, loud-mouth Robinson, you talk too much." Or, "That Jackie Robinson's getting too big for his britches."

Robinson was undaunted. Certainly the glory, the personal satisfaction he got from playing magnificent ball in 1949 was enough to convince him that he could not go back to being the meek, inoffensive rookie of 1947, even if ordered to do so. As a result, there were moments when it looked as if he would be involved in a serious disturbance.

In Ebbets Field in July, 1949, 24,000 fans sat in anxious

anticipation as Schoolboy Rowe of the Philadelphia Phillies strode from the dugout toward home plate as if eager to tangle physically with Robinson. Umpire Art Gore intercepted Rowe, holding up the game for several minutes as the two jawboned back and forth, with the umpire having the last word, as usual.

The near blowup occurred when Robinson came to bat in the late innings with Philadelphia leading the Dodgers, 5-0. Ken Heintzelman was the Phillies' pitcher. As Robinson took his position in the batter's box and cocked the bat high behind his right ear, he heard Rowe yelling from the dugout, "Knock him down, Ken. Bounce one off his noggin."

Robinson began to churn inside, the way he had churned for two years while pitchers threw bean-balls at him, hitting him more times than any other player in the National League. He remembered how he had had to remain silent although it had pained both him and Rachel to have a sports writer comment, "Some pitchers just can't resist that Coney Island urge to throw at Robinson's head."

"Now, with Heintzelman pitching a good clean game and winning by five runs, with no need whatsover to resort to bean-ball tactics, Rowe sits in the dugout telling him to throw one at my head," Robinson said to Stan Lopata, the Phillies' catcher.

"Only a gutless s.o.b. would hit a guy just for the pleasure of hitting him; Rowe ought to know that," Robinson added.

When Lopata went to the bench after the Dodgers were retired, he told Rowe that Robinson was offended by his remarks and had said that only a gutless s.o.b. would throw at a player just for the fun of it.

When Robinson came to bat again in the ninth inning Lopata remarked, "Schoolboy Rowe wants to know why you don't call him that to his face."

Robinson stepped out of the batter's box and turned to the Phillies' bench, shouting to Rowe, "I meant every word I said about you. You're gutless."

Rowe got up and strode toward the plate. As one sports writer put it, "He didn't charge out with the wild abandon of

a man madly infuriated. Rather, he stalked out with measured steps."

In any event, Rowe wasn't so eager to tangle with Robinson that Gore couldn't get him back to the Phillies' dugout.

This rhubarb gave new momentum to talk that Robinson
was a troublemaker, but such whispers went virtually un-
noticed amid the praise that followed his appearance before
the House Committee on Un-American Activities. This was
the peak of his popularity, and at that time not even Jackie
himself saw any real signs that the public which so idolized
him now might quickly be swayed in the other direction. Not
even Jackie could foresee that the man who routs the fears of
an insecure public is today's hero, but he who walks heavily
on tradition, who speaks in desecration of that old public
god, custom, is tomorrow's bum. Today's approbation is tomorrow's censure because the mass public mind is ruled by
emotion rather than reason. It is a mind without direction except that provided by the passions of the hour. Paul Robeson
was the passion of the hour that July day in 1949, and the
public mind absorbed only the fact that Robinson disagreed
with Robeson. Later, much later, the public mind absorbed
the subtler truth: that in the very essence of human things,
Jackie Robinson was more *like* Paul Robeson than unlike
him, for neither would make an easy pact with injustice. Neither was an "Uncle Thomas"—the modern version of a Negro handkerchief-head—willing to accept intellectual, moral
or emotional slavery if given a degree of economic security
and an occasional pat on the head.

It was soon obvious, however, that if Jackie Robinson was
the kind of man adverse publicity could undo, his social conscience would be his undoing, for those who label as a fanatic anyone with strong feelings quickly labeled Robinson a
"fanatic" on the issue of racial equality.

Many sports writers admired Robinson's determination,
his fierce competitive spirit, his daring on the base line, but
they were disturbed by the fact that he took his race seriously,
that he had a vocal sense of concern about social justice, that

he was as likely to start a conversation about a lynching in Mississippi as about one of his batting slumps. Robinson was just too aggressive for some writers. As a result, when some newspapermen were forced to speculate about which Dodger had instigated some outburst, or had been the moving force in some dramatic display of temper, the first inclination was to consider Robinson the culprit.

One thing the resulting controversies did was to produce lively newspaper debate as to how much a Negro ballplayer ought to say under what circumstances, and this forced many sports writers and columnists to do a lot more soul-searching than they had had to do over the basically more simple question of whether Negroes should be permitted to play organized ball.

Ed Sullivan, in his syndicated column, wrote: "The fact that Robinson is a Negro has exposed him to many pressures the white stars escape. It's about time that baseball fans take it for granted that Robinson . . . doesn't intend and shouldn't permit an 'Uncle Tom' attitude. There is no room in baseball or any other area of competition, for this contemptible type of thing."

What Sullivan was obviously pleading for was that Robinson be viewed in the same light as other competitors. This could not be, however, so Robinson's unhappiest experiences during those years involved writers who made him a marked man; used other Negro players to make him look bad; pointed to the most timid players as an example of how a smart Negro ought to act; bestowed honors whenever possible upon the least outspoken of the Negroes; and said to Robinson, sometimes openly, that he would get more recognition if he were not so outspoken. One of the most prominent men in the Baseball Writers Association said to Robinson at the All-Star game in 1951: "Jack, you've been absolutely sensational the first half of this season. I think it's safe to say that all you have to do is stay alive the rest of the season to get the Most Valuable Player award."

Robinson did not get the award, however, although he

batted .338, hit 19 home runs and set a major league record for second baseman with a fielding percentage of .992. This was also the year that he played his most sensational baseball in that Philadelphia game at the season's end to put the Dodgers into the play-off.

Roy Campanella, a fine baseball player, received the Most Valuable Player award. The baseball writer who had predicted in July that Jackie would receive the honor in a walk, confided not only to Robinson but to several others: "I don't want to take anything away from Campanella, but if you ask any impartial observer who is the guts of that Brooklyn team who made it tick this year, nine out of ten people would tell you 'Jackie Robinson.' But Jack has become too controversial. He's too quick to tangle with a newspaperman, to curse him out if he feels he's wrong. Newspapermen are human, too. They hold grudges and have prejudices, not all of them based on race. Some of them who would never have the guts to withhold recognition from Robinson when it comes to writing about him in the newspaper were very happy to get their revenge when it came to voting for the most valuable player. This was particularly so in this case, since they could do it by voting for Campanella, another Negro. That way, nobody was likely to raise any hue and cry that Robinson had been passed over because he is a Negro."

Questioned about this, Robinson says, "I hate to talk about it, because people are so quick to overlook a bigger issue and see only a motive of jealousy. I always tried to point out that it would have been ridiculous for Negro players to get green-eyed over honors won by other Negroes . . . There were enough to go around, and I guess I got my share. Campy was a great catcher, and he was worth his weight in gold to Brooklyn in 1951. For that reason, I could never say that I would have won the Most Valuable Player award, even had I been the most docile, sweet-natured player in the league. Yet the fact that some white writers thought so—and said as much to me—was enough to make me do some serious thinking about what my role ought to be."

By 1951 one thing was clear: Robinson had become one of the most "controversial" characters in baseball, and the reason had been shifted from the obvious and now discredited issue of the color of his skin to that of his temperament. He was being branded as a pop-off, a troublemaker, much more skillfully than ever was the case in his college days. This led Robinson to develop some extremely sharp opinions about the caliber of men who write about major league baseball. Listen to Robinson as he talks about his relationship with the press:

There are a lot of good, honest, sensitive individuals writing about baseball. Yet several sports writers with whom I came in contact were careless and gave no consideration to damage they could do to individuals and their families, either by writing things that they knew not to be true, printing rumors they had not checked, or distorting the facts in a true situation.

From the moment I entered baseball I was aware that I was good newspaper copy. I knew that many newspapermen concluded that if Jackie Robinson, the first Negro in baseball, made a comment it was twice as newsworthy as if a white player with no particular "notoriety" had made the same comment. I never resented that, because I knew that was the nature of news. I was also aware that the public likes to read about conflict, that to the general public as well as to many in the newspaper profession, "good news is no news," yet I never ceased to be amazed that my most casual remarks were often blown up into major rhubarbs, or that a newspaperman standing outside the dressing room would pick my voice out of a chorus of protests by the Dodger team and blow it into a page-one ruckus. Many of the most offending reporters rationalized their actions by maintaining that I was (and am) a headline-seeker, but the truth is that nothing grieved me more than to be involved in some useless controversy.

There are others who consider me naïve in that I always tried to answer newspapermen frankly, especially if they were questioning me on something I felt to be of genuine public concern. I do not regret these controversies, for I had done what I felt was a moral and civic responsibility.

Some writers liked to boast about how decent they were, how instrumental they had been in keeping me in baseball by writing nice stories about me during the first year. I always viewed those writers with suspicion, particularly those who kept injecting sly references that I was too busy fighting various causes and not busy enough playing baseball. I got a true idea of how those writers operate, and how deep their social convictions were, in 1953, when I appeared on a television program, *Youth Wants to Know,* and became involved in one of the biggest blowups of my career. A girl asked me if I felt that the New York Yankees were discriminating against Negroes. I wished that she hadn't asked me that question, for I had felt deep in my heart for years that the Yankees had been giving Negroes the runaround. I knew also that Negro leaders believed this, for they had had so much double talk from Yankee officials that even the most charitable Negro could no longer give the Yankees the benefit of doubt. And several writers had told me of conversations with people in the Yankee organization who confided that they would rather not add Negroes to their squad because it was certain to mean that Yankee Stadium would be "deluged" by Negroes and Puerto Ricans who would chase away all their good, long-standing customers from Westchester. I felt that I couldn't answer that girl dishonestly so I said that I'd played against New York in the World Series and had found the players to be real sportsmen and gentlemen and I did not think that they were against Negroes, but that if she was referring to the Yankee management and the fact that the Yankees were the only New York team without a Negro on the squad, then I did feel the Yankees were guilty of discrimination.

The next day, to my great amazement, a press hurricane had blown up. The Yankees' public relations staff really must have gotten busy; writers who covered the Yankees were devoting reams of copy to stories under big headlines crying, ROBINSON ACCUSES YANKEES OF PREJUDICE, followed by bitter denials by George Weiss of the Yankees. It irked me that the overwhelming majority of these baseball writers were sounding off about alleged comments made on a program that they had not seen. Only one newspaperman, Milton Gross of the *New York Post*, bothered to telephone me to ask what I really had said, why I had said it, and what I meant.

In Cleveland, sports writer Ed McCauley pounded out a long diatribe, which later was reprinted in the *Sporting News*, calling me a "soap-box orator" and a "rabble-rouser." Suddenly I was deluged with mail, the great majority of it unsigned, filled with vicious, insulting remarks, most of them referring to my racial ancestry. Some letters were stuffed with newspaper clippings about Negroes involved in crimes, with penciled notations such as: "Do you blame a nice clean organization like the Yankees for trying to avoid this?"

Some writers went through all sorts of mental gymnastics trying to produce a "motive" for my "slur on the Yankees," but few gave any thought whatsoever to the question of whether or not my remarks were true.

The *Sporting News*, still with misgivings about the presence of the Negro in baseball, said: "Robinson's attempt to play crusader will not be welcomed by [Larry] Doby or [Luke] Easter or Satchel Paige or Roy Campanella . . .

"A reporter contacted Doby, who said: 'I think [Jackie's] about the only one of us who is in a position to say exactly what's on his mind . . . what would I have said? I think I would have gotten around the question somehow. It's a delicate situation . . .' Campanella told a reporter: 'He [Robinson] was just trying to give an honest opinion. But I wouldn't want to be in that spot . . . considering all the confusion.' "

Faye Emerson, moderator of the panel show, telephoned me to say that she was amazed that so much was being stirred up over a casual answer to a question. This bothered me, too, but I was disturbed more by what I regarded as an attempt by some newspapermen to play that old game of "divide and conquer." They seemed to feel that if they could make me eat crow, then they could make all Negroes eat crow, but they were smart enough to see that this had to be done indirectly. So instead of coming right out and saying to their readers, "Jackie Robinson is an uppity nigger who doesn't know his place, so we're going to show him where he belongs," they said, "All we have to do is find some timid Negro ballplayers who will admit that they never had it so good, who are deathly afraid of losing what they have, and we'll hold them up as shining symbols of Negro manhood; the public ought to conclude that, compared with them, Robinson *is* a soapbox orator and a rabble-rouser."

Well, these newspapermen got what some of them were clamoring for. Almost before they could say Jack Robinson I had been called on the carpet before Commissioner Frick. I was working at N.B.C. at the time, right in the same building as the commissioner, so I walked from my office to his.

He was most cordial as he offered me a seat and we exchanged greetings. We chatted a bit about the weather, then before he could get on the subject of the Yankees, I said to him: "Mr. Frick, before we go any further, I want to make this statement: If you've brought me here to tell me that I'm in trouble because I said the Yankee management is prejudiced, we might as well forget it, because if somebody asks me tomorrow if I think the New York Yankee organization is prejudiced against Negroes, the only answer I can give is yes. That is my personal opinion, and it's an opinion that I have reached after weighing all the facts that have come to my attention over a period of years. If the Yankees want me to drop that opinion, all they have to do is give some Negro ballplayers an opportunity to make good. I'd be delighted to have the Yankees make a liar out of me. But I don't intend for the Yankees or anybody else to try to muzzle me to the extent that I no longer have the right of a private citizen to say what I please about what I believe to be racial discrimination. Now, is that what you wanted to talk to me about, Mr. Frick?"

Mr. Frick calmly agreed that that was what he wanted to talk about. He asked me to understand that he had called me in not out of any personal prejudice in favor of the Yankees, or personal opinions about Yankee guilt or innocence of the charges involved, but because it was his job to try to do what was necessary to prevent such controversies from hurting baseball.

I suggested that before he made up his mind even as to who was responsible for the press furor that he ought to get a transcript of the TV program and read what I had said. He said that he intended to, in order to determine whether or not the newspapermen had blown a simple reply to a question into a controversy far out of proportion to what might have existed. After chatting with the commissioner for perhaps half an hour I got up to leave the room.

"Jack," he said, as I started out the door, "I just want you to know how I feel personally about this thing. Whenever you believe enough in something to sound off about it, whenever you feel deep in your heart that you've got to come out swinging, I sincerely hope that you'll swing the real heavy bat and not the fungo."

I thanked the commissioner for his fairness and for what seemed to me to be an understanding that there are things in the world other than baseball, that there are other standards by which even baseball players have to live, else they forfeit all their rights as human beings in a free society. I told him that baseball had been good to me, that it had provided me with income and a national standing that I might never have achieved otherwise, but that all this I would have to give up immediately and gladly if baseball attempted to muzzle me to the extent that whenever I saw evil or wrong I could not speak out about it, or that if I did speak out I would have to do so on the basis of someone else's beliefs rather than my own.

I don't know whether Mr. Frick ever got the transcript,

but to this day I have heard nothing more from him about that incident.

Many newspapermen apparently felt safe in writing all sorts of rumors about me because, with my growing reputation as a pop-off, I might have a difficult time proving that they had really damaged my reputation. It's sort of like a newspaper editor writing boldly and courageously about a man who has been to prison once, kicking him when he's down, making all sorts of allegations against him, many of doubtful veracity, yet becoming woefully timid and afraid to write even a mildly critical editorial about the highly respected businessman in town who may be stealing the public blind through semilegal devices. When I saw how these things operate, I became angry not so much because I was the victim of the moment, but because I realized that so many people were being hurt by this kind of newspapering—people who did not have the financial resources or the accessibility of communications media that would enable them to roll with the punch, or to swing back with that heavy bat that Mr. Frick recommended.

One of the incidents most distressing to me grew out of that crucial game with the Braves in 1951. This was a game that could have changed completely that fateful 1951 season —could have kept us from meeting the Giants in a play-off that broke the heart of the Dodgers and was almost a personal tragedy for a real nice guy, Ralph Branca, who threw that ill-fated pitch that Bobby Thomson hit for one of the most dramatic home runs in baseball history. Late in that Boston game we still figured we would pull it out. However, when the Braves got men on first and third with only one out, we knew we had to keep them from scoring and take a chance of going into extra innings. Manager Dressen ordered the infield in close so that, on a ground ball, we would have to play at the plate. The batter bounced one to me and I pegged the ball to Campanella, who had the plate blocked beautifully. He tagged the runner so hard that he spun him around completely, but to our utter amazement the umpire, Frank Dascoli, shouted, "Safe." Campanella jumped forty feet into the air. Before Campy hit the ground, Dascoli had thumbed him out of the game. This infuriated our team, not so much because of what we considered a bum decision as because of Dascoli's hasty action in throwing out of our line-up a guy whose presence might well have made the difference in our winning or losing not only that game but the pennant.

We lost that game, and I have never seen an angrier bunch of men in my life than the Dodgers as we stalked toward the dressing room. We were even angrier because the umpires had to walk off the field with us, since their dressing room was next to our clubhouse. The Dodgers were shouting everything imaginable at these umpires, and I admit that I was among those shouting some choice remarks about Dascoli's lack of eyesight. Probably the angriest of all the Dodgers was Preacher Roe, who was not only worried about the fate of our team, which had been skidding and skidding, even as the Giants came on stronger and stronger, but was also angry because, if he'd won that game, he could have set an all-time record for pitching percentage.

Finally, as the Dodgers and the umpires neared the dressing rooms, most of the Dodgers strolled into theirs, but Roe paused at the umpires' door and gave it a kick that should have broken his leg. Instead, a big hole was ripped in the door. A few players laughed, because none of us had ever seen the little left-hander so infuriated.

That night after we got dressed and packed I walked into the hotel lobby only to see a big front-page headline declaring that *I* had become infuriated and kicked in the door to the umpires' dressing room. I was stunned. I saw the byline on the story and immediately called the newspaper.

"This is Jackie Robinson. Where the hell did you get that story?" I asked the writer.

"I got it from what I consider an unimpeachable source," he said.

"Well, I just want to let you know that your source is too

damned impeachable to suit me," I said, getting angrier by the moment. "There's not a line of truth in that story."

"Well, didn't you kick that door in?"

"No, I didn't kick that door in, and there are twenty members of the Dodgers who will testify to that fact if necessary."

"Well, I'll tell you where I got the story. A private policeman was near that door and he told me that in all the insults hurled at the umpire he heard your voice and that you kicked the door in. I was already filing a story at the time and didn't have time to check with you or I would have missed my deadline."

"Well, I'm getting pretty goddamned sick of you guys who think a deadline is more important than the truth."

"Well, I'm sorry, Jackie, because you know I've always been in your corner."

"Yeah, that's what a lot of newspapermen go around saying. Well it doesn't make any difference whose corner you're in as long as you write stories that ruin my reputation."

"Well, I'll tell you what, Jackie. I'll write another story indicating that you didn't do it. How about telling me who actually did it?"

"Nothing doing. Why should I tell you who actually did it? All that would mean would be that two players would have their reputations hurt. If you can find out yourself who did it that's your business—all I'm telling you is that I didn't do it."

The next day there was a brief story with a tiny headline saying that "Robinson denies he kicked door in." The writer still didn't have the honesty and the guts to run this information as a correction, to concede that *he* was wrong, that he had written a story only on the basis of hearsay. It was supposed to be a magnanimous gesture on his part to run this small item which was virtually nothing compared with the huge headlines on the story of the day before. Saying that "Robinson denies it" would still leave millions of Americans assuming that he was right but that

I was a liar in denying it. What was worse, the original story had gone out over the wires, leading millions of baseball fans to believe, to this day, that I am a foul-tempered character who takes defeat so hard that I bash in the doors and walls of dressing rooms.

I gave a lot of thought to suing that guy and his newspaper, but I became philosophical and said that it was the price I had to pay for an assortment of factors: being a Negro, having that shrill voice that's easily identifiable, and being what newspapermen and editors all over the country automatically considered good copy because of the circumstances under which I entered baseball.

Still, I never fell in love with the fact that any time I was near trouble, someone was sure to single me out, or to try to involve me in it. There was the time in Cincinnati, in 1952, when the Dodgers were really riding Dascoli because, in our opinion, he was having a miserable day. A few Dodgers even shouted "wop" and "dago," terms that I *never* would shout because I had always made it a policy not to "ride" anyone with references to their racial or national background. Yet I picked up a newspaper the next day and saw that Giles, the League president, had castigated the players who hurled these epithets at Dascoli and told the press that "Robinson was the worst offender."

Luckily for me, Dascoli was fair-minded. He pointed out that they all could recognize my voice and that at no time did he hear me refer to him with any racial insult.

What made me angrier than anything else, however, was that many weeks later Giles came all the way to New York, where they were honoring Campanella as the most valuable player, to stick in some gratuitous praise for me and to talk about how he and others in the National League were proud of me. Actually the guy was apologizing—months late—for a very damaging statement that he should have known all along was not even remotely true. As far as I was concerned his latter-day apology was worse than nothing. The time when I would have appreciated his apology was right after his statement, when I was deluged by letters from Italian people telling me how deeply hurt they were that I should make such insulting remarks about an umpire of their nationality.

Robinson was a target for some newspapermen because they felt that while Reese was the Dodger captain and, in later years, Walter Alston was the manager, it was Robinson who so often articulated the hopes and frustrations of the team. It was Robinson who told sports writers what he thought about various problems that arose, often to find that even writers he thought he could trust would double-cross him and attribute to him information they accepted only as "background material" with a solemn vow not to quote the Negro star.

The result was that, after Rickey's departure, even the Dodger management resorted to using Robinson as the whipping boy when it wanted to beat the rest of the players into submission. One example of this occurred when Dodger President Walter O'Malley made a three-year arrangement under which the Dodgers would play a certain number of games across the river in Jersey City, in the hope of luring a few more buck-toters through the turnstiles. After the first game in Jersey City, some Dodgers were almost livid with rage. They shouted angrily that the park was horrible, the town was bush and the fans were even bushier. They wondered aloud why on earth O'Malley would do that to the team just to get a few extra dollars. As usual, a Jersey City man singled Robinson out as the player on whom he would pin those quotes derogatory to Jersey City. As a result, Robinson found himself in an angry quarrel with E. J. (Buzzy) Bavasi, Dodger vice president and general manager.

In commenting on this episode, Milton Gross summed up rather accurately Robinson's relationship to the press, as well as to the Dodger management: "Despite advancing age and decreasing talent, Jackie Robinson has every reason in the world to believe he still is something special. Events of the first week of the season demonstrated afresh that you may like him or lump him, but you don't overlook him. When he hits they talk about it. When he doesn't hit they still talk about it, and when Jackie talks, his words are immediately translated into a rhubarb which leaves the Dodgers quivering like a plucked string on a hot bull fiddle.

"Anybody else may say anything and it's disregarded. Jackie opens his mouth and everybody rushes to put their feet into it. The tempest evoked by Robinson last week would have been nothing if any other Dodger had said what Jackie did about Walter O'Malley's Jersey City junket. As a matter of fact, they did. There wasn't a Dodger in the clubhouse who didn't pop off as much or more, but it was Robinson who found himself embroiled with a needling newspaperman, exchanging cross words with Vice President Buzzy Bavasi and being falsely accused by another member of the press of wanting to beat up an interviewer as an aftermath of his expression of an honest opinion.

"The sorry conclusion must be that honesty in baseball no longer is a virtue and Jackie's reward will be that he will remain a target for the agitators who, unfortunately, number a number of men in my own business . . .

". . . It was natural that [Robinson] should have popped off about the condition of Roosevelt Stadium. It was lousy.

"It wasn't necessary for Bavasi to have taken a verbal swipe at Robinson just to placate Jersey City's mayor, who was so eager to ingratiate his burg's newspapermen and his constituency. That's politics. But it wasn't politic to remind Robinson not to worry about playing 21 games in Roosevelt Stadium over the three years of the Dodger contract there. Robinson knows he won't be around for three years. However, to have warned Jackie he'd better worry about the next three months rather than the next three years, was strictly a bush league pop-off in keeping with the setup in which it was made.

"Bavasi explained his remarks by saying that he was angry when he made them and that he and Robinson subsequently thrashed it out over the phone and now have an understanding.

"So I ask Bavasi: If he has a right to get mad, does he deny that right to Robinson? The stooges who reported Robinson's remarks to Bavasi certainly reported the general reaction of all the Dodgers to the first of their road-company games. Was Buzzy merely using Jackie as a handy whipping boy to muzzle the rest of the players who recognize the comic aspects of the Jersey jump?"

13....Days of Dissension

Jackie Robinson's troubles with the Dodger front office were more serious than Gross or any of the newspapermen imagined. While his relationship with Bavasi was generally friendly, his differences with Manager Walter Alston were a substantial reason for the difficulties that plagued the Dodgers periodically. Jackie's relationship with Walter O'Malley, the Dodger president, was one of conflict and mutual distrust. More than any troubles with the press, these difficulties with the Dodger brass were leading to what Robinson knew would be the stormiest period of his life. As Jackie tells that story:

I knew from my first meetings with O'Malley that he and I were going to clash. Part of my distrust stemmed from the fact that I felt he had no social conscience, and I was convinced that he would have been a lot happier if Mr.

Rickey had never brought Negroes into baseball. He harassed Mr. Rickey constantly, and whenever possible, I was the excuse O'Malley used for needling him.

My first contact with O'Malley was in 1950, when *The Jackie Robinson Story* was being filmed. Arthur Mann, Mr. Rickey's assistant, tipped off Rae and me that there was serious conflict between O'Malley and Mr. Rickey and warned me that I should be sure to get to spring training on time. Mann said O'Malley was needling Rickey with questions about what would happen to his "prima donna" that year. I felt that if O'Malley was making insulting digs about me behind my back after my greatest year in baseball, what could I expect of him if I had a bad season?

Little did I know at the time that O'Malley and his associates had refused to approve Mr. Rickey's new contract and that he would be forced to sell out and leave the Dodger organization at the end of the year. His departure was a great shock to me, particularly when I saw what a difference one big man can make to an organization or a nation. I never had any real troubles with the Dodger management until Mr. Rickey left; after that trouble of one kind or another became routine.

One of my biggest blowups with O'Malley occurred during spring training in Miami a couple of years later, when I was injured and unable to play in exhibition games. Fearful that fans would not attend if word got around that I was not likely to be in the line-up, O'Malley called Rae and me over to Vero Beach, where we became involved in a heated discussion.

"I don't like your missing these exhibition games, Jackie," O'Malley said. "You know that you're the drawing card. The fans want to see you play. It's not fair to them for you to be out of the line-up.

"Furthermore, Jackie, I've had reports that you've been complaining about having to stay in a separate hotel in Miami. That was good enough for you in 1947. Why do you have to make trouble now?"

"Listen, Mr. O'Malley," I replied, "I took a lot of

things in 1947, not because I felt that they were good enough for me, but because I was convinced that it was important enough to me and to some of the things I wanted to see come about in baseball for me to grin and bear some things that I never was really able to stomach. I happen to feel now, though, that there are a lot of insults being suffered by Negro ballplayers that wouldn't be necessary if the owners would show a little bit more courage.

"And as for my playing in exhibition games, I just want to say that in all my years in sports nobody has ever accused me of goldbricking or giving less than my best for the team. The extent of my injuries can be established very easily by checking with the trainer. I'm not playing because I want to be in good physical condition when the season opens. It's more important for me to be ready to help with the games that count than to risk being out much of the season by aggravating an injury in an exhibition game just to pull in a few extra dollars."

O'Malley bristled. I knew that in talking about "a few extra dollars" I had stepped on his sorest toe.

"You're behaving like a prima donna," O'Malley blurted, "and I don't like it a bit. Other ballplayers, great ballplayers, play day in and day out, and they don't become crybabies over a little sore leg or something like that."

Rae jumped into the fray with both feet. I can't remember ever seeing her so infuriated before as she snapped at O'Malley: "Mr. O'Malley, I feel that I must say a few words here. Of all the things Jackie Robinson is, the one thing he is not is a prima donna. I've seen him play with sore legs, a sore back, sore arms, even without other members of the team knowing about it, doing it not for praise, but because he was always thinking about his team. Nobody worries more about this club than Jackie Robinson, Mr. O'Malley, and I say that that includes the owners. I live with him, so I know. Nobody gets up any earlier than Jackie Robinson to peer out the window to see what kind of day it's going to be, if it's going to be good weather for the game, if the team is likely to have a good crowd. Nobody else spends more time worrying about Pee Wee Reese's sore foot or Gil Hodges' batting slump or Carl Erskine's ailing arm. I know that Jack's heart and soul is with that baseball club and I want you to know that it pains me deeply to have you say what you just said.

"You know, Mr. O'Malley," Rae continued, "bringing Jack into organized baseball was not the greatest thing Mr. Rickey did for him. In my opinion, it was this: having brought Jack in, he stuck by him to the very end. He understood Jack. He never listened to the ugly little rumors such as you mentioned to us today. Rumors you listen to are things Mr. Rickey ignored completely. If there was something wrong, or if he heard there was something wrong, he would go to Jack and ask him, 'Is this so?' or 'Are you unhappy about this, Jack?' He would talk to Jack, and they would get to the heart of it like men with a mutual respect for the abilities and the feelings of each other."

While the white players were quartered at an air-conditioned hotel in Miami, the colored players were staying at a Negro hotel. The rumors O'Malley had heard about me complaining about our hotel involved not so much the fact that we had been segregated as the fact that the hotel had not arranged adjoining rooms, with the result that the two children, who were mere tots, slept across the hall where Rae and I could not hear them if they awakened at night. Now, with O'Malley taking it upon himself to reprimand me for complaining, I had decided to let go full blast.

"Mr. O'Malley, my only complaint up to now has involved this intolerable situation in which my family is placed. But I *could* have complained about the fact that it's a very crummy hotel. I could have complained about the fact that these reservations were supposedly made many weeks in advance, yet we end up in this kind of situation. And I *can* say today that it doesn't strike me too well to have people who sit in comfort in an air-conditioned hotel lecture to me about not complaining about where I live."

O'Malley seemed surprised by the response he had re-ceived, at the fact that neither Rae nor I was frightened or awed. O'Malley shifted his tactics and became diplomatic as he asked, "Well, Jackie, no harm meant. But won't you just *try*—won't you just try to come out and play today?"

Rae and I left that meeting in a most unhappy mood, for we had concluded that while O'Malley had resorted to diplomacy, he really had not taken that session too well. O'Malley wanted "yes men" around him, and he would ap-preciate a Negro only if he were the smiling, congenial, hat-in-hand kind.

I was later warned that O'Malley had a burning dislike for Rickey people, and I certainly was one. On more than one occasion O'Malley had made anti-Rickey outbursts in my presence—so much so that once, when I felt that I was being goaded, I said: "Mr. O'Malley, I suppose it's best for all concerned if we get a few things straight about Mr. Rickey. You're perfectly free, as you know, to hold what-ever opinions you desire about him. But your opinions are not going to change mine. I happen to think Mr. Rickey is a great man with a big heart as well as a big mind, and I say this without regard for the fact that I owe him an everlast-ing personal debt of gratitude. So, no matter whom it dis-pleases, whenever the occasion arises I shall always speak out with the utmost praise for this man."

Even after this, almost every reference to Mr. Rickey that O'Malley made to me was catty, corny, even childish in many instances. Also, instead of ignoring rumors, or com-ing to me to talk about them, he took them more seri-ously all the time. When Pee Wee Reese was thrown out of a game in Milwaukee, angry Dodger players shouted from the dugout at the umpires, waving towels at them. I had a towel wrapped around my head and under my chin. I didn't say a word, but my gestures said emphatically that I thought the umpire had choked up. The umpires glared at me, but did not throw me out of the game. Later, as we took our showers the Dodger players discussed this rhubarb rather heatedly and here I expressed my opinion about what a lousy decision I thought the umps had made, and how unjustified I thought they were in throwing Reese out of the game. The partition between our shower room and the dressing room of the umpires did not go to the ceiling, so they could hear us. The next day I received a telegram from National League President Warren Giles informing me that I'd been fined $75 for my conduct in the dugout and for carrying the argument into the locker room after the game. I found that I was the only Brooklyn player punished, and I fumed.

I showed the telegram to O'Malley, and really sounded off because I knew that in the dugout I had done much less than half a dozen other players. "And what about this business of fining a man for a conversation in the clubhouse? Does that mean that a player is liable to be fined if he expresses his personal opinion in his living room?" I asked.

O'Malley asked me not to say anything to newspapermen about the fine. I did not know whether he planned to discuss it with Giles or what. Later, however, I was sitting in a hotel coffee shop with a New York sports writer when a Dodger executive joined us and began to talk about the fine. When the story showed up on the paper O'Malley assumed that I had leaked it because I liked to see my name in headlines, and he needled me for some time. Finally, he found out that I was not to blame.

Also, O'Malley disappointed me by becoming concerned about some second-hand rumors printed by Dick Young in the *New York Daily News* about five young members of the Dodger team who were supposedly making disparaging remarks about me in Brooklyn bars. Young did not hear the remarks. Someone went to him claiming to have heard them and Dick wrote a sensational yarn about this being an indication that Dodger players resented me and some of my activities, particularly the aggressive manner in which I protested plays and "acted as if I were running the team."

I felt that O'Malley should have known it was inevitable that some players would resent me and the publicity I had received—that they would have resented my position on the team even if I weren't a Negro. Yet O'Malley made several small remarks about this unpleasant gossip.

What it all boiled down to was that I was not O'Malley's kind of Negro. After the Supreme Court outlawed school segregation, hoodlums in the South figured they could intimidate Negroes and decent whites by bombing churches and synagogues. Several bombings occurred in the Miami area, so some newsmen figured they could get a story by asking Negro ballplayers what they thought of the bombings. Naturally, I blasted these church bombers as the sick criminals that they are, and I felt that even the federal government ought to take steps to apprehend them. The writer then informed me that Campanella had said the way to prevent this kind of trouble was for Negroes to stop "pressing to get too far too fast."

I was irked that Campy, a Negro with children, should blame the bombings on Negroes who were asking only for their Constitutional rights, but I was doubly irked when, after stories were printed about my reaction, O'Malley went around accusing me of making "ill-timed and intemperate" remarks. With the future dignity and well-being of my children involved, could he really expect *me* to more or less exonerate these bombers by urging Negroes to take it easy?

I could no more do that than I could have gone on forever living in a Jim Crow hotel in St. Louis. I had gone to the Adams Hotel quietly at first, for the same reasons that I kept my mouth shut in the face of other provocations, but after Mr. Rickey told me the gag was off I felt compelled to express my dislike at being treated differently in terms of living accommodations from other members of the team. Aside from any feeling of racial insult, players sleeping in air-conditioned rooms at the Chase Hotel were likely to give better performances than those trying to sleep in hot, second-class facilities.

The Chase finally relented and I announced immediately that henceforth I would stay with the team. To my surprise and deep concern, the other Negroes were reluctant to move.

"Well, they didn't want me at first, so I'm not going over now. I've got my pride," Campanella said to me.

"We've all got pride," I said to Campy. "Organized baseball didn't want you at first, but you're in it now. Speaking of pride, I'm gonna be mighty proud that we finally reached the point where a Dodger is a Dodger and there are no second-class members of the team when we come to St. Louis. Furthermore, I'll wager that within a short time after we start staying at the Chase the hotel management will concede that accepting other Negro guests won't mean crap games and cutting scrapes in the corridors every night. We've got a chance to make a contribution outside the area of baseball."

"I'm no crusader," Campy said disdainfully.

I went to the Chase and the manager assured me that there would be no dining or other restrictions on Negro players. Dodger officials then ordered that all the team stay at the Chase.

Meanwhile, a minor press blowup about the hotel situation had occurred, and as usual O'Malley seemed to blame me as the "crusader" who had refused to let well enough alone, who had created a press ruckus when other Negro players were "happy" in the segregated setup.

I did not regret my differences with O'Malley, but I hated to see that his attitudes and feelings were rubbing off on Walter Alston, who became Dodger manager in 1954. Shortly after becoming manager, Alston came to me to express his hope that I would put out for him the way I had for Charlie Dressen, whom I had praised without reservation on several occasions. I wondered why Alston should have any doubt about my putting out for him. I told Alston that I was a great admirer of Dressen but that he need never worry about my giving my best for him because that was the only way I played the game. Yet I soon found that

Alston could not get over the notion that, because of my high regard for Dressen, I *had* to resent him.

I soon found Alston to be a nice, quiet man, but I never really respected his ability as a baseball manager, and neither did some other members of the team. I rated Dressen number one of the four managers I played under because he knew baseball and was always thinking ahead of the play at hand. After Dressen, I rate them in this order: Durocher, Shotton and Alston. The only way I can separate Dressen and Durocher is to say that if you have a winning team nobody is better than Durocher. He had the knack of stimulating winning ballplayers, pushing them to heights that were sometimes beyond their abilities. But with a losing team, Durocher would lose his composure. He got upset, he made players angry, causing some to play below their ability. Dressen was steady day in and day out, win or lose. One of the first things I learned from him was the positioning of players, which is extremely important for a base runner to know. If you keep in mind the picture of where the fielders are playing you know once a ball is hit to the outfield how many bases you can take. Always, when I would get on third, Dressen would point to the fielders, and when that ball was hit you'd know what to try and what not to try. With Alston it was completely different. When he was coaching at third he'd get a runner hung up between home plate and third base as often as not. Once I was on second when the batter hit a line drive to right. I had noticed that the right fielder was playing in close, so ordinarily I would have stopped at third, knowing I couldn't make it home. As I steamed into third, however Alston waved to me to keep going. I figured the fielder had fumbled the ball or let it go through his legs, but as I wheeled around third I saw the fielder's arm move forward as he pegged the ball toward the plate. Alston ran down the base line with me and, to my shock, as I got three-fourths of the way home, threw up his hands telling me to stop. There I was, all dressed up and no place to go. I was an easy out. Two days later Alston took himself off the third-base coaching job.

I place Shotton third, but not because he wasn't a sound baseball man. He was quick. Shotton's only trouble was that he almost never came out of the dugout. I like a manager who goes out to fight the team's battles the way Dressen did. Old Charlie would battle for you whether you were right or wrong. He might tell you later that you were wrong, but he'd never embarrass his players on the field. Charlie would fight your battles even to the point of being thrown out of the game, and the next morning, after he'd slept on it, probably give you hell for being wrong.

At one point there was real trouble on the Dodger team. I was a major factor in the dissension of 1955, and as I look back on that year I often regret that I let my desire to win, my temper, provoke me to make remarks that might best have been left unsaid. I realize that I should have done something to change the situation in 1954, when tension and conflict began to build up rapidly between Alston and me. Perhaps it was foolish pride that made me convince myself that I couldn't talk things out with Alston, so I kept waiting for him to make some move to ease the tension. Had I discussed the situation frankly with Walt, perhaps we could have avoided a situation where players were airing their gripes and criticisms privately and I was going around with little irritations festering inside me.

But it kills me to lose—it always has—and although that may not be justification for helping to cause open dissension on a team, it is the only excuse I can offer in this instance. Perhaps Alston was eating his heart out every time we lost, but I got the impression that it didn't bother him as much as it did me, and this feeling overruled every inclination I had toward what I am sure many of my friends would call "better judgment."

The biggest rhubarb began in 1954, during a game with the Chicago Cubs in Wrigley Field. We were trailing by two runs in a game that meant an awful lot to us when Duke Snider caught hold of a fast one and pulled it deep into right field. The ground rules at Wrigley Field were that a ball hit against the right field wall, but interfered with by a spectator, was an automatic two-bagger. If the ball was hit over the wall, of course, it was a home run. I watched eagerly as Snider's ball soared toward the seats beyond that wall, for I knew that if it was a home run it would put us within easier striking distance of the Cubs. I saw the ball clear the wall and hit a spectator, who doubled up as if in pain. The ball bounced back over the wall onto the field. Umpire Bill Stewart assumed that the ball had bounced off the wall and ruled that it was a double. I leaped out of the dugout and dashed toward Stewart, shouting that it was a home run. The two players beside me jumped up, too, and I assumed that they were right behind me, joining in the protest. When I got to second base, however, I realized that not one Dodger soul was out there but me. Alston stood at third base, hands on hips, staring at me as if to say: All right, Robinson, all the fans see you. Cut out the grandstand tactics and retire to the dugout. I looked at Jake Pitler, the coach, standing calmly at first base, looking to Alston for his cue. I felt like a fool, for I knew that this embarrassing situation would fit the rumors that I was a hothead, the guy always eager to rush out and beat my gums with the umpires when everyone else knew there was nothing to argue about. I mumbled a few words to the umpire and walked off the field. As I passed Pitler I mumbled, "No wonder this damn baseball team isn't going any place." Then I walked back to Pitler and said, "I'm sorry, Jake. Here I am cussing you out, when it's really Walt that I want to tell what I think."

The fellows in the dugout knew that I was angry, for many had discussed Alston with me. After the next inning, when I went back to the dugout, a couple of guys kidded me. One shouted, "You should have heard what Walt said when you were out on the field, Jack." It didn't take much to get me going, because I was still pretty sore. "If that guy didn't stand out there at third base like a damned wooden Indian, you know, this club might go somewhere.

Here's a play that meant a run in a tight ball game, so whether I was right or wrong, the play was close enough for him to protest to the umpire. But not Alston. What the hell kind of a manager is that?"

The next day one of the Chicago newspapers carried a photograph of the fan doubling up and clutching his midsection as that baseball hit him in the belly, showing conclusively that it was a home run.

Someone told Alston what I had said, but Alston made no comment about the situation for the rest of the year, in which we lost the pennant to the Giants.

I seriously considered quitting baseball after the 1954 season, even to the point of writing part of an article for *Look* magazine, which had purchased rights to the first story of my retirement. But there was still too much baseball in my blood, so I tore the retirement article up, as I was to do a couple more times in the months ahead.

I knew that because of the feelings of Alston and O'Malley, I would have to be the best third baseman on the squad beyond any doubt in order not to lose my job in 1955. Alston had commented that he hoped Don Hoak would show him enough to win the third-base job. I made up my mind early that I wasn't going to let anyone take that job, so I eased off the winter knife-and-fork circuit and went to spring training in unbelievably good condition, considering my age. Even in the earliest days of spring training I was playing well, fielding beautifully and getting lots of wood on the ball. The only thing I feared was that Alston would not allow me to play regularly. With one day in the line-up and two or three out I knew that I would get rusty because it would take me two days to get my timing back after each day of sitting on the bench. Just as I feared, Alston left me hanging in suspense. One day I was in the line-up, the next day I wasn't. As we started north after breaking camp I was deeply concerned as to how far Alston might go to make his point that he didn't consider me a vital cog in the Brooklyn setup.

When we got to Knoxville, Tennessee, for an exhibition

game and I found that I was out of the line-up again, I was really burning, because this was the fourth or fifth day that I'd been on the beach.

Here I made the mistake of not talking to the man responsible—Alston. I rationalized that all he would give me was meaningless double talk when probably I was just burning a bit at the thought of having to ask a manager whether I would get to play any baseball. I was egotistical, perhaps, to feel so confident that I was the best man they had for third base. The more I thought about it, the more hostile I felt toward Alston, who, I was sure, was paying me for that "wooden Indian" crack in 1954.

I knew that if I stayed anywhere near Alston I would get into a squabble with him, so I left the dugout and went to the bullpen to sit with the pitchers and catchers. Dick Young of the *Daily News* was there. I had a hunch that the front office always tipped him off on any Dodger development as soon as, or sooner than, other reporters traveling with the team, so I said to Dick (and this was a big boner): "You newspapermen usually know more about what's happening to the team than those on it. Tell me, am I going to play any baseball this year?"

"Well, that's one I can't answer, Jackie," replied Young. "Why do you ask?"

"Well, it's obvious that in my old age I can't play one day and sit on the bench four and expect to be ready on opening day."

Dick chuckled and strode away. Later I learned that he had gone to Alston and said, "Jackie wants to know whether or not he's going to play baseball for you this year."

Alston exploded, telling Young that any player who wanted to know anything about the team should come to him and not ask newspapermen.

The next thing I knew this rhubarb was being played up in the press. In Louisville, Alston called a team meeting at which he talked angrily about "players who run to newspapermen with their problems." He seemed to avoid mentioning me deliberately so I refused to say a word. But the more Alston talked, the angrier he got. I knew that he was trying to get a rise out of me, and my refusal to jump was really irritating him. When he couldn't move me with his talk about Young, he hopped back to 1954 and said, "And another thing—this business of players going around shooting off their mouths about who's a wooden Indian and all that stuff, that's the kind of business that's got to go."

That did it. Reason flew out the window. Soon Alston and I were shouting at each other almost at the top of our voices, and it seemed that we might come to blows. However, Gil Hodges tapped me on the arm. "Take it easy, Jack. Take it easy," he said.

I knew that Gil, one of the nicest guys in the business, was right. I didn't say another word.

The sports writers soon learned that there was something less than harmony on the team. Two days after I asked Young whether I would play or not, pitcher Russ Meyer complained to other players and a few sports writers: "Alston only pitches me against Chicago and Pittsburgh. If he doesn't let me have a regular turn, why doesn't he send me where I'll be appreciated?"

In fact, the writers had heard so much complaining from so many different sources that on April 6, in Washington, the reporters began to needle Alston about the fact that Hodges, one of the best first basemen in the business, was in left field, Reese, one of the great shortstops of all time, was playing second base, and I was not playing at all. Alston blew his top again. "I don't see why I should tell the damned press anything," he shouted, ". . . and as for Robinson, if he has any complaint, why the hell doesn't he come to me instead of the writers?"

I suppose I didn't fully appreciate the difficulty of Alston's position. He joined the Dodgers with no career as a major league player behind him and was taking over a team of old pros, so I suppose it was natural that he might feel insecure to some extent, might resent the thought of veterans on the club second-guessing him, or talking to newspapermen about who should be played when and where. I didn't appreciate these factors at the time, I guess, because I was too irked at the thought that Alston kept singling me out in his moments of anger.

Alston was fuming at me, and although he knew that the complaints were many (a week later in Brooklyn, Campanella was snarling mad after being dropped to eighth in the batting order. "That's fine encouragement he's giving me, having me hit with the bat boy," Campanella snapped), Alston was following the pattern (laid down by a few sports writers, a couple of the umpires and O'Malley) of picking me out to be made a "lesson" for the rest of the players. Luckily, we got off to a fantastic start, winning twenty-two of our first twenty-four games to open up a ten-game lead on the league. Some of us were so blooming mad that the only thing we could do was to take it out on the other teams.

Robinson remembers these troubles as making 1955 the worst year he had in baseball. First, he played in just over two-thirds of the Dodger games, and he learned the bitter truth of what the old-timers and the second-stringers always said about its being impossible to keep your batting eye sharp sitting on the bench. He hit only .256 and drove in just 36 runs, a paltry figure compared with the 124 that he'd socked in in 1949. Even his fielding had fallen off. He made 10 errors and fielded at an average of .966, a far cry from the .992 with which he set an all-time record for second baseman in 1951. Robinson wondered how much he could attribute to that feud with Alston, to his knowledge that the relationship between him and O'Malley bordered on open contempt. He recalled the many times that the sports writers had hauled out their funeral orations for "the old gray fat man" who, at thirty-six, was in the twilight of his baseball career. In the fading days of that 1955 campaign, his ninth in the majors, he had felt that the sports writers were correct. He was an old gray fat man with aching legs—but more than that, a man with work problems that would have destroyed the will to win in almost anybody else.

Yet when that 1955 World Series came along, the baseball world saw once again that even though old and creaking, the spring supposedly gone out of his legs, Robinson was the heart of a Brooklyn team that walked onto the baseball field with an inferiority complex, with a feeling that it was useless for them to try to defeat the New York Yankees. For two days the Dodgers played the Yankees the way the Dodgers were expected to play, and with the Yanks off to a lead of two straight victories, yawning sports writers predicted that the Bronx Bombers would humiliate the Dodgers by winning four in a row. But on the last day of September, Alston gambled with a young left-hander, Johnny Podres, to hurl against Bob Turley, a young fireballer whom many were calling the new Bob Feller of the American League. Podres pitched a marvelous game and went on to become the pitching hero of that series, but almost everybody in Ebbets Field that September day knew that, as Bob Wolfe of the *Milwaukee Journal* put it, "A creaky old man of thirty-six convinced the Brooklyn Dodgers Friday that they could beat the hated New York Yankees after all.

"Jackie Robinson, forgetting for this day at least about the silver in his hair and the age in his legs, rallied the Dodgers almost single-handedly from the coma that had gripped them the first two days of baseball's World Series. He batted and fielded and ran them to an 8-3 victory as 34,209 fans yelled themselves hoarse.

"Technically, it was Johnny Podres who beat the Yanks. The youthful lefty, by way of celebrating his twenty-third birthday, pitched a strong 7-hitter and struck out 6. Actually, however, the guy who did the job was Robinson, the one Dodger who everybody was sure was nearing the end of the major league line."

On that day the creaky old man provoked the sports writers to haul out their choicest gems of praise by proving once again that in a crisis, when the big chips were down, Robinson was a peerless competitor.

While newsboys outside Ebbets Field were hawking afternoon newspapers with front-page headline blaring, YANKEES

BORN TO WIN, the pigeon-toed warrior strode to the plate amid speculation that he was using his bat as a walking cane. The score was tied 2-2 and heartsick Dodger loyals sat hoping for the best, but secretly waiting for the Yanks to bust it wide open. Then Turley came in with a fast one and Robinson lashed a single to center. Jackie danced three steps off first and crouched over as a fan along the first base line turned to his wife and mentioned that Robinson now had a belly paunch that sagged a bit. Jackie danced off four steps, then five, then slid back to first as Turley fired over a fast one trying to pick him off. When the first baseman returned the ball, Robinson danced off again, swaying toward second. As Turley went into his motion, Robinson leaned mightily toward second as if about to steal. Flustered, Turley hit the Dodger batter, Sandy Amoros. Podres stepped to the plate, and Robinson saw the sign flash for the pitcher to bunt. Jackie dashed off second, chattering, "Come on, Johnny boy, smash it down his craw! Heads up, Johnny boy, I may take third on this pitch," and he leaned toward third as if determined to steal. Podres bunted perfectly, beating Turley's throw for a single. Now, the bases loaded, Junior Gilliam stepped to the plate. Each time the fast-balling young Yankee pitcher threw that foot high in the air and wound up for the pitch (he later dropped the windup so as to get better control), that old gray fat man on third would come rocketing down the base line as if on his way to steal home. The more Robinson danced, the more irritated Turley became. He threw four straight balls to Gilliam, forcing in a run. Shrewd old Casey Stengel stood disconsolately at the edge of the Yankee dugout, then strode methodically out to the mound, where he took the ball from Turley. A creaking old man had danced his pitcher out of the game. Tom Morgan came in to pitch for the Yankees, but before he could get organized he had walked Pee Wee Reese to force in another run. The Dodgers had scored two runs and taken a 4-2 lead and only one ball, Robinson's, had been hit out of the infield.

Nobody rested easy, however, even when the Dodgers stretched their lead to 6-3, because the Ebbets Field faithful had seen in years past that the Yankees could come back. In the seventh inning, however, Robinson reached into his speedy past to show that, if only for a few fleeting moments, he could still play baseball in the Ty Cobb tradition, and he sewed that game up for the Dodgers. With Tom Sturdivant pitching, Robinson sent a sharp-breaking curve screaming down the left-field line. It hit the screen that protects the Yankee bullpen and bounded back on the field, where Elston Howard, the Yankee left-fielder, grabbed the ball. As he looked up, Robinson was steaming into second, but he was rounding second as if he thought Howard had lost the ball. A second later, however, Robinson skidded abruptly, as if he intended to return. Howard, completely outfoxed, rifled the ball to second, only to find that Robinson's skid was temporary and that he had continued to third. Billy Martin grabbed Howard's throw and fired it to Gil McDougald at third, certain that he would nab Robinson, whose speed wasn't what it used to be. But Robinson was in a direct line between Martin and McDougald, forcing the Yankee short-stop to throw high in order not to hit the runner. Mc-Dougald reached up and the ball plopped into his glove, but when he reached down to make the tag, Robinson was resting between his legs, his feet anchored safely on third. A few moments later Robinson jogged safely home with an insurance run when Amoros singled. As Roger Birtwell of the *Boston Daily Globe* put it, "The old gray fat man had done what he wanted. He had shown the Dodgers, he had shown the Yankees, he had shown the world—that the Dodgers can beat the Yankees."

The Dodgers got the point, and they never stopped fighting, winning the series from the Yankees, four games to three. There was bedlam over all Flatbush.

14....A Farewell to Feuds

It was midnight. In the countryside of Fairfield County, Connecticut, the silence was heavier than the snow that weighted down the branches of the evergreens around the Jackie Robinson property. The forest that began with the adjacent property line was a blur of darkness, the thickly matted trees impenetrable to the cold light of a late autumn moon.

The slam of a refrigerator door broke the silence, and a prematurely graying man, noticeably heavy at the waistline, dished up a heaping portion of ice cream and drenched it with grape juice as he peered out the kitchen window at the tiny flakes of blowing snow dropping gently, then disappearing, into the lake behind his home.

Nobody knew better than Jackie Robinson that he stood

at the brink of one of the winters of his life. The spring had gone out of his legs, and it was more and more difficult to fire himself up through the sheer will to win. No getting around the fact that he was not a young man any more. In fact, he was ancient as baseball players go, except for those who seemed able to coast, to save a little something, as he never could, and except for those phenomenal characters like Enos Slaughter and Satchel Paige, who seemed to have joints made of butter, muscles impervious to strain, and bones unable to hold a pound of fat.

Jackie thought about old Satch and smiled wryly as he wallowed a lump of ice cream around in his mouth, remembering how his own bones had ached and creaked in the closing days of the 1955 season. And he had ached mentally because the season had been a bad one. But then the World Series had come along and he was in love with baseball and the world again, for he had played the way he knew he could. He was convinced that in just one more year, 1956, he could re-establish himself at the pinnacle. Then he would walk out of baseball the way he came in: to the tumult and the shouting of the crowds.

Robinson laughed as he said to himself: "Baseball is just like a poker game. Nobody wants to quit when he's losing; nobody wants you to quit when you're ahead."

Well, 1956 wasn't as easy as he had hoped it would be. His joints seemed stiffer than ever, and getting off the bench every inning became more and more of an ordeal. His legs were less willing to carry his weight around those bases. Weight—fighting weight was half the story of his baseball life, it seemed.

Age had taken its toll, but the turn of events also robbed Robinson of the challenges that had fired him up in years past. Only rarely was he the daring gladiator, the inspiration, that he had been to the Flatbush crew in years past.

But as it turned out, the occasional fires that Robinson lit were enough to rob the Milwaukee Braves of what seemed destined to be their first pennant. Some will remember

Jackie for his courage at Montreal as a Dodger rookie; some will speak of his base-running exploits during the 1947 World Series; others will point to that Philadelphia game in the dying hours of the 1951 season as the ultimate performance in baseball. But for sheer courage and determination, for clutch performance where it is desperately needed, Robinson may well have been at his greatest in a midsummer series that broke the backs of the Braves in 1956.

The young and frisky Braves, spurred on by a frenetic new major league audience, had rolled into Flatbush on July 30 to whip the Bums and open up a five-game lead on Brooklyn, which was in third place behind Cincinnati's crew of weight lifters. Brooklyn was a lethargic team, spiritless, indifferent, seemingly playing just to finish out the schedule.

On the night of July 31, with the scene shifted to Jersey City, Walt Alston looked at his bench as if finally concluding that the man who might help was there—sitting out games while Alston experimented with men he hoped would replace him. Alston put Robinson at third base—and the Dodgers were a new team. As one writer put it, where they "had been spiritless; now they snarled. They had slouched; now they strutted."

The reason for the change was soon obvious. The Braves took a 1-0 lead in the second inning when big Joe Adcock poled a long homer off Carl Erskine, but in the Dodger half, Robinson bashed one of Gene Conley's pitches even farther, with Carl Furillo on base, and the Dodgers led, 2-1. Then, in the ninth inning, Eddie Matthews smashed one out of the park to tie the score—but when the Braves filled the bases, Jackie snuffed out their dreams of victory by starting an inning-ending double play.

In the Dodger half of the ninth, Reese led off with a single and was sacrificed to second. Relief pitcher Dave Jolly was ordered to walk Furillo and set up a double play.

Robinson strode to the plate, a grim, portly figure, and watched two pitches whiz by without a twitch of his bat. On the next pitch he swung mightily and began his churning strides toward first. Billy Bruton, the Braves center-fielder, was off almost at the crack of the bat, moving back, back, back with frantic strides. But the ball screamed past him and hit the distant fence on one bounce. By this time, the Little Colonel was crossing the plate with the winning run.

The following day, the now-snarling Dodgers beat Lew Burdette in a 2 to 1 chiller, then the next day Don Newcombe (the guy they later said could never win the big ones) threw a 3-to-0 shutout at the stunned Braves.

As far as Milwaukee was concerned, the season ended with that series; the newly inspired Bums came on to take the pennant.

By the time the Series was played, Robinson was a walking reservoir of liniment and bandages. In one glorious moment, he rapped a line drive over the head of leaping Enos Slaughter to give Brooklyn and Clem Labine a 1 to 0, 10-inning victory over Turley in the sixth game, tying up the series at three games apiece. But the following day, in spite of all the liniment and bandages, the Yankees took the game and the championship.

The shouts of the series crowd were still reverberating throughout the Bronx when Robinson said to himself, "Maybe I've had enough of baseball."

He knew that the old challenge wasn't there any more. He still had the sporting instinct, the competitive spirit, to fire him up, but no longer was he a lone Negro spitting in a sea of prejudice, as if trying to make it run over. Negroes were now not just the backbone of several major league teams, but were being cheered with rebel accents in Florida, Georgia, Texas. How many years since he entered the National league had a Negro been named most valuable player? Six? Seven. Who ever would have guessed when a nervous young Negro played his first game in Jersey City that less than a decade later white southerners would be shouting in behalf of Negro members of their home-town teams?

Yes, who ever would have thought in 1946 that a decade later a Negro flier would be commanding the nation's air forces on Formosa, or that a Negro would help to set public school policy in the largest city in Georgia, or that one would serve at cabinet level in Washington, and another on the President's staff in the White House? Who would have believed that, after generations of Jim Crow, Negroes and whites would attend college and/or public schools together in Arkansas, Tennessee, Oklahoma, Texas, Louisiana, Missouri, West Virginia, Virginia, North Carolina, Kentucky, the District of Columbia—and that the nation would be turning itself inside out trying to find a way to make the practice meet the preaching in many other areas of life.

The big fight now was in education, housing, employment, and Jackie wanted in it. But was he far enough ahead to quit that poker game called baseball? The time to make up his mind was now, when he was between contracts with the Dodgers.

One morning in December, Jackie told Rae he had made up his mind to retire from baseball, an announcement that Rae did not greet with whoops and cartwheels; she had heard much the same declaration every December since 1953, but spring always found Jack heading for the ball fields of the South.

This time Robinson was more than serious. Dave Alber, publicity man for the Chock Full O' Nuts restaurant chain, had telephoned him to say that the firm's president, William Black, wanted to meet Jackie. Sensing that a job offer might be involved, Robinson expressed to Rae the hope that it would be a real job and not just some scheme to use him as a publicity gimmick. Jack wanted to feel that he was carrying his share of the work load, the idea load, in any firm with which he took a position, and he had emphasized this feeling by quitting a job at N.B.C. where he had a big office with all the mahogany trimmings, but little in the way of responsibility or work to do.

Later, when Black himself telephoned Jack to say that he would like to have him on the Chock Full O' Nuts team, Robinson's hopes rose that this might be the job opportunity he was waiting for. He called his friend and adviser Martin Stone to ask him to accompany him to a meeting with Black, which had been set for December 10.

Jackie walked from the telephone conversation with Stone and stared sadly out the big window at the rear of his house. Rae sat on the fireplace hearth, looking wistfully at her husband.

"Well, I've got a feeling this is it," Jack said softly. "As far as my career in baseball is concerned, I guess we've reached the final put-out."

Rae said nothing.

"I'd better call Bavasi," Jack continued. "Although this out-fit hasn't gone out of the way to make life pleasant for me since Mr. Rickey left, Buzzie's always been a decent guy. I'd hate for him to peddle Ransom Jackson on the assumption that I'll be around next year."

"You can't tell Buzzie you're retiring. You aren't even sure you'll want what Mr. Black has in mind. Furthermore, you've got an agreement to do an article for *Look* announcing your retirement."

"I'll just tell him that I'm doing some serious thinking about my future and that he shouldn't let Jackson go till he hears more from me."

"Well, if you feel the moral obligation, go ahead, but you know that if you tell any of them in confidence it will be leaked to the press. I can see that the honorable thing to do is to protect Buzzie, but you also have an obligation to *Look*. And the people at *Look* have been decent all the way."

Robinson called Bavasi's office and learned that he was in Chicago.

"I guess we've got to tell the kids sooner or later," Jack said, "so it might as well be now."

"Let's wait until things are more definite," said Rae. "We don't want to burden them with the responsibility of keeping any secrets."

The December 10 meeting with Black was a great success. Robinson was offered, and accepted, a vice presidency in the firm and the job of personnel director. About three-fourths of the chain's employes were Negroes, Jack was told, and there were some problems with rapid turnover, absentee-ism and the like. Jackie was convinced that he could iron out these problems, so December 12 was agreed on as the date for contract signing and for a meeting with *Look* editors to discuss the retirement article.

On Tuesday evening, December 11, Red Patterson, Dodger public relations man, telephoned Robinson to say that Bavasi had something important to discuss with him and wanted to see him at 11 o'clock the next day.

"I'm sorry, Red, but I have a couple of important conferences scheduled for tomorrow and won't be able to see him at that time. What's so important?"

"I don't know, er—uh—I'm sure Bavasi wants to talk to you about it."

"Well, I'll phone him tomorrow. That's the best I can do."

When he hung up he said to Rachel, "That was Patterson. Says Buzzie has something important to discuss."

"Do you suppose they would pick this time to come up with a managing job for you? Wouldn't it just be our luck to have this kind of timing?"

"Could be. It could also be that they've traded me."

"Oh, don't be ridiculous."

"Ridiculous my eye. I wouldn't put it past them."

It was 3:00 P.M., December 12, the day after Patterson called, before Robinson finished his discussions at *Look*— where he told the editors that he would prepare immediately the article he had promised on his retirement—and was able to reach Bavasi.

"Jack, I've got something important to talk about, and if it's no inconvenience I'd like to come by your house tonight."

Having decided that he would honor his obligation to *Look,* Robinson was reluctant to have Bavasi come by for an evening; he didn't want to get into a long conversation in which he might announce his retirement prematurely.

"Is it something we can't discuss by phone?" he asked.

"I'd rather not, but if you can't arrange a meeting, I guess we can discuss it by phone."

"I'll see what I can work out."

At 5:00 P.M. Robinson went to Black's office and signed a two-year contract. Afterwards he telephoned Bavasi again to say that a face-to-face meeting seemed entirely unlikely and that he'd like to discuss whatever was on Bavasi's mind by telephone.

Bavasi was silent for a while. Then he said, "Well, what I wanted to tell you, Jack, is that you're now a New York Giant." The Dodgers had sold him for $30,000 and a left-handed pitcher, Dick Littlefield.

I was stunned momentarily. I had heard rumors for months that I might be traded to the Giants—and to a lot of other clubs—but I never put too much stock in those rumors. Somehow, I just didn't believe it could happen. So much of me was wrapped up in the Dodgers that I suppose I wanted to believe—foolishly—that a lot of the Dodger organization was wrapped up in me. Buzzie went on to say briefly that trading me was a tough thing for him, but that the Dodgers felt they had to do it in line with their new plans for rebuilding the team. He expressed hope that it would work out to my benefit. Buzzie then asked, "What will you do?"

My first impulse was to tell Bavasi that I would offer him a coin so he and O'Malley could flip it to see who got the privilege of going to hell with those transfer papers, but I remembered my obligation to *Look*.

"I'll have to think about it, Buzzie. I'll have to think about it for a while."

As I put the receiver down I couldn't help smiling about the irony of my having quit baseball a half-hour before one segment of baseball was ready to quit me. I couldn't help uttering a few words of thanks that I had made my move before organized baseball made me a vagrant.

The Robinsons knew that to Jackie, Jr., news of his father's trade to the Giants would be horrible.

"You'll have to explain this to Jackie immediately," Rae said. "We can't afford to let him find out from the radio or newspapers."

"I'll tell him as soon as we get home," Jackie said.

He took the boy into his bedroom and told him about the trade. Jackie, Jr., bawled freely, unable to comprehend the lack of sentiment, the callousness of baseball, that could permit an organization to trade away not just the man he considered the best player in the world, but a man who was a Dodger institution.

"Don't worry, son. Everything is going to work out all right," Jackie consoled him. He wanted to tell him about the Chock Full O' Nuts contract, but he and Rae agreed that the burden of keeping a secret of this importance was too great to place on a nine-year-old.

"Don't worry, son. This is all going to work out all right," Jackie consoled him.

Meanwhile, Robinson had called Charles (Chub) Feeney, vice president of the Giants, to ask him not to make a public announcement of the trade. Robinson did not want the Giants to get out on a limb, but he could not explain his request to Feeney. So the trade was announced.

Now the Robinson household was being overrun by newspapermen, out to get another story from the player who had been their best single source of copy for a decade. Robinson gave them an assortment of vague answers which they interpreted in an amazing variety of ways.

With the press out of the way, Jackie and Rae sat quietly poring over the hundreds of letters and telegrams that came in offering Jackie advice as to whether or not he ought to play with the Giants. Two of the most interesting came from Dodger officials. Bavasi mailed Robinson's official release notice with the following letter:

Dear Jackie:

Enclosed herewith please find your Official Release Notice indicating your assignment to the New York Giants. This is something I never thought I would ever have to do, and as a matter of fact, I want you to know it was done with a great deal of reluctance.

Some time ago, I believe just before the season started, you wrote me a letter which I still have in the files. I appreciated that letter, just as I appreciated everything you did for us both on and off the field. I want to put this in writing, that you were a great deal of assistance in our scouting . . . on numerous occasions you helped us sign boys whom we would have lost. There is a great deal more to baseball than just playing the game on the field. I think you know what I mean.

I certainly enjoyed our association over the past six years, and I hope we can continue that association. Please remember me to Rachel, and to you both, our door is always open.

Sincerely,
(Signed) Buzzie
E. J. Bavasi
Vice President

A day later O'Malley wrote:

Dear Jackie and Rachel:

I do know how you and the youngsters must have felt. It was a sad day for us, as well.

You were courageous and fair and philosophical on radio and television and in the press. It was better that way.

The roads of life have a habit of recrossing. There could well be a future intersection. Until then, my best to you both.

With a decade of memories,

Au revoir,
Walter O'Malley

Robinson smiled. "I suppose Bavasi is sincere, but I know O'Malley isn't. He's the 'big' man being magnanimous when he's sure he's outsmarted you." Robinson knew things would be lively when word of his retirement was released, and he suggested facetiously that maybe they ought to go to Europe for a few weeks when the *Look* piece came out.

"No, I wouldn't miss the fireworks for the world," said Rae.

"You—the one who has flinched for ten years every time I got in some controversy?" said Jackie teasingly.

"Yes, but this one I think I can stand."

"Seriously, Rae, if the decision wasn't already made, I'd have to give serious thought to playing with the Giants. Stoneham has made a marvelous offer. And some of these messages coming in are real touching. I guess not as many people are angry at me as some writers would have you believe."

He showed Rae a postal card. It was addressed to "Jackie Robinson, one of baseball's greatest—*Stampford*, Conn.," and said, "Dear Jackie—For the sake of the many school children or New York, City. Please do not quit baseball they all love you so much. You have a few years left to play. We will be out there rooting for you next summer. Money means a lot; but it isn't everything. Please, please please. Signed —All the children."

"Doggone it, Rae, a card like that makes you hate to think of retiring. Every time I got a letter from some white parent telling me how proud he or she was to overhear his youngster shouting in the pasture nearby, 'I'm Jackie Robinson, I'm Jackie Robinson,' or to hear some other white youngster declaring himself to be Willie Mays, it gave me a good feeling, it made me think that indirectly I might be contributing a little something to the country by helping youngsters like that to lose their concern with race. Makes you kind of wish that you could stick around in baseball forever."

"It does give you a strange feeling. I feel sort of lost and your retirement hasn't even been announced," said Rae.

There were some experts who were convinced it never would be. Jimmy Powers had written: "We wish Jackie Robinson the best of luck in his new job with the Giants. We've always admired him as a player and a man and hope he can play for Horace Stoneham at least a couple more years. Jackie actually can't afford to retire. He came up to the majors in the era of high taxes and his top salary was $39,000. He purchased a nice home for his family in Stamford, Conn., and some of that mortgage still has to be paid off.

"Jackie never failed to give his best to the Dodgers and will go down in history as the man who broke the color barrier in baseball. Whatever he has left as a player, you can bet he'll give it all to the Giants."

As he read this, Robinson's high-pitched laughter bounced off the walls of his house.

"Same old Jimmy Powers," he said. "You'd think I wore glass trousers the way some of these guys pretend to know how much money I've got, and what I can afford to do and what I can't afford to do."

2

After the press furor about his sale to the Giants had died down, Robinson and his family left to visit their West Coast relatives while waiting for the *Look* story announcing his retirement. The story hit the nation's sports pages with a splash in early January, three days before *Look* was on the newsstands, because some subscribers got their copies early. A *Look* executive asked Robinson to rush to New York to be on hand for what was certain to be another hullabaloo. One of the first to leap into the new controversy was Bavasi, who called Robinson's retirement "typical of Jackie."

"This is the way he repays the newspapermen for what they've done for him," said the Dodger vice president. "He tells you one thing and then writes another for money. You writers will find you've been blowing the horn for the wrong guy."

Several newspapermen quickly adopted the line that Robinson had betrayed them, that he had misled them with remarks indicating that he would play for the Giants. Others who had no legitimate reason, even by their own estimate, to expect Robinson to give them first crack at the story of his retirement, argued simply that it was a violation of some vague code of ethics for Robinson to sell such an important story to a magazine and keep quiet about it until that magazine appeared on the newsstands.

Gene Ward of the *New York Daily News* wrote: "The best you can say for Jackie Robinson is that his exit from baseball has generated the same type of rhubarb as did his entrance. As the game's first Negro major leaguer, he was a controversial figure when he arrived on the scene . . .

"He spoke as he played—from a competitive heart the size of the diamond on which he displayed his talents. But the Jackie Robinson who covered up the fact of his definite retirement, who still acted and talked as though he would be in a Giant uniform come spring training even though his article for *Look* magazine had long since been written—that Jackie was not the same man.

"He may not have lied, but he skirted the truth . . .

"Speaking of his son, 10-year-old Jackie, Jr., 'he cried,' Jackie, Sr., said. The very small can cry when something happens to one of their idols, but not grown men, and definitely not sports writers who see them come and go, failures and successes, big men and little, guys with guts and character and guys with shortages of both. But we must confess a throb of disappointment in the case of Jackie Robinson. The manner of his leaving did not befit him."

Another strong attack on Robinson was made by syndicated columnist Red Smith, who asserted that: "If it's true that Jackie Robinson has, for a price, deliberately crossed his friends and employers, then it requires an eloquent advocate to make a convincing defense for him. From here it appears true and no defense at all is discernible."

Smith said Jackie "embarrassed the Dodgers, dislocated the plans of the Giants and deceived the working newspapermen whose friendship he had and who thought they had his confidence in return."

Robinson was disturbed by the comments of newspapermen, and he conceded publicly that Bavasi's remarks hurt.

The still hopeful Giants offered Robinson a one-year contract which, including some benefits after Robinson's playing days ended, would have meant well over $60,000 to him. Robinson agreed to meet with Feeney, vice president of the Giants, as a matter of courtesy, but he told news men that there was no chance whatsoever that he would delay his retirement.

"If I ever had any thought of changing my mind, Bavasi ended all that with his slurring remarks about my character," said Robinson, who pointed out the irony of the fact that Bavasi's remarks completely contradicted his letter of praise of a few days earlier.

"Buzzie's remarks hurt me more than anything that ever happened during my baseball career. I have always prided myself on my honesty with newspapermen and to have him say that I betrayed them is so utterly unfair and untrue that I can never forgive him."

Robinson was not without supporters. Sam H. Day, managing editor of the *New York Journal American*, said: "We have been chafing all week while we waited our turn to get indignant at Jackie Robinson. We felt we had to join his critics in scolding him for the way he announced his resignation.

"We know he must be wrong. Buzz Bavasi, his boss, has said so, and he represents the club owners.

"As a fan, we know owners are always right.

". . . We're still unable to get indignant at Robbie, darn it.

"On the contrary, we wish he would glance at the name of his new employer, the Chock Full O' Nuts Co., select the so-suitably-appropriate word, direct it to the attention of his critics, and then sing it out, loud and clear."

John Hanlon, of the *Providence Evening Bulletin*, took his fellow sports writers to task for giving Robinson what Hanlon called "a bad rap." Hanlon was particularly irked by the wail of certain newspapermen that Robinson *owed* them something because of favorable stories written about him in previous years. "Just what, specifically, an athlete owes to a man who in the course of his daily job is supposedly telling what a Robinson does right or wrong is completely lost on me . . .

"In the case of Robinson, his debt is very small. The boys got tremendous mileage out of him. For a decade, he was the bell-cow of the Dodgers, and it was almost ridiculous the way the reporters made for Robinson's cubicle after the critical games. Others may have starred, but Robinson, all knew, was the one who talked.

". . . Furthermore, and partly because of his lucidity, a good many of the working newspapermen cashed in handsomely on Robinson by doing magazine pieces about him. His story always sold and so he was not only bread and butter to the reporters' daily menu, but frequently their steak and wine, too."

Yet there were writers who spread far and wide the owners' propaganda that baseball had made Jackie Robinson, that without the Dodgers he would have been nothing. True, of course, in the same way Babe Ruth and Joe DiMaggio would have been nothing without the Yankees, Bob Feller nothing without the Cleveland Indians, Stan Musial nothing without the St. Louis Cardinals and Ted Williams nothing without the Boston Red Sox.

What those sports writers forgot to add in their exuberant efforts to give Robinson the rap was that, to a great extent, these teams would have been next to nothing without the stars involved. Certainly, as subsequent events have demonstrated so pathetically, the Dodgers, who were pennant winners or strong contenders for ten consecutive years, would not have been so without Jackie Robinson. In the fifty-seven years before Robinson came onto the scene, there were only four when the daffy Dodgers lured more than a million customers through the turnstiles. With Robinson as the drawing card, the Dodgers performed before more than a million customers at home for ten consecutive years. Yet in 1947, when the Dodgers drew 1,807,526 fans, largely because of Robinson, the Negro was paid the minimum salary a rookie can be paid. His peak salary was around $45,000, whereas Ruth, Williams, DiMaggio and Musial all earned $80,000 to $100,-000 a year, and more.

Robinson has told newsmen that he knew all along that he was being underpaid, but several times he went along with the Dodger management without stirring up a public furor by becoming a holdout because he had a deep feeling of gratitude toward the Dodgers for opening the door to the Negro in baseball.

How great was Robinson's "gift" to the Dodgers? Look at 1949, when Robinson beat out Musial and Enos Slaughter in a three-way, down-to-the-wire battle for the National League championship and went on to win the Most Valuable Player award? When contract time came, the Cardinals offered Musial a reported $80,000 and the aging Slaughter $35,000; Robinson signed for about $30,000.

Yet even to this day there are those in baseball, particularly in management, who would have the public believe that Robinson is an ingrate who took much from baseball and gave little. In 1958, for example, at a sports dinner, Robinson said: "I will always consider baseball a great part of my life, but it hasn't been my whole life." Frank Lane, now of the Cleveland Indians, followed Robinson to the dais and uttered this barb: "I'd say that Mr. Robinson owes everything he has to baseball. Without baseball he would never have been in a lucrative job as he is today."

Irked by this remark, Harold Weissman wrote in the *New York Mirror:* "When he copies the sentiments of the un-sentimental industrialists who operate the contemporary baseball cartel, Mr. Lane is caught way off base. As measured against the blood he contributed to an anemic sport, Jackie Robinson took an eye-dropper's portion out of the game. If there is an unfulfilled obligation in the case of Baseball vs. Jackie Robinson, the debt belongs to Baseball, which can never pay off in full."

3

Jackie Robinson, now steeled to controversy, walked out of the institution to which he had given a great part of his life, and which he was quick to admit had given so much to his life, regretting only that he had had to be in the midst of such controversy. Yet there was the consolation of the cards, letters and telegrams from the thousands of Americans who had no particular ax to grind. There were nice letters from ballplayers like Erskine and Brooks Lawrence—and, just as when he entered baseball, Canadians to stand solidly behind him.

The *Toronto Daily Star* said: ". . . Rickey has said Robinson's character was the key to their success. A fierce competitor, Jackie had in the early days to curb his angry pride. He ignored insults, and won recognition as a baseball player, on equal terms with others, whether white or black. Today ability is the key, not pigmentation. This will be the eventual result elsewhere: stone-throwing at buses, picketing of schools, will go the way of the cruel racial heckling on the diamond. And some day Jackie's greatest honor will come when he is simply a name in a record book, when, because there was a Jackie Robinson and others like him, future generations have forgotten there was ever a need for a Jackie Robinson.

"He has had a thrilling final season, an electrifying stretch drive, a brilliant series. His fierce self-respect has driven Jackie to retire, afraid of becoming a run-of-the-mill player, traded from team to team. We'll miss seeing him at the plate, or dancing down the third base line. But we're glad he took this course. Legends should not be degraded. He is a proud man; few men are more entitled to be."

Robinson considered that one of the nicest compliments ever written about him.

And there was Horace Stoneham of the Giants—Stoneham, who had had so much more to lose when Robinson retired, invalidating the deal, than the Dodgers—Stoneham, who had been a perfect gentleman as compared with Bavasi and O'Malley. "I know you had a big decision to make and I am sure only you could decide, so it must be the right one," Stoneham wrote. "All of us wish you success and happiness in your new career, but I can't help thinking it would have been fun to have you on our side for a year or two."

As he read that note, there was a lump in Robinson's throat. How would it have been playing for the Giants? he wondered. It might have been fun. Then he remembered the pain, the bruises, the charley horses, the creaking joints, the salves and the rubbings of those last two years, and he knew that his decision had been the right one. He reached into his pocket and clutched a handwritten note "from the desk of William Black" that he had received in the midst of the controversy:

"Dear Jackie—All I can say at this point is that I am proud—very proud—to have you on my team. I'll do everything possible to make you happy with us."

15.... Gentlemen's Disagreement

A fierce, frigid wind raged out of the northwest, hurling cascades of soggy snow before it. Chicago's State Street was all but deserted now, its neon signs a multicolored maze of blurs against an ugly, ominous night. Chicago was catching the brunt of one of those vicious midwestern blizzards that strike swiftly to paralyze great cities.

As the train sloshed to a halt at Lake and State, the dark, husky bareheaded man stepped to the platform, his massive shoulders hunched, his neck rammed down turtle-like as he sought to shrink inside his overcoat. Robinson's face showed weariness and strain, even beyond the permanent wrinkles of his brow, as he walked in a pigeon-toed gait now familiar to millions of Americans toward a friend who awaited him.

"Well, if it isn't the all-American soft touch!" said the friend joshingly. "Is America's most newsworthy sucker frozen to death?"

"Boy, this is rough," Jackie replied as he dashed inside the station, stamping the snow off shoes over which his wet socks had begun to droop. "What a stinker of a night."

"Yes, and you look punch-drunk with tiredness," scolded the friend. "Why do you do it, Jackie? You ought to get an agent, or somebody to say no for you. A few nights ago you braved a snowstorm to get to Waukegan for a speech, and all you got was some more lumps from the press. Now, with every newspaper in the country hounding you, with Rachel worried sick, I'm sure, because of the abuse the writers are heaping upon you, and with a rehearsal for the Perry Como show scheduled in New York tomorrow, here you are traipsing through a blizzard after giving another speech. Why the devil do you do it, Jack?"

"I promised them, Dave," Robinson said in a voice edged with irritation. "I promised those youngsters 'way back during the baseball season, and the fact that some writers are roughing me up a bit was no reason to disappoint them."

David Wallerstein looked at Jackie and shook his head. "No, Jack, I guess it really wasn't," he said quietly.

Wallerstein and his wife, Carolyn, had known Robinson intimately for ten years now; they had agonized with him during batting slumps, been angered by the bean balls thrown at him, jeered at umpires with him, shared his hurts and triumphs; so Dave Wallerstein didn't have to guess what was on Jackie's mind. Jackie was irked when friends or relatives accused him of being a soft touch, of letting too many people take advantage of his position as a celebrity. It irritated him to have people lecture about the "special hardships" suffered by those in the public limelight, primarily because Robinson knew that neither he nor any other celebrity was trying very hard to get out of the limelight. What if he did give more than he got on occasion? He was still a pretty lucky guy—a lot luckier than the people who tapped him for favors, for a handout or a free speech. Wallerstein also knew that no amount of argument would change

Jackie's views on the subject, so he decided not to pursue that line of conversation. The two walked to the automobile in which they would go to television Station WBKV, where "good Joe" Jackie was going to do another favor by appearing live on the station after the showing of *The Jackie Robinson Story*, the movie in which he had played himself.

As Robinson and Wallerstein entered the station, sports commentator Jack Drees approached them with a sheaf of wire-service copy.

"Say, Jack," Drees yelled, "since you let loose with such a hot one in Waukegan the other night, maybe we ought to talk some about that."

"Hot one?" chuckled Jackie, assuming Drees was praising his speech. "I was so blooming cold that speech never got off the ground."

"No, I mean your revelation about the Braves. Boy, is that stirring them up."

"Oh, that," Robinson said as a half-sick feeling surged through his chilled body. How had it happened? Yes, after the speech the youngsters had asked questions. One, apparently knowing that he neither drank nor smoked, asked if he thought it made a lot of difference in an athlete's performance. A thousand times before he had answered that same question by declaring emphatically that athletes cannot dissipate generally, or abuse their bodies with drink and smoke, and give a top performance every day. But this night, for some reason, he had been specific; he had said that some people close to the situation believed that the Milwaukee Braves lost the 1956 pennant because some of their key men were breaking training rules by carousing in the wee hours during the crucial days of the pennant stretch drive. As usual, a newspaperman had gotten wind of these remarks and was making them sensational copy across the nation.

"Are they still on that?" Robinson asked. He looked at the copy and saw that already a half-dozen people had gone on record assailing him as a "gossip," a "cheap character assassin," a practitioner of "Joe McCarthy scattergun tactics" in which everyone is assumed guilty because no one is named.

Wallerstein could see that Jackie was upset, as these press rhubarbs always upset him. "It's the same old story, Jack," he consoled. "Everyone close to baseball has heard that the Milwaukee manager dished out some fines to players who were violating the curfew. Several people know about one key Brave who was arrested at 3:00 A.M. for a traffic violation. The writers know the true story. But you mention it innocently in trying to impress upon some teen-agers the necessity for clean living and it becomes headline news. You'd just as well face it, Jack, as long as you live you'll be good copy—and as long as you live some newspapermen will criticize you."

In the wake of that ugly January blizzard, Jackie Robinson rode home from Chicago chagrined by the fact that another storm had blown up around his personal life. He gritted his teeth in disgust and asked himself over and over why on earth he had made those remarks about the Braves. Rae would be irked, and even though what he had said was the truth, he would not be able to defend his actions in the same way he had in the past. He felt that the moral issue involved here did not require him to point a finger at any particular Brave.

Robinson thought of Rae, of all they had gone through since that first painful, hopeful, humiliating, exhilarating trip to Florida in the spring of 1946. Perhaps it wasn't right that she should have to suffer through controversy after controversy. But now, with unprecedented fury surrounding his announcement in *Look* magazine of his retirement from baseball, with dozens of newspapermen moaning that he had "sold them out" by not giving them the retirement story, why did he have to add this new hullabaloo?

Rae, and even Jackie, Jr., would have to flinch under another welter of sly invectives: "pop-off," "hothead," "racial agitator," "troublemaker"—some reporters would write all this for their newspapers, and later, over their Scotch and sodas, they would talk more plainly. They would call him a big-mouth, smart-aleck nigger.

Riding home, Robinson tried vainly to sleep. He reminisced briefly about that glorious opening day in New Jersey in 1946. He tried to concentrate on that day in Washington when he became the "patriot of the hour" by denouncing Paul Robeson's assertion that American Negroes would never fight against the Soviet Union. How the press had loved him then, for he was not the prodding, demanding, exhorting American the public was to know later, but a Negro celebrity professing his devotion to "the American way."

Still, memories of these things were crowded out of his mind by recollections of his fading years as a big leaguer, of fans booing him in Jersey City and even at Ebbets Field, the home park; of Milwaukee fans filing lawsuits after a bat slipped from his hands and flew into the stands; of sports writers trying to play him off against more timid Negroes, of his differences with Walter O'Malley.

"And now this," he thought. "What the devil can I tell Rae? How can I explain to her or anyone else why I *have* to speak out, why I *can't* dodge questions that I think are of importance to the nation or to other Negroes? Why did *I* have to say that the New York Yankee management was discriminating against Negroes? Most people knew the Yankees were discriminating. The newspapermen knew it. Some admitted it to me, but wouldn't write it. Why did *I* have to denounce the dynamiters of those synagogues and churches down in Florida when I could have been labeled a "nice guy" by asserting that 'I'm a ballplayer, not a crusader'?"

Robinson thought of the letter that he had just received from another Negro major-leaguer and he felt nauseated. In a short handwritten letter, this Negro colleague thanked Jack of all the things he had stood for, for blazing the trail for other Negro players—yet, in conclusion, he had begged Jack to keep secret the fact that he had written.

I admire your guts and the way you stick up for us po' colored folks, but you're a controversial character and I don't want no trouble, so this word of praise is just between us colored folks: that, in effect, was what his Negro colleague had written, Robinson knew, and he asked himself rhetorically: "Why can't I live a nice, peaceful, cowardly life like this?"

Jackie had to speak out because deep in his heart he knew that no Negro, however famous, however great his contributions, was safe from the poison darts of racial bigotry. Crowds could cheer him, clubs could heap their choicest honors upon him, business tycoons could offer him great chunks of money, but as long as *any* Negro was unfree every Negro was unfree, for in the minds of millions the most accomplished black man would remain "just another Negro," as vulnerable to attitudes of racial superiority as any Mississippi sharecropper.

It took no special bitterness or suspicion for a Negro to see that throughout history wherever one group of men oppressed another the oppressors used a privileged few in the oppressed class to squelch any notions of rebellion among the masses of the downtrodden group. Jackie was determined not to be "used" in any games of "divide and rule."

As Robinson recalls, one of his most spirited—and most interesting—hassles with newspapermen was over this very issue. After an exchange of unpleasantries, Dick Young set out to tell Jackie what was wrong with him. Robinson relates what followed:

"The trouble between you and me, Jackie," said Young, "is that I can go to Campy and all we discuss is baseball. I talk to you and sooner or later we get around to social issues. It just happens I'm not interested in social issues."

"Well it just happens that I am," I replied. "If I've got to stop talking about race relations or discrimination against Negroes or injustices that exist in baseball just to stay on good terms with you, then we can't be on good terms."

"Well, I'm telling you as a friend that a lot of newspapermen are saying that Campy's the kind of guy they can like but that your aggressiveness, your wearing your race on your sleeve, makes enemies."

"O.K., Dick, we'd just as well get this straight: I like friends just like other people do. But if it comes down to the question of my having a choice between the friendship of some of these writers and their respect, I'll take their respect. I know that a lot of them don't like me because I discuss things that get in the way of their guilt complexes, but I'll bet you they respect me."

"Personally, Jackie, I put it this way: when I talk to Campy I almost never think of him as a Negro. Any time I talk to you I'm acutely aware of the fact that you're a Negro."

"Tell me this, Dick, what do you think of when you think of me as a Negro? I want to be thought of as a Negro, because I'm proud of my race; I'm proud of the accomplishments of Negroes. So the fact that you think of me as a Negro is fine with me. If you tell me that when you think of me you think of a whining, cringing handkerchief-head standing before you with his hat in his hand expressing eternal gratitude for the fact that you only had nine little digs in yesterday's story when you could have had ten, that's one thing. If you think of me as the kind of Negro who's come to the conclusion that he isn't going to beg for anything, that he will be reasonable but he damned well is tired of being patient, that's another thing. I want to be thought of as the latter kind of Negro, and if it makes some people uncomfortable, if it makes me the kind of guy they can't like, that's tough. But that's the way the ball bounces these days."

It irked me that Dick would expect me to swallow the talk about never thinking of Campanella as a Negro. People thought of him as a Negro when he was Jim Crowed at the Adams Hotel down in St. Louis just like the rest of us. They thought about him as a Negro for decades before Branch Rickey had the guts to break baseball's color line. They think of him as a Negro when he goes on spring training in the South and has to take racial abuse just like the rest of us. They think about him as a Negro when he goes to buy a house. And they'll think about his children as Negroes if he tries to enroll them in the school of his choice in many places in this nation. Young meant that he didn't think of him as a *certain kind* of Negro.

Dick and I parted amicably with him inviting me to join him at dinner soon. I felt that, irritating as it might be at times, Dick knew what I was saying—and deep in his heart he knew that I was right.

2

Rae Robinson looks back on those turbulent days of Jackie's retirement from baseball and remembers that her worry was less than Jackie feared. There were moments when she thought at length about the rhubarbs, moments when she wished Jackie had not spoken so hastily, and she told him so, but she never had to guess *why* he had spoken out. The one thing that did disturb her on occasion was the knowledge that these controversies had created a distorted public image of her husband, had become an invisible wall blocking millions from any knowledge of the real nature of Jackie Robinson. As Rae warms up to this subject she says:

Jack walked through it all without whimpering, but how little the public knew about the ways in which it mattered to us, and mattered deeply, to read the nasty, cutting comments. You could never get callous enough not to care, not when you knew that the world was populated by so many mentally lazy human beings, easy to propagandize, and by no small number of individuals who seemed by nature to want to believe the worst in others.

There is no use pretending that Jack and I or those close to us were indifferent to the furor in the press, because we learned during those ten years that individuals in the public limelight are to a great degree at the mercy of those who control and work for the mass communications media. To the average man in the average American community, Jackie Robinson was just what the sports pages said he was—no more, no less. He was the first Negro to play baseball in the major leagues. Everybody knew that. But beyond that, there was this tradition of Jackie as the aggressive competitor, the most cantankerous member of a notoriously cantankerous team, a bellicose, arrogant man with a penchant for arguing with umpires and shooting off his mouth at the most inappropriate moment.

Perhaps this is part of the price one has to pay for fame, or notoriety, or whatever it is that Jack has experienced. Perhaps it was inevitable that writers who, in their daily work, dealt heavily with the notion that Jack was a great competitor, should be unable to draw that fine line of distinction between being courageous and being pugnacious. There can be little doubt that millions of Americans were unable to make this distinction, and the one thing I hoped for during all these years was that something would happen to make the public realize that the real Jackie was not a belligerent individual carrying a permanent chip on his shoulder.

Although we lived in a fish bowl for a dozen years, the public really knows so little about Jack. They know the aggressive, fiercely competitive, courageous side of the life of a sports figure, a man many of them assume to be vindictive and bitter because of the obstacles he has faced, the rebuffs he has received. But so few know Jackie as I know him: a gentle, infinitely shy man who meets obstacles and rebuffs with aggressiveness and courage only because he views them as a challenge, only because he believes that the true measure of a man is the degree to which he can meet the obstacles and rebuffs of life and maintain emotional balance. Only a few people really understand that rather than view racial difficulties with bitterness and vindictiveness, Jack looks upon them as a special challenge to Negroes to become wise and strong and morally courageous enough to help give the nation and the world some of the leadership it seems to need so desperately now.

So many people view Jack as a man difficult to reason with, an individual knowing no compromise. How silly can they be? How little they know the extent to which Jack compromised when he felt that it was necessary for the achievement of an end beneficial to great numbers of human beings. There were dozens of times that Jack went to Cincinnati with the Dodgers and made himself a virtual prisoner in his room at the Netherlands-Plaza Hotel, never venturing to the dining room or to the other facilities in the hotel because a Dodger official had indicated to him at the outset that the movement of the Negro into organized baseball might go more smoothly if he would not press for equality in service and treatment at certain hotels. The official told him that Cincinnati was virtually a southern city, and that it would help all concerned if he would not assert himself too much too soon in this community.

The Negro was a long-accepted figure in major league baseball when Jack—at my urging—decided to pay the Netherlands-Plaza dining room his first visit. As we walked in the head waiter strode toward us with a broad and effusive grin as he said in an embarrassingly loud voice: "Mr. Robinson, finally you honor us by coming to eat in our dining room. We have wondered why you never came in with the other members of the Dodger team. We have been so afraid that there was something wrong with our food or our service. We are so glad to have you, Mr. Robinson."

How foolish Jack and I felt. How acutely we realized that so many rights and privileges available to Negroes go begging because someone has fed us the old cliché that people who "push too fast" do "more harm than good."

No, the public doesn't know the Jackie I know: a man made acutely sensitive to the needs and struggles of others because of a past so full of need and struggle and trouble that he could never become hardened to the difficulties of his fellow human beings. Those who write of him as an athletic madman and a social firebrand eternally wearing his race on his sleeve apparently know little about the Jackie who, if not watched, would quickly give the family's last nickel to the poor and hungry of the world. Jack is so tender-hearted that about the only way someone less close to him than I would describe him would be to say that he is naïve, a patsy, a sucker for someone with a real good hard-luck story. I remember the time in Pittsburgh when a man approached several Dodger players, complaining that his family was hungry and desperately in need of money to get home to New York. As the man introduced the dirty, ragged, apparently underfed members of his family, several Dodgers turned away, a few made token gifts, but Jack gave every nickel he was carrying to the man. No one could convince Jack that he had probably been the victim of one of the oldest rackets going until he left Ebbets Field a few weeks later to find the same man and his family approaching players with a story that he was desperately in need of money to feed that same dirty, ragged, hungry family and get it home to Chicago. Yet this incident did not transform Jack from a "soft touch" to the cynical, coldly calculating character that some sports writers sought to lead the public to believe he was, or that Mr. O'Malley apparently had in mind when he told a newspaperman that every time Jackie involved himself in a rhubarb it was because he had calculated coolly as to how to get some more publicity.

I remember sharecroppers coming out of the Deep South, trudging up to Jack with their pleas for help in adjusting to the cities of the north; relatives of Negroes in the bitterly embattled South, coming to Jack with the plea that he help the folks "down home" to get out from under the economic pressure of the White Citizens Councils —even the man who occasionally wrote a really nauseating plea for help, explaining that the damp spots on the paper were saliva, there because he was without arms and legs and "am writing my merciful plea for help with a pencil between my teeth."

Jack believes the best about everyone, sees great and ultimate good in everyone. When offered a long-wished-for opportunity to buy certain merchandise wholesale, Jack can't wait even a few days to spread the opportunity around to even casual acquaintances. Why? Is he the glory-seeker, the man with the ailing ego seeking to appear important, with his broad pronouncements that "I can get it for you wholesale"? No. It stems directly from the fact that Jack has struggled against poverty, has lived through the grim ordeal of economic want, has battled up that rugged road to something approaching economic security, and he has seen in so many instances that breaks, like the opportunity to buy a suit, a dress, a golf bag wholesale, all too often are available only to those who least need to save money. So this is Jackie Robinson protesting, in his way, that long-established law of society that "them as has gets, them as has not begets."

3

But it is not enough to say that the real Jackie Robinson is not pugnacious, not as reckless, as daring, as uncompromising as his athletic exploits have made him appear to be. It is not enough to say what Robinson is not; in our time of world ferment, of ideological and racial passion, it seems of ultimate importance to know what Robinson *is*. If people can understand what motivates Jackie Robinson, what makes him appear in moments of crisis to be consumed by rage, to be swept up in the imprudence of passion, then Americans may also find a better understanding of the forces with which they grapple throughout the world today.

As has been true throughout the history of man, personal rage often produces imprudence, particularly in the eyes of those comfortable enough and powerful enough to think theirs is the right to define prudence.

Robinson's retirement from baseball was dictated in part by the fact that he was unable to live with his rage against injustice, was obsessed with a desire to become a part of the conflict and turmoil over race relations that has produced for our nation a critical time of troubles. One thing that bothered him especially was to pick up the newspaper day after day and be struck by the stories of juvenile delinquency among Negro youth—to realize that he was reading about youngsters whose lives were being warped and twisted by their environment. Jack thought of these youngsters, cooped up in the dirty, smelly, rat-infested tenements of our big cities, north and south, of the crime, corruption, frustration and aimlessness that surrounded them, and he thought how hopeless it was for society to expect more of these youngsters without making it possible for them to grow up in a more wholesome environment.

"How easy it would be," Jackie says, "for me to find satisfaction in the fact that my children have escaped the ghetto, that my children live on five acres in the Connecticut countryside where a lake is nearby for swimming, fresh air is everywhere for breathing, and the opportunity exists for them to live their whole lives without fully realizing the plight of so many Negro youngsters. But only a fool would seek that kind of contentment. All you need do is pick up almost any issue of *U.S. News & World Report* to see that an effort is being made to discredit all Negroes because of the delinquency, the antisocial behavior, of a few. As long as any substantial number of Negro youth is trapped inside that web of violence and delinquency, with Jim Crow blocking the exits, the struggle of all Negroes for complete equality, for a position of respect under the American banner of democracy, is jeopardized."

Robinson believes that thinking white people of America realize this. What is more, they have begun to see what is happening to their cities, to see that the nation is much the poorer because of these wretched slums that stand as squalid monuments to the ignorance of men. Yet some strangely different psychology rules when they read of a Negro criminal. It touches emotional chords that are completely dormant when the criminal is white, and even the well-educated white man finds himself straining intellectually to keep from saying: "Well, that's what you expect of Negroes." Even if they succeed in fighting back the urge to make this comment, few can so suppress the recurring doubts that they will not ask themselves: "Why is it that every time they arrest a dope peddler in our town, it's a Negro?" Or, "Why is it that there are so many stabbings on the South Side of Chicago, or the North Side of Minneapolis, or the Jo Johnston district of Nashville?"

Robinson knows that the Negro is paying a double burden for Jim Crow housing. Sure, *thinking* white people know and understand, but who can be sure *how many* white people are thinking in this period of tension and emotions? Despite the rising clamor for an end to discrimination in housing, great numbers of people express disbelief that there is need for "agitation" against Jim Crow housing.

"Oh, you don't have any trouble getting housing, do you?" How many times Jackie has been asked that question by whites who apparently wanted to believe that only Negro "riffraff," only Negro dope peddlers and prostitutes, are denied access to decent neighborhoods. These people with basically decent motives would point quite eagerly to his home in North Stamford as an indication of the white man's willingness to give equality to "Negroes who deserve it."

Well, Jackie could tell them a few things from first-hand experience. So could Willie Mays, Ralph Bunche, Marian Anderson, Harry Belafonte and nearly every other Negro who ever tried to buy a house outside the so-called Negro neighborhoods. They had all found that, whatever their professional distinctions, to the power structure of the real estate industry, and, for an unbelievable number of years, to those federal officials who wield so much influence upon the nation's housing programs, each of them was "just another Negro" in the sense that they lacked the freedom to buy and live where they pleased.

Robinson remembered how pleasant it had been securing an apartment in Montreal with no difficulty, no trace of racial opposition, and the contrasting experience of looking almost without hope in Brooklyn, finally to have to settle in a miserable, drab excuse for an apartment.

But at least those miserable days of poor housing and very little money in Brooklyn had provided them with an opportunity to meet some wonderful people. Jack Semel, a New York businessman, gave them some extremely pleasant moments when they needed most to find things to take their minds off the racial experiment in which the family was involved. It was Semel who took them to a Broadway theatre for the first time—"It was *Brigadoon*," Jackie recalled, "I can remember it just as if it were last night." Semel was also one of the organizers of the first "Jackie Robinson Night," when the Negro star was given an off-white Cadillac which he and Rae received with the joyous knowledge that no longer would they be at the total mercy of subways and buses.

Finally, that second year in Brooklyn, they were able to rent half of a nice, sunny duplex where they didn't have to share a bath or the living room. But the acquisition of this apartment also enhanced their knowledge of what it means to be a Negro seeking decent shelter. Petitions had been circulated in the neighborhood seeking to block the sale of this duplex to the Negro woman who now owned it, and Robinson recalls that their moving into the duplex did not seem to lessen in the slightest degree the fears of white residents that utter calamity was about to befall them.

This is how Rae remembers their experiences:

Jackie, Jr., was about eighteen months old when we moved into that duplex. He turned out to be our good-will ambassador, for every time I turned my back he would disappear into a neighbor's yard where he would rap on doors to ask if anyone wanted to give him a cookie or pretzel. Usually my first contact with our neighbors arose out of my searches for Jackie, Jr., and I was pleased to note that once these neighbors got over their initial shock, they were quite pleasant. There was a family behind us, however, with a boy about eight or nine named Sidney who, although he was a great admirer of Jackie Robinson, baseball player, always waited to heckle and taunt Jackie Robinson, Negro resident of his neighborhood. Jack figured the child was seeking attention the only way he knew how, so he spent time with the youngster each day, with the result that they became good friends.

Our days in that duplex were made all the more enjoyable by the fact that here we met Sarah and Archie Satlow and the Covington family—people who did so much to make life pleasant for us and who have remained our dear friends down through the years.

Like most parents, however, we wanted a home of our own with a lawn and all the things that go to make for good family living, so we could hardly wait to buy our first place. As soon as we got enough money, we bought a house in St. Albans on Long Island. We had many houses to choose from, because this neighborhood was in the throes of what has been the traditional pattern in so many cities of the north: a few Negroes had moved in and great numbers of whites, fearing for their property values and their social status, had become panicky and begun a wholesale exodus. In turn, housing-hungry Negroes were flocking to this area in such numbers that one can only term it wholesale invasion. We selected an old house—badly in need of repairs, however—because it seemed to have wonderful possibilities as far as repairs and redecoration were concerned. I had studied interior decorating, and was eager to try my hand at the job.

A white couple lived next door to us, and I was delighted that they showed no signs of hostility. In fact, the man was unusually kind and helpful and almost fatherly in giving me advice about various problems connected with half-rebuilding a house. He volunteered his services and the comforts of his home when I was waiting for delivery of furniture, food, and so forth. I mentioned this to a Negro schoolteacher who lived across the street from us and she told me that this same man, at the time when she moved in as the first Negro in the area, was president of the block association formed with the purpose of keeping Negroes out. She said that he had called the police when her son began to practice his piano lessons and that he had done everything imaginable to make life miserable for her family. But after a few years, the teacher related, he had come to her and apologized for his previous behavior and said to her, in effect, that he now realized that he and the community would have been much better off through the years if every white family in the block had been as good neighbors as that Negro family. He also expressed appreciation for the fact that for the first time in his life he had the opportunity to know and understand a portion of his countrymen who until then had been total strangers to him.

I listened to the story of my neighbor and realized that, had I ever had any doubt, this incident was reason enough for feeling that racial segregation is a terrible thing in that it prevents human beings from having an opportunity to get to know each other and to develop the kind of understanding so necessary if there is to be peace either in our own communities or in the world. It created a feeling of both sadness and hope as I realized what contact (or, as Mr. Rickey would put it, proximity) had done for this man, and speculated as to how many millions more Americans might be rescued from the ugly seas of prejudice if selfish, irresponsible politicians would only permit them the freedom of association necessary to relieve them of the ignorance and passions handed down to them for generation after generation.

After five years in this neighborhood, we began to look for a place to build. We had come to love our home in St. Albans and to value the friendships that we had made there. We were particularly pleased that in the vast majority of cases where Negroes had bought homes in the area they had poured money into the property, redecorating inside, painting outside, relandscaping, and generally making those properties far more valuable and attractive than when they moved in. Yet there was one development that concerned us. As the community grew in Negro population we saw that young families with several children were replacing older families with few or no children, with the result that not only was the school becoming overcrowded, but it was becoming virtually an all-Negro school. Many people may ask, "What's wrong with Negro youngsters going to an all-Negro school?" We would say, "Nothing," if these Negro youngsters lived in an all-Negro country and an all-Negro world, but we were unwilling to ignore the fact that Jackie, Jr., Sharon and David were growing up in a predominantly white country and in a world populated by a great variety of people. We felt that if they were to

succeed on merit, to work out for themselves careers satis-
fying not just from a money standpoint, but in terms of
their own egos and emotions, they needed every possible
benefit of schooling and of social and cultural contacts. Only
a fool would deny that there are many intangible, but extremely important, benefits that accrue from going to
school with the people against whom one eventually must
compete. We wanted our children to have these intangible advantages—not to mention many very tangible advantages—of living and working in an integrated community and school.

We feel that not only do Negro children suffer from
going to an all-Negro school because, as the Supreme Court
said so eloquently, forced attendance at such a school
gives them feelings of inferiority and impairs their ability
to learn, but that white youngsters going to an all-white
school suffer in a great many instances.

Still, we knew that if we found the kind of property
in the country that we desired, it was inevitable that someone would say that we were going to the other extreme
of living in an all-white community where our youngsters
still would not receive the benefits of an integrated society. The simple truth is, as every Negro knows, that
there are few, if any, ideally integrated communities. Many
that are created do not remain that way for long, simply
because the pathetic but almost inevitable pattern is for
one Negro to move in, like a soldier securing an advance
beachhead, to have white exodus and Negro invasion turn
what for a brief period was an integrated community into
an all-Negro one. That is what we had seen in St. Albans.
To say this is not to blame the Negroes who flock in, for
these are people desperate to improve their social status
and the environment in which their children grow up, and
their housing opportunities are sorely limited. To say this,
however, *is* to blame the power structure that prohibits
Negroes from spreading out, from moving into residential
areas freely, with the result that the pattern of white exodus and Negro invasion would not be repeated time after

time. To say this *is* to blame real estate operators, Negro and white, who operate like conscienceless leeches, moving into neighborhoods where the Negro has made a quiet, modest entry, and using all sorts of scare tactics to convince white residents that they ought to panic, that they ought to "flee the black tide," which actually never would exist if whites refused to panic.

Knowing that the ideal situation was difficult, if not impossible, to find, we had a choice to make which, for us, was not difficult at all. We were convinced that the disadvantages of bringing our children up in a predominantly white community would be far less than the disadvantages of bringing them up in an all-Negro community. We also felt that someone had to lead the way in this struggle for integrated housing, and that if we lacked the courage to do it then we had no right to ask others to bemoan our plight.

We began our search for more living area, more privacy, more outdoor space for the children, and preferably a view of water, by answering ads in the *New York Times*. I found that house-hunting soon becomes something close to a disease, for I read ads with a passion and could hardly wait for the papers to be delivered on Sunday. My enthusiasm began to wilt at the edges, however, after I answered the first few ads. Some real estate agents gave me the familiar, time-worn alibis like, "I'm sorry, but I'm sure we just closed the deal on that house two hours ago." Others were more resourceful. They would invite us to make an offer on the house, warning us at the same time that "two or three other offers had been made," and that our offer would be submitted for the owner's approval at the same time as the other offers. It was here that we began to understand that in the purchase of housing the Negro has no bargaining power whatsoever. If the real estate agent told us he was submitting other offers, he quickly called back to say: "Your bid was too low. Why, one of my other clients made an offer two thousand dollars higher, and the owner even turned that down." We tried not to be suspicious, knowing that in instances of this kind we Negroes all too often go in with a chip on our shoulders, but after a few such occasions I began to feel that a chip was more than justified, for I was convinced not only that there were no other bids on the houses in question, but that our offers never were submitted to the owners. We decided, as Negroes must do in almost every instance, that the only way to find out whether we *could* purchase a particular piece of property was to attempt no bargaining whatsoever, so as to leave the agent and the owner no easy "out." So when on two occasions—one in Purchase and the other in Bedford Hills—we offered the total asking price, the agent simply said curtly: "That property is being taken off the market."

In our case, as seems to be the pattern wherever a Negro becomes audacious enough to attempt to buy a home outside the Negro neighborhood, word spread through the real estate industry like a whirlwind. There were all sorts of rumors about where we had tried to buy, what we had offered, who turned us down and why.

The events leading to our building in North Stamford were finally put together as if they were part of some great plan for us—just as had been the case in every instance where we had had to make a difficult decision as to which path to follow. Just when we had become most discouraged, indeed angered, by the walls of prejudice and guile devised to hem Negroes in, a reporter from the *Bridgeport Herald* telephoned us to say that his newspaper was doing a series of articles on discrimination in housing and that he had been told by two brokers that we had been refused housing in Westchester and in various parts of Connecticut. I confirmed this and gave him some of the details of what we had been trying to do, and of the rebuffs and evasions we had run into.

When the story came out it dealt largely with North Stamford, which surprised me in view of the fact that our "troubles" had arisen in a great many other areas. I was pleased, nevertheless, to see that there were people in

North Stamford who resented having the label of "bigot" pinned on them, even by suggestion, and who were determined to show their resentment by action rather than argument. Shortly after the article was published a man named Tom Gaines led the formation of a group of clergymen and laymen in Stamford with the purpose of doing something about housing discrimination. A member of this committee was Mrs. Richard Simons, who later was to become one of our dearest friends. Actually, we know very little, other than what we picked up through hearsay, about the actions of this committee. We were told that a petition was circulated in which residents pledged not to become parties to discrimination. We heard also that several ministers used their Sunday service to talk with their congregations about the un-Christian aspects of housing segregation. We never saw the petition, although we were told that many members of the community signed it as a pledge that they would not be a party to any discriminatory action.

The first we knew of what was taking place was when Mrs. Simons called and told me that a committee in North Stamford would like to meet with me because they had been trying to make amends for the housing rebuffs we had received, but that a broker had notified the committee that we really weren't interested in buying a house because I had rejected several places which she had shown me. The implication here, of course, was that the Robinsons weren't really interested in finding housing, but were only "troublemakers," stirring up various neighborhoods, or acting as advance agents for "blockbusters." When Mrs. Simons told me who the broker was, I remembered the places to which she was referring—two huge white elephants in Greenwich. I explained to Mrs. Simon that a Negro seeking housing in the open market faces two hazards: first, the prejudiced agent who poses the threat of rebuff and humiliation; second, the slick, insincere agent who views the Negro as a desperate customer upon whom he can push property no one else is willing to buy. I agreed to come to

Stamford to meet with the committee at Mrs. Simons' summer home.

She met me in her car at the North Stamford turn-off from Merritt Parkway and led me to her house. As I followed her I was conscious of my great apprehension about the meeting, of a great many doubts about the sincerity of the people with whom I was going to meet, but Andrea Simons acted quickly to restore my sagging confidence in human beings. As I got out of the car at her home, she came forward with a rush to offer a warm greeting and a handshake. I have never made friends too easily, but with Andrea I got the immediate feeling that she had deep convictions and courage, and I said to myself, "Here is someone I am sure I am going to like."

I found that not only were ministers and local residents waiting at Mrs. Simons' house, but also a real estate broker whom Mrs. Simons had asked to bring some listings and to be prepared to take us both out that afternoon. The broker had come with a list of about six houses for us to see. At each place, Andrea and I would confer and I would explain to her why the particular place did not meet my requirements. Finally, at the last place, the broker said in a voice of semidesperation: "I think I have a place that answers all your requirements, and I am going to take you there. But I want to be honest with you. Don't fall in love with this place until I talk to the builder, because the last time I spoke to him he said that he would like to be able to sell that home to the Robinson family but that he was financially dependent upon the banks and local merchants, so he would have to check with them first."

As we drove to this place, I kept saying to myself: "Here it is again. The power structure in the community dictating policies of Jim Crow. Bankers and businessmen feeling for some reason that their financial stability depends on "keeping the Negro in his place." This is why most of our communities are in need of some kind of fair housing law comparable to the laws enacted in the field of employment. We need laws to make it possible for men like this one to sell to whom they please without fear of being penalized by bankers and businessmen.

When we drove up to the place, which was barely beyond the foundation stage, and I looked at the spacious, rocky land overlooking a lovely little lake, at the thicket of trees surrounding it, at the little evergreens weaving in the brisk wind, I knew that the broker was right. This place met all my requirements. Andrea and I scampered over the foundation and the land, exclaiming over the sight. Meanwhile the broker huddled nearby with Ben Gunnar, the builder. When she told us that he was willing to sell, Andrea and I became so excited that the casual observer might have thought he had given us the property. I don't think I can ever forget the sensations that surged through me when I realized that after more than a year of searching I had found, and most of all was able to purchase, the home of my dreams. I don't know that I ever have felt closer to being a real American, closer to having lifted from my shoulders the nagging doubts and insecurities that are the heritage of the American Negro, than on that day when this broker, this builder, this woman, Andrea Simons, representing Connecticut citizens of courage and integrity, said to me in effect: "This house is for sale; you want it and you have the money; it's yours." It seemed so simple now, that for a moment it seemed hard to believe that these words were so impossible for some men to utter, so completely beyond the hearing of so many Negroes.

For a year and a half we went through that frustrating ordeal known as building a house. The Simonses had been gracious enough to let us move into their summer house in September so we could enroll our youngsters in school in North Stamford at the start of the school year. Instead of being in the Simons' place three weeks, as we had expected, we were there for six months. While there, we began to go through the experiences that many Negroes run from, to find ourselves thrust into unpredictable situations where there can be either embarrassment or great pleasantness. We realized why many Negroes preferred to continue in segregated situations rather than run the risk of embarrassment, and that this aspect of human nature was to a great degree responsible for the fact that the Negro had not knocked down many of the barriers—the fact that many whites could argue with conviction that "Negroes prefer to be with Negroes."

When the time came for me to take Jackie, Jr., to school I was worried. First of all, he had spent two years in an extremely progressive private school in Long Island where he had learned almost nothing. He could print, but he couldn't write, and he could barely read, so I knew that in addition to the social adjustment made necessary by the fact that he would be the only Negro in his school, he would probably be at a distinct disadvantage academically. Thus I began to understand a little better the heart-pangs of Negro parents in the South who are faced with decisions as to whether to send their youngsters to white schools where there are not only problems of social adjustment but problems of competing with white youngsters whose better previous schooling, facilities, cultural and economic backgrounds placed them in positions of advantage.

That first morning when I held Jackie, Jr.'s hand and led him into the little fieldstone school called Martha Hoyt, I was acutely conscious of the neat rows of children lined up on the front walk. I felt as though I was taking him past a firing squad of curious eyes, and I wondered to what extent he was aware that he was "different," that he was being scrutinized in the minutest detail. Someone whispered a little too loud, "Oh, look at the little colored boy," and I tensed up inside, but I did my best to give no indication that I had heard. But that moment has come back to me often in the past few years when I have read of courageous Negro youngsters in Little Rock marching proudly past a mob toward Central High School, or of Negro parents in Nashville leading their children past jeering hoodlums; and I have wept unashamedly at my realization that the pain and worry of these parents is infinitely greater than what seemed to me to be a monumental struggle that day in Connecticut.

I was relieved when Mrs. Riordan, the assistant principal, came forward to greet us, for it gave me someone to talk to. I felt even better after I meet Miss Carlucci, the wonderful, dedicated teacher who not only made Jackie, Jr., feel at home, but who saw to it personally that he made two grades in one year.

Sharon was to enter kindergarten in another school. My pleasant experiecnes at Martha Hoyt School did not lessen my apprehension in the slightest degree when the time came to take her to school. Happily, as we got out of the car in the parking lot a very attractive woman walked over to me with a big smile and said, "I'm Sandy Amussen. Will your little girl be in kindergarten with my son, Chris?" I sensed that here was more than contrived politeness, and it pleased me greatly to know that Sharon had a pal even before entering school.

When finally we moved into our new home (although it was still far from completed), at least one adult member of practically every family on our road came to call and to welcome us to the community. It was a unique and thrilling experience, especially in view of the old saying about a person living in New York for decades without ever knowing his next-door neighbor. Even in Brooklyn and Long Island there were many neighbors whom we had seen only when we called to pick up our children. We got the feeling of really being welcomed to the Stamford community.

The only adverse comment we heard was from one neighbor who expressed fear that we would hurt the value of his property. Another family panicked and sold their house at a sacrifice price before we moved in. No doubt a great deal more was said. Indeed, it is unreasonable to assume that white people could be a party to what really is a basic change in their neighborhood pattern and perhaps ultimately a basic change in their way of thinking without a great deal of discussion, any more than Negroes could participate in such change without discussing it. What was important to us was that we became part of the community in every way that we found time to be. We were invited to and subsequently joined North Stamford Congregational Church because we wanted a church home and religious instruction for our children. We began to participate quite fully in community activities. Jackie, Jr., took on Cub Scouts and Little League affiliations, and Sharon joined the Brownies and a ballet group. David found his own circle of little friends.

This is not completely a "they lived happily ever after" story, however, because both Jack and I were disturbed when a Negro newspaperman accused us of "running away" from the problems of the great masses of Negroes by seeking to "escape" into the suburbs of Connecticut. Nothing could be farther from the truth, and anyone with the remotest knowledge of Jack must understand that no amount of wealth, no kind of position or status in any white society would make him cease to identify with the great mass of Negroes struggling for equality of opportunity. Likewise, anyone who knows Jack knows that we form our friendships strictly on the basis of common interests, of mutual respect and admiration, and that the race, religion, economic status or social level of an individual plays no part whatsoever in our selection of friends. We do not want our youngsters to grow up with an aloofness toward the problems of the great mass of Negroes, so we have made a conscious effort to provide them with Negro friends. We are not so naïve as to be unaware of the fact that as soon as our youngsters reach the teens many of their white playmates of today will probably be less "available." At the same time, we are making a subtle but persistent effort to instill in our children a racial pride as well as a national pride, to give them an understanding and appreciation of the great barriers that the American

Negro has to overcome. We want our children to be familiar with Negro history, to be proud of Negro personalities and achievement, to know and love those things that are part of the Negro's special culture and have become a part of American culture.

Our ultimate desire, of course, is that our children have the same opportunities and benefits that white parents want for their children. We are attempting to help our youngsters develop the necessary tools for dealing with life in all its complexities, for we never want them to feel that they must use their race as an alibi for mediocrity. We want them to be prepared to meet such opportunities as may come to them. We don't want them to feel mistreated and bitter when they are rejected, but to feel unafraid and challenged.

Our years in Stamford have convinced us that they will be far better equipped to do these things as a result of having been exposed to all kinds of people, rather than to have spent all their young lives within the confines of a Negro world only to find that as adults they will have to compete with groups of people whom they have never had a chance to know. Even now I see signs in my children of poise and confidence as they move among others in a variety of settings, and I am pleased to note with certainty that they are far more poised than I was at their age. We have seen, of course, that to expose a youngster to white society must expose that youngster, also, to little barbs and sly innuendoes, but this has not bothered us because we have been able to provide them with the answers necessary to prevent any diminishing of their self-respect. The only really difficult explanation I have had was when I had to explain to Jackie, Jr., the reason why his father wasn't "good enough" to play golf at a country club owned by the father of one of his classmates.

Rae was referring to one of the most hotly discussed "racial" incidents ever to occur in the Stamford area. This is how Jackie tells the story:

It all began when Carl Rosen, a long-time golfing buddy of mine, asked me to be his guest at the High Ridge Country Club, which is only a couple of good wood shots from my house. I was delighted to do this, first of all because I am an ardent golfer, and secondly because I felt proud of what members of this club were trying to do. It was less than two decades ago that this was one of those "we're-all-native-born-Protestant-Gentiles" clubs. In that period, I understand, there was no place in the Stamford area where a Jewish person could play golf. Then Milton Friedman bought High Ridge, which had disbanded a few years earlier, and fixed it up. He turned it into what was to be the area's first nondenominational, nonracial club. It was agreed that the club would have a board of governors one-third Jewish, one-third Catholic and one-third Protestant. At the time I first went up with Rosen I was told that about seventy-five percent of the members were Jewish, with a mixture of Italian Catholics and Protestants of various national backgrounds.

I learned months later of an incident in which Rosen was involved shortly after I began golfing with him there. As Rosen tells it, after one of our outings I had to dash away quickly for another appointment. When he neared the club house he was accosted by a member who said, "Say, Carl, this Robinson has been a guest every week for more than a month now."

"Yes, I know," Rosen replied.

"Well, you know what the guest rules are," the member continued. "The same guest can come only once a month."

"I know, but this is after Labor Day and there's no one on the course, so what does it hurt if Jackie plays more than once a month?"

"Yeah, but he's colored, and it looks kind of strange for him to come here every week."

Rosen bristled at this mention of my color. He stared at the member and replied sharply, "To hell with you!"

"Wait a minute, Carl," said the member. "We're friends,

and I just thought I'd mention it to you in case you hadn't figured that it might look strange."

"Are you mentioning it as an individual or as a member of the club committee?" Rosen asked.

"As an individual."

"Thanks. All right, so the rules say I can't bring Robinson here that often. I'll bring Ralph Bunche next week, is that O.K.?"

The complaining member flushed redder. Angered by Rosen's sarcasm, he snapped, "Yeah, you bring Bunche. I'll bring my maid."

Rosen spat on the floor by the protester's feet and walked away.

For weeks, Rosen didn't mention this incident to me. He did tell me, however, that several members of the club had suggested that I be asked to become a member. They felt, though, that since my baseball kept me away most of the summer, it wasn't fair to make me pay regular membership fees. I agreed, especially in view of my knowledge that we would be joining this club only for my golfing convenience, because Rae had stated emphatically many times that she had no social desire whatsoever to join a country club. She had said that she preferred to entertain her friends at home.

However, when club members told Rosen that it wasn't fair for me to be his personal guest at his personal expense each week and suggested that I be permitted to come each week as a guest of the entire club, I told Rosen that I wouldn't like sponging off the members of the club, that I could afford to pay and felt I should do so just as the others did.

"O.K., Jack," he said. "I'll tell the boys that you prefer to be a paying member."

Rosen, John Hammond and a few other members went to Irving Krassner, the new owner of the club, and told him that they were proposing me for membership. Krassner said he'd be delighted to have the Robinson family, and that if it was O.K. with the club's members it would be fine with him, but that the application ought to be put before the board of admissions.

Rosen reported that when the matter went before the board, one ex-southerner came to the meeting to object, but he was quickly silenced and my membership was approved unanimously. A few days later I was playing golf with Rosen at the club when I heard a member yell to Rosen from an adjoining fairway, "Did you give Jackie that application?"

Rosen yelled back that he hadn't yet, but that he would do so promptly.

As we walked off the eighteenth green I noticed that, as usual, I was late for an appointment and would not have time to sit around. Rosen went to the clubhouse alone to find Krassner awaiting him, "white as a sheet," as Rosen put it.

"I don't know what to do," said Krassner. A group of women (later reported to be eight) had come to him to say that they didn't "give a good god damn what the men want," but that "if the Robinson family comes into this club we go out."

"You know, I'm losing money with this club now," Krassner said to Rosen, "so I don't know what to do."

"You'll lose with Robinson? Hell, you'll gain members!" Rosen replied.

"All I know is that I'm losing money now. I know I've got those eight members now, but I don't know what I'll get if they pull out."

Rosen told me that Krassner had "chickened out." He said that one zealous anti-Negro member had gathered a handful of women and swayed the whole club.

I talked to Krassner, telling him that I had not been campaigning to get into the club, but that I simply felt I was able to pay my own way, and if he felt his financial investment was more important than the issue at stake, that I was not the one to lecture him. Certainly I had no intentions of harassing him because of this decision. Several weeks later, however, the story of what had happened at High Ridge leaked out when John Hammond mentioned the incident to a reporter on the *New York Post*, explaining that he (Hammond) had resigned because of this. When the *Post* called me to ask if Hammond's story was true I confirmed it. The next thing I knew the Stamford papers and Walter Winchell had picked it up.

This set in motion an almost comical round of semi-apologies and rationalizations from friends and acquaintances, many of whom felt constrained to tell us that they would resign in protest, too, but that they thought it best to stay in the club and "work at the problem from the inside."

At first we were tempted to tell our friends that they need not offer us excuses for any pacts they felt they had to make with snobbery. As we thought about it, we realized that these were friends who loved golf, who had long been barred from other clubs, and we wondered how much right we had to ask them to resign, to give up what they had now achieved, as a gesture of friendship for us.

Knowing that we had no legal or moral right to *demand* membership in High Ridge, we decided not to pressure our friends (some of whom did resign), but to see what toll time might take on the consciences of the club's members.

It would be nice to conclude this chapter with a report that the High Ridge controversy was resolved happily in the same way that the controversy over Negroes entering baseball was resolved, but that is not possible. The minority of objectors won, some members resigned and Robinson ceased to play golf at High Ridge. Some members of the club continued a campaign to open up membership to the Robinsons, or to any other couple meeting membership standards that are not based on race or religion.

"We do not, and will not, press this issue," Rae explains. "We realize that no legal or constitutional right is involved, so we simply recognize this as a situation where someone can say with validity: 'We'll just have to wait for time to change the hearts of men.' "

16....The Citizen

Now that he was deeply involved in the Negro's fight for equality outside the area of athletics, Jackie Robinson realized that the closer the Negro got to first-class citizenship, the fewer his supporters were. Some of the people who had led the crusade, who had won national and international reputations as humanitarians when the demands were only that Negroes not be lynched or allowed to starve to death—ran for cover when an attack was launched on segregation itself.

Seeing that the Negro could count on only limited white help in the more crucial stages of his struggle, Jackie was determined to mobilize new Negro strength, and at the same time to solidify white support by helping white Americans to understand that the Negro's new quest for dignity, his demands for freedom from the stigma of Jim Crow, were even more deserving of support, than his material demands for food and shelter.

Toward this end, Jackie undertook a lengthy tour for the National Conference of Christians and Jews, seeking to arouse in Americans a living concern for the principle of man's brotherhood under a just God. Later he crisscrossed the nation speaking in behalf of the NAACP, exhorting Negroes to buy their freedom with dollars and courage, warning them that even a just God would help only those determined to help themselves.

At the same time, Jackie knew that more is involved in the Negro's winning first-class citizenship than lawsuits and legislation. He had seen, as have all proud, ambitious Negroes, the extent to which the misbehavior of one Negro is made the burden of all, so he knew that it was foolish to assume that the Negro would ever be free beyond his display of responsibility. Thus it was but another facet of the crusading spirit within him that he gave so much time to the Harlem YMCA, teaching youngsters citizenship, self-respect, the meaning of ambition, offering them hope for the future and at the same time a warning that the future would be no more than they might make it through struggle and sacrifice.

Jackie was honest enough to say aloud what troubled Negro leadership privately: that the Negro masses had not gone to bat for their freedom. Perhaps this was a mere reflection of the fact that whites had used the bonds of paternalism to chain Negroes to an old order, had employed the shades of ignorance to hide from them any vision of better things to be had. Or perhaps what ailed the Negro masses was also what ailed white America: they never had it so good. A people used to fatback and molasses had found the paradise of ham and eggs, and that full-stomach feeling was good enough.

Robinson went to the national convention of the NAACP in Cleveland and created a furor by asserting that Negro leadership had failed to gain the confidence of the "little man in the street"—a man watching to see if Negro leaders were really going to risk personal loss to stand behind policies beneficial to the Negro masses. Citing the relatively small membership of the NAACP, of which he became a director in 1957, Jackie challenged the organization to get the masses interested in the fight for freedom.

Even while these activities consumed almost his every thought, controversy dogged Robinson's trail. On the NAACP tour, St. Louis newsmen confronted him with a news dispatch in which Roy Campanella had blasted him for allegedly saying that Campy was "washed up." Dick Young of the *Daily News* had gone by Campanella's liquor store in Harlem to quote Jackie as making such a statement, provoking Campanella to do quite a bit of talking. "When it's my turn to bow out of baseball, I certainly don't want to go out like he did. It just wasn't the dignified thing to do," said Campy.

Young went on to quote the Dodger catcher as saying that his relations with Robinson had been "kind of cool" in recent years. "You can play with a guy and not want to live with him," Campanella allegedly told Young. "I always steered clear of him when he was doing that popping off in the clubhouse. Jackie has made quite a few remarks and cracks since retiring and I'm not surprised he said something like that about me. He's been shooting his mouth off about everybody, and most of the time he doesn't know what he's talking about. A guy like Jackie should have gone out of baseball with a lot of friends. Instead he made a lot of enemies. He always was stirring up this club and in the clubhouse, too, making a lot of trouble. Instead of being grateful to baseball, he's criticizing it. Everything he has, he owes to baseball.

"He better learn to talk differently to those people who are working for him in that director of personnel job of his. If he talks to some of them the way he talked in baseball, they'll wrap something around his neck and walk out."

According to later dispatches, Campy was surprised to see these words in print. He said that he "thought it was all off the record," and that he expected a "wingdinger" of a reply from Robinson.

Jackie was of a mind to give a wingdinger of a reply, but the quality that had stood him in good stead for years—the ability to take advice—prevailed. Frank Williams, the young

NAACP executive traveling with him, persuaded Jackie to make no reply in St. Louis and to take time to think the situation over.

Later, at the Chicago airport, Jackie gave this statement to the press: "Friday night in St. Louis a dispatch from New York, allegedly quoting Roy Campanella, was called to my attention. It said, among other things, that I had expressed the opinion that Roy was 'washed up.' I have never made such a statement! I have said, in response to a reporter's inquiry, that the Dodgers were understandably concerned as to whether Roy's hand had completely recovered from last year's operation.

"I'm sorry that Roy 'popped off,' apparently without bothering to check the accuracy of Dick Young's statement to him as to what I was supposed to have said. Campy is also quoted as saying that our relationship had 'cooled off' over the past few years. Absolutely no good would be served by my saying why it 'cooled.' I have no argument with Campy and I don't want one. In addition, I'm too busy as chairman of the NAACP Fight for Freedom campaign to concern myself with arguments of this type.

"I have no apology for the manner in which I left baseball. I am confident that I left many warm and loyal friends behind me both in and out of the Dodger organization. Ever since leaving, I have told the press and the public of my deep gratitude for the opportunities which baseball gave to me and I shall continue to express and feel such gratitude."

Several Negro newspapermen hopped into the dispute, however, and aired what they called the true story of the Robinson-Campanella feud. A. S. (Doc) Young, one of the best-informed and most respected sports writers in the Negro press, wrote: "Background for this feud is found in the differences in personalities between these two stars. Campy is a Dale Carnegie disciple who believes in 'getting along' at all costs, in being exceedingly grateful for any favor, or any deed interpreted as a favor.

"Jackie, on the other hand, is an aggressive individualist who is willing to pay the price, and once having paid it in full does not believe that effusive 'thank yous' are a necessary tip.

"Campy believes Jackie owes baseball everything. Jackie knows that baseball was ready to put the skids under him without his knowledge after having lived handsomely on him for years. Jackie knows that baseball never has been overly concerned about its unpaid debt to all the great Negro players who lived from 1887 to 1945 without a mere look-in on organized ball.

". . . This whole business leaves me with a bad taste in my mouth. I like both players, and I'm sorry this kind of thing must come up to further mar Jackie's retirement. I'm sure Campy would eat those words, if he had a chance."

Writing in the *Pittsburgh Courier*, William G. Nunn said: "Negroes who still look upon Robinson as the man who 'broke the color line' in organized baseball just aren't ready at this stage of the game to turn thumbs down on their hero. This fact has been accelerated by the knowledge that Robinson is even now on a twelve-city tour of the nation, heading up a million dollar . . . campaign for the NAACP . . .

"Robinson talks a lot . . . but investigation has proved. . . . He's usually right when he 'pops off'! . . ."

In the midst of this furor, Branch Rickey wasted no time letting the public know where he stood. He was with Robinson. When Jackie visited Pittsburgh on his NAACP tour, Rickey introduced him before a standing-room-only crowd of more than 2,500 people. Rickey told the throng that if he had it all to do over again, Robinson would still be his choice as the man to break baseball's color line; that in his opinion Robinson had been right on every occasion when he had "popped off"; that he, Rickey, could appreciate Robinson's resentments against insults hurled at him and the injustices he had to face; that Negroes in that audience had better take their cue from Jackie and "fight with every resource at your command, short of violence, to achieve full citizenship rights."

Some observers believe that although Robinson clearly won the battle of words with Campanella as far as the Negro public is concerned, among white sports writers, especially those who dislike Robinson's aggressiveness, Campanella will laugh last.

After Campy's injury, for example, dozens of writers not only produced reams of praise of Campanella and wished publicly for his recovery; they included comments like, "Robinson was the aggressor who paved the way for other Negroes, and Campanella made the friends." Or, "Robinson was the more colorful star, but he made enemies. Everybody liked Campy."

"Other Campanella comments were recalled as the entire sports world prayed with Roy for his complete recovery," wrote Joe Reichler of Associated Press.

" 'It's nice up here. Don't spoil it.'

"That was an impulsive remark by Campanella early in his National League career, during an altercation with an umpire in which the fiery Jackie Robinson was involved.

"Campanella was happy to be in the major leagues after so many years of struggling in the Negro leagues and he didn't want anything to jeopardize his chances of remaining there.

" 'I'm no crusader. I'm a baseball player.'

"That was Roy's reply to Robinson, who once accused him of not feeling strongly enough about racial matters . . .

"If Campy has one regret it is that Robinson, and not he, was the first Negro to play in the majors. . . ."

Jackie was unhappy because so many sports writers appeared to be trying to create the impression that everyone considered Campy the nice, considerate guy while Robinson —because he protested, was a crusader—was a hot-headed ogre. Robinson wrote his old friend Reichler asking him to cite the time or place Campy had said to Jackie, "It's nice up here. Don't spoil it." Reichler did not know, of course, because no such conversation ever occurred—still Jackie smarted with the irritating knowledge that this myth would die hard because a lot of people apparently wanted to believe it.

How far would the tide run? How much would Jackie Robinson pay eventually for being aggressive and outspoken? Nunn figured the tide had only begun. In 1958, he wrote:

"Roy Campanella may beat Jackie Robinson into baseball's Hall of Fame after all. If Campy is unable to return to the game, a group of baseball writers will campaign to have the five-year retirement rule waived so he can be voted into baseball's shrine during the next balloting. Speaking of the Dodgers, it is interesting to note that while officials of the team have retired Campanella's number, they refuse to retire Jackie Robinson's number 42. Jackie's old number is assigned to anyone it will fit. Currently Jackie's white shirt is being worn by Dodgers Scout Al Campanis. The gray one went to Johnny Dixon, a free agent catcher who is only in camp to help out in batting practice."

Anyone wondering how much this means to Robinson can find the answer in several places. On Dec. 8, 1956, upon receiving the forty-first Spingarn Medal from the NAACP for his contributions to Negro progress, Jackie said: "Today marks the high point in my career. To be honored in this way by the NAACP means more than anything that has happened to me before. That is because the NAACP . . . represents everything that a man should stand for: human dignity, brotherhood, fair play . . .

"I am now quite convinced that [my past conduct] has been right . . . I was so often advised not to press issues, not to speak up every time there was an injustice. I was often advised to look after the Robinson family and not to worry about other people . . . If I did so, many honors and awards would come my way, but [I would not get these awards] if I insisted on continually speaking out for what I thought was right.

"Well, I don't know about all those honors and awards. But I am pretty certain now that what I have tried to do was in keeping with the spirit which the Spingarn Medal represents."

A month later, in Los Angeles, he told an overflow crowd at an NAACP fund rally: "The fight has just begun . . . If I could choose between being named to baseball's Hall of Fame and getting first-class citizenship for Negroes, I would not hesitate a second to take the latter."

The one place where Jackie Robinson has pulled his punches has been where writers have sought to draw him out on his differences with Campanella. Why has Jackie refused to sound off on this subject? He explains:

I have never felt that there was any dispute between Campanella and me as individuals. The thing that separated us is an issue far more important than either of us as individuals, for it goes to the heart of the question of how we Negroes can best assure some measure of liberty and dignity for our children.

I admired Campanella the ballplayer, for he was one of the greatest. I admire him even more for the courage he has shown in the wake of his tragic accident. He is a symbol of inspiration to millions.

Still, it never has been a secret that Campy and I are poles apart in our views on how to deal with racial injustice. We have strongly conflicting views as to the role that should be played by Negroes who, by the grace of God and the struggles of Negroes before us, are now thrust into positions of prestige and wealth. I cannot for a moment pretend that I was pleased to see Campy write in the *Saturday Evening Post:* "I've never had much trouble with white or colored folks anywhere . . . That's because I never tried to push things too hard or too fast."

I must even confess that one of the few times I've felt like weeping was when I read in Campy's book, *It's Good to Be Alive,* this paragraph: "I've had a struggle all my life. I'm a colored man. I know there are lots of things that I can do and things that I cannot do without stirring up some people. But a few years ago there were many more things that I could not do than is the case today. I'm willing to wait. I believe in not pushing things; in giving the other fellow a chance. A man's got to do things the way he sees them. No other way."

I wanted to weep, not for Campy, but for his children and mine who will have to battle the defenders of the status quo whose primary argument is and always has been that the Negro is trying to push "too hard or too fast." Campy had played into their hands so completely, had uttered the words that the segregationists want most to hear from Negro leaders: "I'm willing to wait." I wanted to cry aloud, asking Campy if he had forgotten that the career in organized baseball that he cherishes so would never have been his but for Negroes and whites who pushed, hard and fast, to knock down the barrier of Jim Crow; I wanted to remind him that we both might still be fighting to escape the back slums of America but for those courageous forebears who were never beaten so low or soft-soaped into enough self-satisfaction for them to say, "I'm willing to wait." Both Campy and I played our hearts out for the Dodgers because something in us made it impossible for us to accept that age-old Brooklyn slogan, "Wait till next year." I know that in this area of human freedom we Negroes must also play our hearts out, must speak up with responsible militancy, or another generation will be telling Campy's and my great-grandchildren, "Wait till next year."

I'm tired of waiting and I know that deep in his heart Campy is tired, too. In fact, he speculates in his book that the segregation to which we were subjected during spring training in Havana gave me stomach trouble and adds: "I wasn't happy either, but felt I was getting that big opportunity. Nothing else mattered."

I believe that we Negroes are a lost people, that all our talk about democracy and civil rights is in vain, so long as our own personal gain and opportunities are all that matter to the more fortunate ones among us. This belief lay behind the fact that I was frequently irked to have writers repeat the phony story that Campy once warned me not to talk too much and ruin things in baseball for the Negro, with Campy supposedly adding: "I like it up here." I kept hoping that sooner or later Campy would squelch that canard and inform the writers that no such incident ever took place, even though Campy and some of the writers probably did feel that I spoke out too often.

Still, I shied away from invitations to air publicly my differences with Campy because I did not want anyone to get the mistaken notion that personal antagonism was involved. Nor did I want it to appear that I was trying to play God and decide how other Negroes should think and act.

Campy said in *Ebony* magazine, "I'm not a man for controversies. I stay away from them like the plague." Now, I feel that the Negro's plight would be unmitigated hell if all successful Negroes ran from controversy, but I concede to Campy the right to feel the way he does. Not all of us are equipped or disposed to articulate the Negro's grievances—and, in fact, Campy may want to argue that in his "noncontroversial" way he is advancing the Negro more than the militant ones among us who file suits, make speeches and protest in other ways.

In any event, that gives me no special quarrel with Campanella, for thousands of people, black and white, apparently feel as he does. At times I have felt that it has become a mark of American society for people to run from controversy "like the plague." Everybody wants to conform. I have wondered whether too many of us have become so soft in our high standard of living, so preoccupied with raising it even higher, that we have lost the time or the will to be concerned with the social problems that beset us.

I say all this to say that my quarrel never has been with Campy the individual, but with timidity. I may be wrong, but I'm staking my children's future on the belief that first-class citizenship will come only when the Robinsons, Campanellas, Belafontes and Poitiers walk shoulder to shoulder in determination, speaking with a clear voice the Negro's determination to be free. Sure, the worshipers of the status quo will criticize us, but I am certain that in the secrecy of their souls they will respect us.

Americans can remember, then, that the Jackie Robinson who "sounds off" on many issues speaks not from bitterness, but from this conviction. Few Americans are more aware of their blessings than Jackie; few more proud of the fact that this country is the kind in which a Negro minority can move from peonage and virtual illiteracy to one of education and burgeoning self-respect—all within the mere four decades Jackie has lived. He wants the United States to remain the kind of country in which the weak may continue to have reasonable hope of becoming strong, the shackled continue to believe that freedom is within their grasp, the impoverished maintain faith that abundance will be theirs. He believes that the way to assure this is to spend more time removing remaining injustices, more time battling whatever forces nibble at the freedom of the people, and a lot less time gloating over, giving thanks for, the gains of the past. This belief is so strong that Robinson repeatedly risks financial loss and the disfavor of close friends by taking actions that he thinks will deepen the freedoms of the nation's less privileged groups.

His liberal friends were aghast, but this did not force Jackie to soft-pedal his pro-Nixon feelings. His friends snorted that "Tricky Dick" was a reactionary beyond conversion, but Jack stuck by his belief that Nixon had learned from experience, from his journeys to the Far East and Africa, and that the Vice President had developed real principles and convictions in favor of racial equality.

Nor did fear of public reaction prevent Robinson from blasting the Los Angeles Urban League when it gave a plaque to O'Malley for the Dodgers' "enlightened leadership in opening the door to employment of Negro athletes in major league baseball."

It was just too much for Robinson that Dick Young was laughing in print in the *Daily News* about how the Urban League had "goofed."

"If Robby gets to see this, he will fall right off the chair laughing," Young wrote. ". . . O'Malley is something less than a champion of the Negro, in baseball or anywhere else . . .

"Last year, even while going through the motions of negotiating with New York officials for a piece of downtown Brooklyn, O'Malley was setting up his alibi for pulling out of the borough—lock, stock and ballclub.

" 'It's an interesting statistic,' he said then, and repeated often, 'that during the month of May, 60 percent of all the children born in Brooklyn were Negro or Puerto Rican.'

"I wonder whether the Urban League would like to present him another plaque inscribed with that quotation."

Robinson quickly called the Urban League action "preposterous" and a "farce," leading the executive secretary of the Los Angeles Urban League to explain that the award was given to the entire Dodger organization and that O'Malley simply had accepted on behalf of the organization.

This provoked an exchange between O'Malley and the *Los Angeles Sentinel*, a Negro newspaper, in which O'Malley repeated the statement that his only disagreement with Jackie was over "ill-timed and intemperate remarks."

Jackie fired off a letter to O'Malley in which he said:

We know what the relationship is between your organization and myself and why. I am sorry after ten years of association we parted as we did. However, I believe we are both happy the relationship is over. I may have been one of your all-time greats as far as my play on the field is concerned, but we know why we personally never had much in common. It had nothing to do with what you called ill-timed and intemperate remarks. I am aggressive where I feel my rights are being jeopardized, and no amount of praise or awards will ever change my desire that we be recognized solely on merit alone.

I am honored my friends at the *Sentinel* feel as they do. It's pretty evident to me they, too, know pretty much what the score is. Personally, I feel it would have been better for all concerned had the trade to the Giants occurred when Mr. Rickey left the Dodgers which in my opinion sums up the cause for our relationship.

There is certainly no need to disguise our feelings. It's pretty commonly known what they are.

O'Malley then sent Jackie a telegram saying:

Jackie, think back. Your letter has to be very wrong. Someone is wrapping [apparently the word was warping] your thinking. Let's talk it out some day. Regards to Rachel, youngsters and to you.

Jackie then wrote:

I have thought back, and although I would like very much to feel differently, I find no reason to do so . . .

I think you know, and Mrs. O'Malley knows of the deep and sincere respect I have for her and the fondness for Terry and Peter, but there has always been an invisible barrier where you and I were concerned. I feel certain it's because you refused to accept me as I was even though you knew there wasn't a man in your organization who put out for it any more than I did. I did so because I felt I was a part of the organization, and whatever I did for it, I was also helping myself. I knew, in my salary talks with Buzzie, that had I demanded more money I could have gotten it, but again realizing some of the problems, it wasn't hard for us to agree to terms.

So, you see, Mr. O'Malley, although I don't usually feel this resentment over such a long period of time, one does not or cannot easily forget some of the things that happened . . .

I have passed along your remarks to Rachel. She certainly doesn't feel as I do, but she resented as much as I did what happened [when Jackie was traded to the Giants].

I did appreciate your wire. I wish I could find reason to think differently.

This kind of outspokenness has left Jackie with a small army of detractors, still there is considerable evidence that in circles where men think and admire integrity, Robinson is respected. Politicians with an eye on the White House seek his help because they know that endorsement by a Negro with guts, a Negro whose convictions cannot be sapped by prosperity, is worth the praise of a hundred Uncle Toms. These politicians have found that Jackie symbolizes the "new Negro" when he demands more than the case of whiskey or the handful of dollars that was so long the "price" of the Negro "leader." Jackie's price, as Nixon has now found out, is bold, concerted action toward securing the Negro's rights.

When Attorney General William Rogers announced publicly in late 1957 that the Eisenhower administration would not press for additional civil rights legislation in the next session of Congress, but would allow "a cooling-off period," Robinson fired off a Christmas Eve letter of protest to Nixon.

The Vice President replied that the administration was not relaxing its efforts toward equal opportunities for all citizens but that time was needed to see the effect of present legislation before pressing for more. "While all great movements of reform started slowly and encountered bitter opposition, they soon gathered an irresistible momentum and gained rapid acceptance," he wrote. "I fervently believe this will be the case in the battle for equal rights."

Robinson replied that he knew "Rome was not built in a day," but that Negro leaders would be "repudiated by the Negro masses if they attempt to justify 'a breathing spell' in the fight for integration at a time when the total Negro South and the best elements of the white South are looking to the government for leadership and protection from disaster at the hands of the White Citizens Councils and white office-holders in the South who are determined that the Supreme Court's mandate will not be obeyed in our lifetime."

Five months later, Jackie was in Washington with other Negro leaders, asking what kind of leadership they could expect from the administration. Mr. Eisenhower spoke to the Negroes, urging them to show "patience and forbearance." Many Negroes came away disillusioned, asserting that the President's speech was "an insult—he acted as if he were lecturing kindergarteners."

Jackie wrote the President:

My dear Mr. President:

I was sitting in the audience at the Summit Meeting of Negro Leaders yesterday when you said we must have patience. On hearing you say this, I felt like standing up and saying, "Oh, no! Not again."

I respectfully remind you, sir, that we have been the most patient of all people. When you said we must have self-respect, I wondered how we could have self-respect and remain patient considering the treatment accorded us through the years.

Seventeen million Negroes cannot do as you suggest and wait for the hearts of men to change. We want to enjoy now the rights that we feel we are entitled to as Americans. This we cannot do unless we pursue aggressively goals which all other Americans achieved over 150 years ago.

. . . I respectfully suggest that you unwittingly crush the spirit of freedom in Negroes by constantly urging forbearance and give hope to those pro-segregation leaders like Governor Faubus who would take from us even those freedoms we now enjoy. Your own experience with Governor Faubus is proof enough that forbearance and not eventual integration is the goal the pro-segregation leaders seek.

In my view, an unequivocal statement backed up by action such as you demonstrated you could take last fall in dealing with Governor Faubus if it became necessary, would let it be known that America is determined to provide—in the near future—for Negroes—the freedoms we are entitled to under the Constitution.

Respectfully yours,
Jackie Robinson

Still later, feeling that proper leadership was not emanating from the White House, Jackie decided to make a return visit to Washington. This time not so many reporters were there to meet him, not so many newspapers carried glowing editorials about his mission, as a decade earlier when he had gone to vow the Negro's loyalty to America. This time Jackie was in the Capital to join white and Negro youngsters in a march on the White House to dramatize their desire to see school integration achieved this generation. Still, this return to Washington was a happy occasion, for Jackie did not walk alone. Harry Belafonte, the Reverend Martin Luther King and many other prominent Negroes walked in proud dignity, saying to Negroes and the world that it demeans no man to march in the name of freedom.

Some Americans cringed at this spectacle of rich and famous Negroes leading a protest march. One Florida columnist thought it "odd" that the protest leaders were men who seemed to have least to complain about. "Jackie was given his chance by white men. Does he hark back to that?" asked another writer.

Jackie did hark back to the fact that white men had given him some breaks—and realized happily that those white men stood behind him and the cause for which he protested. One of these, Branch Rickey, saw Jackie's role in that march on the White House as further evidence of the courage, the unselfishness, that had prompted him to select Jackie as the guinea pig in one of mankind's great social experiments.

"Surely, God was with me when I picked Jackie," says Rickey. "I don't think any other man in the Negro race or any race could have done what he did those first two or three years. He really did understand the responsibility he carried . . . Then he had the intelligence of knowing how to handle himself under adversity. Above all, he had what the boys call 'guts,' real 'guts.' "

William Black, president of Chock Full O' Nuts, who had given Jackie a real job and found that Robinson had more to offer than a name—that the workers trusted and respected him because he had lived their kind of life and had their kinds of problems—also stood unflinchingly behind him. In fact, few things have made Jackie prouder than Black's response when a group of Long Island citizens threatened to boycott "Chock" after Robinson lashed them publicly for advocating school segregation.

"I cannot speak for all the stockholders of Chock Full O' Nuts, because I now own only one-third of the company," said Black. "Speaking for my third, if anyone wants to boycott 'Chock' because I hired Jackie Robinson, I recommend Martinson's coffee. It's just as good.

"As for our restaurants, there are Nedick's, Bickford's and Horn and Hardart in our price range. Try them. You may even like them better than ours."

So Jackie's return to Washington in 1959 was no journey of despair. He saw in the marchers themselves a reason to be happy: they represented a new sense of unity, a new dedication to freedom on the part of the American Negro. And the wealthy, famous Negroes there were symbols of a phase of American progress no casual observer would see: the day was passing, perhaps had passed, when Negroes need fear that cringing timidity was the price for holding a job.

In the difficult days ahead, Jackie Robinson and those inspired by him will protest—and be subjected to the criticism that squeamish men heap upon the bolder ones among them. Jackie and his admirers are sustained by the consoling fact that neither baseball fans nor historians build monuments for those who merely wait. Man's march away from barbarity, his struggle to achieve a just, civilized social order, have been the work of the pushers, those impatient men of zeal and vision. Our most hallowed legends are about "crusaders," those brave souls who dared to rock the boat. Without the pushers and the crusaders, the waiters wait in vain; without people like Damon Runyon and Branch Rickey, Wendell Smith and Isadore Muchnick, Jackie and the Negro might still be waiting for their hour in organized baseball.

For years to come, whenever a Henry Aaron lashes one off the boards or an Ernie Banks hits one into the seats, baseball fans north and south will give silent thanks to Jackie, the pioneer "whose wounds you cannot see or feel." Remembering him as baseball's trailblazer, not all of them will lose sight of the broader effect he has had . . . A Pullman porter on a train that hurtles through the moonlit Florida night, a porter who has harbored unhappiness for years because his college training brought him no better job, confides to a writer for a national magazine: "I can't rightly explain what Jackie did for me. I guess you'd say he renewed my pride, my self-respect. He made me believe again that a black man can be a real man and still get ahead. Jackie gave me a reason for ceasing to think of myself as a failure, for at worst I am able to tell myself that part of my situation arises from the fact that there was no Branch Rickey of my day and calling."

Or a teen-age lad sits in a high school in any one of a thousand American towns, buoyed up by the subconscious, perhaps conscious, knowledge that his books mean more today than yesterday. No longer are the barriers that remain in business, medicine, engineering and other fields to be considered insurmountable. Jackie planted a black man's flag atop one of the highest, craggiest barriers of them all and in doing so freed these thousands of brown-skinned lads from the astigmatism of outlook, the hopelessness bordering on despair, that have shadowed the lives of Negro boys and girls for generations.

Burning pride, an indomitable competitive spirit, a sense of responsibility, intelligence—just plain guts—these are the qualities that made Jackie Robinson perhaps the greatest all-around athlete of his generation. They also are the qualities that make great men. You will please Robinson if you speak of him as a ballplayer's ballplayer; you touch the wellspring of his soul-force when you call him a freedom lover in an age when many are afraid of freedom. Because of the thousands of lives he has touched—Caucasian, Negro, African, Asian—future generations will remember him, not as the base runner who worried pitchers to their doom, but as the proud crusader against pompous bigots and timid sentinels of the status quo—as the symbol of a new Negro American.

In 1956, at the age of thirty, CARL T. ROWAN became the only newspaperman ever to win three consecutive awards from Sigma Delta Chi, the nation's foremost professional journalistic organization. He won its coveted medallion for the best foreign correspondence of 1956 for his articles on Southeast Asia and his coverage of the historic Bandung Conference. A year earlier he had won the foreign correspondence medallion for his articles on India. (These foreign experiences were described in his second book, *The Pitiful and the Proud*.) Sigma Delta Chi had also, in 1954, cited his articles on the school segregation cases then pending before the United States Supreme Court as the nation's best general reporting of 1953. The same year his first book, *South of Freedom*, appeared. In *Go South to Sorrow* (1957) he evaluated the progress of integration since the historic Supreme Court decision.

Since 1950, when he became a staff writer for the *Minneapolis Tribune* after a two-year stint on the copy desk, Rowan has won awards from many other organizations, including the Sidney Hillman Foundation, the American Library Association, the Capitol Press Club, and the National Conference of Christians and Jews. He has also been awarded honorary degrees from Simpson College and Hamline University.

After graduation from Bernard High School in McMinnville, Tennessee, Mr. Rowan spent three years in the Navy during World War II. At the age of nineteen he won one of the first fifteen commissions granted to Negroes. He studied at Tennessee State University; Washburn University; Oberlin College, for a bachelor's degree in mathematics; and at the University of Minnesota, for an M.A. in journalism.

Mr. Rowan lives in Minneapolis with his wife and three children.